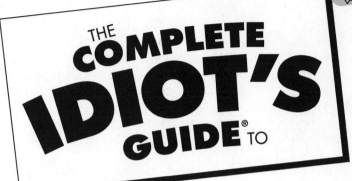

THE COMPLETE IDIOT'S GUIDE® TO

Computer Basics

Fourth Edition

by Joe Kraynak

ALPHA

A member of Penguin Group (USA) Inc.

To my kids, Nick and Ali, who constantly inspire me to keep up with the latest technology.

ALPHA BOOKS

Published by the Penguin Group

Penguin Group (USA) Inc., 375 Hudson Street, New York, New York 10014, U.S.A.

Penguin Group (Canada), 10 Alcorn Avenue, Toronto, Ontario, Canada M4V 3B2 (a division of Pearson Penguin Canada Inc.)

Penguin Books Ltd, 80 Strand, London WC2R 0RL, England

Penguin Ireland, 25 St Stephen's Green, Dublin 2, Ireland (a division of Penguin Books Ltd)

Penguin Group (Australia), 250 Camberwell Road, Camberwell, Victoria 3124, Australia (a division of Pearson Australia Group Pty Ltd)

Penguin Books India Pvt Ltd, 11 Community Centre, Panchsheel Park, New Delhi—110 017, India

Penguin Group (NZ), cnr Airborne and Rosedale Roads, Albany, Auckland 1310, New Zealand (a division of Pearson New Zealand Ltd)

Penguin Books (South Africa) (Pty) Ltd, 24 Sturdee Avenue, Rosebank, Johannesburg 2196, South Africa

Penguin Books Ltd, Registered Offices: 80 Strand, London WC2R 0RL, England

Copyright © 2007 by Joe Kraynak

International Standard Book Number: 978-1-59257-597-8
Library of Congress Catalog Card Number: 2006932990

09 08   8   7   6   5   4

Interpretation of the printing code: The rightmost number of the first series of numbers is the year of the book's printing; the rightmost number of the second series of numbers is the number of the book's printing. For example, a printing code of 07-1 shows that the first printing occurred in 2007.

Printed in the United States of America

Publisher: *Marie Butler-Knight*
Editorial Director: *Mike Sanders*
Managing Editor: *Billy Fields*
Acquisitions Editor: *Tom Stevens*
Development Editor: *Michael Thomas*
Senior Production Editor: *Janette Lynn*
Copy Editor: *Keith Cline*

Cartoonist: *Shannon Wheeler*
Cover Designer: *Bill Thomas*
Book Designer: *Trina Wurst*
Indexer: *Heather McNeill*
Layout: *Brian Massey*
Proofreader: *Aaron Black*

Contents at a Glance

Contents

Introduction

A funny thing happened on the way to the twenty-first century. Computers became more human. By "human," I don't mean "humanoid." I only mean that the computer has evolved from being a stodgy office tool to a revolutionary home appliance and entertainment system, a device designed to help us manage and enjoy our lives more fully.

Sure, you can still use a computer to type and print a letter, but the latest computer technology can completely revolutionize your professional and personal life. Here's just a glimpse of what you can do with a computer, an Internet connection, and some additional equipment:

- Compose letters and create custom publications.
- Decorate your documents with professional clip art and other graphics.
- Shop at mega-malls and specialty shops without leaving your home, and save money, too!
- Send and receive mail electronically—no postage, and same-day delivery.
- Carry on conversations with friends, relatives, and complete strangers anywhere in the world—without paying long-distance charges.
- Plan your vacation, get medical advice, and find maps to nearly any location.
- Copy music clips from the Internet and from your CD collection and burn your own custom CDs.
- Take photos with a digital camera, transfer them to your computer, make prints, or e-mail photos to your friends and family.
- Create your own websites or blogs (web logs) to express your views, communicate with family and friends, or market your products and services.
- Edit your home videos and copy your video clips to CDs, DVDs, or VHS tapes.
- Find a mate. (I do recommend meeting in person before you make any commitments.)

Sounds pretty cool, huh? Well, it is—assuming, of course, that you know what you're doing. To master the high-tech world of computers and electronic gadgets, you must first master the basics. You need to know your way around a computer, how to point and click with a mouse, how to run programs in Windows, and how to enter commands. After you've mastered a few basics, as explained in the first few chapters of this book, you will be well-prepared to explore and exploit the full power of your computer and the Internet as you proceed through later chapters.

Welcome to *The Complete Idiot's Guide to Computer Basics, Fourth Edition*

Most computer documentation is based on the assumption that you, the user, are the computer's servant. The documentation lists the parts of the computer and explains how each part works, as if you purchased a computer to impress your friends and neighbors rather than to perform a particular job.

The Complete Idiot's Guide to Computer Basics, Fourth Edition, is different. Instead of installing the computer as your master, this book places *you* in charge of the computer. This book assumes that you want to do something practical with your computer, and it shows you how to use your computer as you would use any appliance in your home to perform practical, hands-on tasks. You'll learn how to do everything from typing and printing letters to editing your own videos.

What You Will Learn in This Book

You don't have to read this book from cover to cover (although you might miss some savvy tidbits if you skip around). If you just purchased a computer, start with Chapter 1 to learn how to get your computer up and running. If you need a quick lesson on using Windows, skip ahead to Chapter 3. If you need to get wired to the Internet, check out Chapter 18. To provide some structure for this hodgepodge of computer skills and techniques, I've divided this book into the following six parts:

Part 1, "Firing Up Your Computer: Bare-Bones Basics," covers the bare minimum: setting up and turning on your computer and using your mouse and keyboard to make it respond to your every command.

Part 2, "Navigating Microsoft Windows," shows you how to take control of the Windows desktop (a virtual desktop on which you create documents and play games), install and run programs, share your computer peacefully with others, manage and secure your documents, and network your computers so that they can share valuable and often expensive resources.

Part 3, "Getting Down to Business with Office Programs," teaches you everything you need to know to type a letter and other documents, add clip art and other graphics, and print your letter. You also learn your way around spreadsheet programs, databases, and personal finance programs.

Part 4, "Tapping the Power of the Internet," launches you into the world of telecommunications. In this part, you find out how to install a modem, connect to an online service, surf the Internet, send and receive electronic mail, wander the World Wide Web, chat online with others, and much more.

Part 5, "Going Digital with Music, Photos, and Video," takes you on a tour of the wonderful world of digital audio, imaging, and video. Here you learn how to copy music clips from CDs and from the Internet to burn your own custom CDs and transfer music clips to a portable music player; buy a digital camera and use it to snap and print photos and e-mail them to your friends and family; and use video-editing software to splice your home movie clips into a full-length motion picture.

Part 6, "Maintaining and Upgrading Your Computer," acts as your computer maintenance guide. Here, you learn how and when to clean your computer, how to give it regular tune-ups to keep it running like new, how to troubleshoot common problems, and how to find additional technical support when all else fails.

Conventions Used in This Book

I use several conventions in this book to make it easier to understand. For example, when you need to type something, it appears in **bold.**

Likewise, if I tell you to select or click a command, the command also appears in **bold.** This allows you to quickly scan a series of steps without having to reread all the text.

A plethora of margin notes and sidebars offers additional information about what you've just read. These boxes are distinguished by special icons that appear next to them:

Whoa!

Before you press that button, check out the Whoa! icons for precautionary notes. Chances are that I've made the same mistake myself. Let me tell you how to avoid the blunder.

def•i•ni•tion

In the computer industry, jargon and cryptic acronyms rule. When a computer term baffles you or an acronym annoys you, look to the Definition icon for a plain-English definition.

Panic Attack

You did everything right, but the same error message keeps popping up on your screen or, worse yet, nothing happens. When your computer or program does the unexpected, look to the Panic Attack icon for an explanation and a fix.

Inside Tip

When you've been in the computer business for as long as I have, you learn better ways to perform the same tasks and pick up information that helps you avoid common pitfalls. To share in my wealth of knowledge, check out my Inside Tips.

Computer Cheat

Do the steps required to perform a simple computer task seem convoluted? Then they probably are. Software programs commonly have hidden shortcuts that help you perform a task more efficiently. Check out the Computer Cheat icon for tips from the masters.

Acknowledgments

Several people had to don hard hats and get their hands dirty to build a better book. I owe special thanks to Tom Stevens for choosing me to author this book and for handling the assorted details to get this book in gear. Thanks to Michael Thomas and Keith Cline for guiding the content of this book, keeping it focused on new users, ferreting out all my typos, and fine-tuning my sentences. Jan Lynn deserves a free trip to Aruba for shepherding the manuscript (and art) through production. The Alpha Books production team merits a round of applause for transforming a collection of electronic files into such an attractive book. I also owe special thanks to my agent, Neil Salkind, and the rest of the staff at Studio B for expertly managing the minor details (like paying me).

Special Thanks to the Technical Reviewer

The Complete Idiot's Guide to Computer Basics, Fourth Edition, was reviewed by an expert who double-checked the accuracy of what you'll learn here, to help us ensure that this book gives you everything you need to know to get up and running with your computer. Special thanks are extended to Valerie L. Bird.

Valerie Bird is an Associate Professor at Wytheville Community College in Wytheville, Virginia. She has a Bachelor of Science degree in Math from Western Michigan University (1972) and a Master of Arts degree in Computer Education from Empire State College, NY (1997). She has an IC3 Certification, a MOS Master Instructor Certification, and a Master CIW Designer Certification. She is an ACM member and an ACM Club Faculty Advisor at WCC. She has been using and teaching computers for over 20 years.

Trademarks

All terms mentioned in this book that are known to be or are suspected of being trademarks or service marks have been appropriately capitalized. Alpha Books and Penguin Group (USA) Inc. cannot attest to the accuracy of this information. Use of a term in this book should not be regarded as affecting the validity of any trademark or service mark.

Part 1

Firing Up Your Computer: Bare-Bones Basics

Right after you purchase a car, the salesperson sits you down behind the wheel and shows you how to work the controls. You learn the essentials, such as how to tune the radio, activate cruise control, adjust the seat, and work the headlights and windshield wipers.

When you purchase a computer—a much more complicated piece of machinery—you're on your own. You get several boxes containing various gadgets and cables, and it's up to you to figure out how to connect everything, turn it on, and start using it.

To make up for this lack of guidance, this part acts as your personal tutor, leading you step by step through the process of setting up and starting your computer and using the controls (the keyboard and mouse) to run programs and enter commands.

Chapter 1

Kick-Starting Your Computer

In This Chapter

- ◆ Preparing a home for your computer
- ◆ Unpacking your computer's fragile components
- ◆ Plugging stuff in
- ◆ Turning everything on in the correct sequence
- ◆ Following the startup instructions (if there are any)

Bringing home your first computer is nearly as exhilarating and worrisome as adopting a puppy. You're excited, but you really don't know what to expect or how to get started. Where should you set up your computer? How do you connect everything? What's the proper sequence for turning on the parts? How do you respond to your computer the first time you start it?

This chapter shows you what to expect. Here you learn how to prepare a space for your computer, set it up, and turn on everything in the correct sequence. This chapter also provides plenty of tips and tricks to help you be sure that you received everything you ordered, to test your computer, and to deal with the unexpected the first time you start your computer.

Finding a Comfortable Home for Your Computer

Your home seems spacious until you take delivery of a new sofa or entertainment center. Then you just can't figure out how you'll wedge that new piece of furniture into your existing collection. Likewise, few people spend much time considering where they're going to place their computer until they bring it into their home or office. In their haste to get the computer up and running, they might place the computer on a rickety card table in a dank room, where it teeters precariously until they get the time and money to set it up properly.

This is a risky strategy. Perching your computer on unstable furniture in a damp or dusty room can significantly reduce its life expectancy—not to mention your enjoyment of your computer. Think ahead and prepare your computer area *before* you start connecting components:

♦ Think about how you'll use your computer. If you intend to use it as a tool for the family, don't stick it in the basement next to that treadmill you never use. Place it in a room that's convenient for everyone and where you can supervise your kids.

Inside Tip

If you're in an old house and you're not sure if the outlet is grounded, go to the hardware store and buy an *outlet tester*; it has indicator lights that show whether the outlet is properly wired.

♦ House the computer next to a grounded outlet that's *not* on the same circuit as a clothes dryer, air conditioner, or other power-hungry appliance. Power fluctuations can damage your computer and destroy files.

♦ Keep the computer away from magnetic fields created by fans, radios, large speakers, air conditioners, microwave ovens, and other appliances. Magnetic fields can mess up the display and erase data from your disks.

♦ Choose an area near a phone jack, or install an additional jack for your modem. (If you purchased the computer mainly for working on the Internet, consider installing a separate phone line for your modem.) If you plan to connect to the Internet through your cable company, contact the cable company to install a cable connection near the computer.

♦ Place your computer in an environment that is clean, dry, cool, and out of direct sunlight. If you have no choice, cover the computer after turning it off to keep it clean. (Don't cover it when the power's on; it needs to breathe.)

◆ To reduce glare on the monitor, be sure it doesn't directly face a window or other source of bright light. Otherwise, the glare will make it difficult for you to see the screen.

◆ Give the computer room to breathe. The computer has fans and vents to keep it cool. If you block the vents, the computer might overheat.

Whoa!

To prevent lightning damage to your computer (which is usually excluded from manufacturer warranties), plug all your computer components into a high-quality surge suppressor. The surge suppressor should have a UL rating of 400 or less, an energy-absorption rating of 400 or more, and a warranty that covers damage to the surge suppressor *and* to your computer. If possible, use an outlet located on an inside wall to further reduce the likelihood that lightning will strike your computer.

Unpacking Your New Toys

When you bring your computer home (or when it's delivered), you will be tempted to tear open the boxes and unpack everything. Before you do, read the following list of precautions for unpacking and connecting your equipment:

◆ Take your time. It's easy to get flustered and make mistakes when you're in a hurry.

◆ Clear all drinks from the work area. You don't want to spill anything on your new computer.

◆ When unpacking your equipment, keep the boxes on the floor to avoid dropping any equipment from up high.

◆ If your computer arrives on a cold day, give the components 2 to 3 hours to adjust to the temperature and humidity in the room. Any condensation needs to dissipate before you turn on the power.

◆ Don't cut the boxes. Carefully peel off the packing tape. This serves two purposes: it reduces the risk of your hacking through a cable or scratching a device, and it keeps the boxes in good condition in case you need to return a device to the manufacturer.

◆ If you have trouble pulling a device, such as a monitor, out of the box, turn the box on its side and slide the device out onto the floor. Don't flip over the box and try to pull the box off the device.

♦ Save all the packing material, including the Styrofoam and bubble wrap. Many manufacturers accept returns only if you return the device as it was originally packed. The packing material is also useful if you need to move your computer to a different home or office later.

Inside Tip

As you dig through the boxes, find the warranty forms, fill them out, and mail them in. This ensures that if a device goes belly-up within the warranty period, the company will fix or replace the device. Taking time now to complete the forms could save you hundreds of dollars down the road. Stuff your computer instructions, warranty, and other paperwork in a folder (I prefer using one of those oversized, sealable plastic bags) and store it in a safe place for future reference.

♦ Read the packing list(s) thoroughly to be sure you received everything you ordered. If something is missing, contact the manufacturer or dealer *immediately.*

♦ Find all the cables. The cables are often stored in a separate compartment at the bottom of the box. They're easy to overlook. (Some cables, including the all-important printer cable, might not be included.)

♦ Inspect the cables. Look for cuts in the cables, and check for bent pins on the connectors. Although you can straighten the pins using tweezers or needle-nose pliers, you can easily snap off a pin, voiding the warranty. If you find a bent or damaged pin, call the manufacturer. The manufacturer probably will instruct you to straighten the pin; but then if it breaks, it's the manufacturer's fault.

♦ Remove any spacers or packing materials from the disk drives and printer. Cardboard or plastic spacers are commonly used to keep parts from shifting during shipping. To avoid damaging your new equipment, remove these spacers before you turn on your computer.

♦ Unlock any devices that might have been locked for shipping. Some scanners, for instance, have a switch that locks the scanner's carriage in place. That switch might be at the back or bottom of the scanner.

♦ Don't force anything. Plugs should slide easily into outlets. If you have to force something, the prongs are probably not aligned with the holes they're supposed to go in. Forcing the plug will break the prongs.

♦ Don't turn on *anything* until *everything* is connected. On some computers, you can safely plug in devices when the power is on, but check the manual to be sure.

Identifying Your Computer's Parts and Appendages

A computer is not a single entity, like a refrigerator or a TV set. A typical computer consists of several components that contribute to its operation and performance. As you work through this chapter to connect the components, you must be able to identify each component and know its common name. Figure 1.1 points out the key parts.

The central component of all computers is the *system unit*, which contains the brains and memory of the computer and the disk drives where data is stored. All other components are considered *peripheral devices*, and they plug directly or indirectly into the system unit. These include the keyboard and mouse that you use to enter commands and data; the monitor, which enables you to see what you're doing; the speakers that provide audio feedback; the printer, which enables you to make paper copies of the documents you create; and the modem, which connects the computer to the Internet. (The modem may be built right into the system unit.) Peripheral devices also include joysticks for playing games, digital cameras, scanners, and a host of other electronic gadgets.

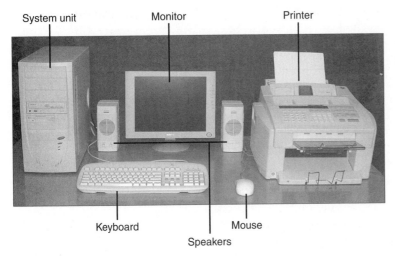

Figure 1.1

A computer consists of several parts.

Making the Right Connections

When everything is unpacked, arrange all the devices on your desk. If you connect the devices before arranging them, the cables get all twisted up when you begin moving things around. If you have a mini-tower or full-tower system unit, you can set it on the floor to conserve desk space. (If the floor is carpeted, set the unit on an anti-static pad to prevent static buildup that could damage the sensitive components inside the system unit.)

After everything is properly positioned, you can connect the devices. This is where life gets a bit complicated. Connections differ depending on the computer's design and the types of components you're connecting. For example, although most computers include a central system unit into which you plug the monitor, keyboard, mouse, and printer, some newer computers combine the system unit, monitor, and speakers as a single device into which you plug other devices. In addition, newer computers make greater use of USB (Universal Serial Bus) ports, special receptacles that allow you to connect a string of up to 127 devices to a single receptacle. If your computer comes with a USB mouse and keyboard, you need to plug them into the USB ports instead of into the standard PS/2 mouse or keyboard ports.

If you have a USB keyboard, chances are that the keyboard itself has USB ports; you plug the keyboard into a USB port on the system unit and then plug your mouse into the USB port on the keyboard. If your keyboard has an extra USB port, you can plug an additional device, such as a USB joystick, into the keyboard, too. This frees up additional USB ports on the system unit.

To figure out where to plug things in, look for words or pictures on the back (and front) of the central unit (the system unit or combination system unit/monitor). Most receptacles (ports) are marked, and many systems even have color-coded cables. If you don't see any pictures next to the receptacles, try to match the plugs with their outlets, as shown in Figure 1.2. Look at the overall shape of the outlet to see whether it has pins or holes. Count the pins and holes and be sure there are at least as many holes as there are pins. As a last resort, look for the documentation that came with your computer.

Panic Attack

If your mouse or keyboard has no cable, don't panic. Wireless technologies used in many new keyboards, mice, printers, and other peripheral devices enable them to connect to the system unit via radio-frequency or infrared signals. Devices typically connect automatically when they are within 30 feet of the system unit. Wireless keyboards and mice require batteries. Wireless printers typically plug into an electrical outlet, just like standard printers, but require no data cable to connect them to the system unit.

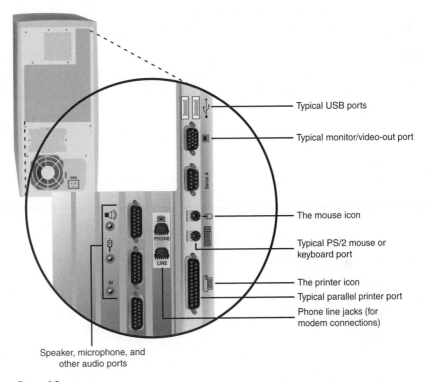

Typical USB ports

Typical monitor/video-out port

The mouse icon

Typical PS/2 mouse or keyboard port

The printer icon

Typical parallel printer port

Phone line jacks (for modem connections)

Speaker, microphone, and other audio ports

Figure 1.2

Look for clues on the system unit to figure out where to plug in devices.

Bringing the Beast to Life

Dr. Frankenstein must have had a real rush just before he flipped the switch and sent that mega-volts jolt through his monster's patchworked body. You get a similar thrill just before you turn on your new computer. What will the screen look like? What sounds will it make? How fast will things pop up on the monitor?

Well, you're about to have all your questions answered as you perform the following steps to start your computer:

1. Press the button on the monitor or flip its switch to turn it on. Computer manufacturers recommend that you turn on the monitor *first*. This allows you to see the startup messages, and it prevents the monitor's power surge from passing through the system unit's components. (On many newer computers, the monitor turns on automatically when you turn on the system unit.)

Panic Attack

If this is the first time you're turning on your printer, you must install the ink or toner cartridge. Check the printer manual for instructions.

2. Turn on the printer if it has a power button or switch. (Many new printers have no power switch.) Be sure the online light is lit (not blinking). If the light is blinking, be sure the printer has paper, and then press the online button (if the printer has an online button).

3. If you have speakers or other devices connected to your computer, turn them on.

4. Be sure the floppy disk drive is empty. If it has a floppy disk in it, press the eject button on the drive and then gently remove the disk. (Don't worry about removing any CDs from the CD-ROM drive.)

5. Press the power button or flip the switch on the system unit. (On notebooks and some newer desktop models, you must hold the button for 1 or 2 seconds before releasing it.)

What happens next varies from one computer to another. Most computers perform a series of startup tests, load a set of basic instructions, and display text messages (white text on a black background) on the monitor. These messages typically disappear before you have time to read them, so don't worry if things seem to rush by too quickly. Your computer then runs its *operating system*. The operating system provides the basic instructions your computer needs in order to function.

def·i·ni·tion

A **user account** is an identification badge that enables each user to log on to Windows XP and set it up to suit his or her own tastes. It also provides some low-level security by requiring each user to sign on using a unique password (if a user chooses to do so). Skip to Chapter 7 for details.

Windows XP (the most popular operating system) prompts you to log on by clicking your user name, as shown in Figure 1.3. If this screen does not appear, your computer is set up for a single user and does not require a password to log on. If this screen does appear, click your user name and then, if requested, enter the password that has been assigned to this *user account*.

After you log on, your monitor should display the Windows desktop. Figure 1.4 shows the Windows XP desktop. If you have a different version of Windows, such as Windows 2000 (commonly used in business settings), or Windows Me (Millennium edition), the log on screens and desktop look different but function in much the same way. You might also encounter different displays on startup if your copy of Windows is set up to run additional software when it starts.

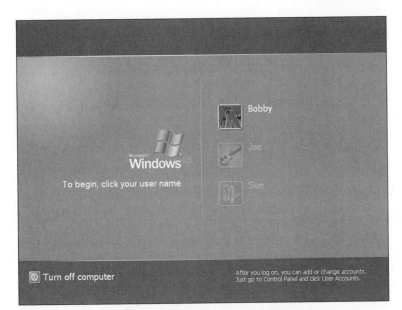

Figure 1.3

Click your user name.

Figure 1.4

When your computer finally settles down, it should display the Windows desktop.

Installing the Software That Runs Your Hardware

You're not the first person to have turned on your computer. The manufacturer or dealer turned it on right after it came off the assembly line to test the computer before shipping it. However, the manufacturer typically tests the computer without the printer and other accessories connected, so the first time you run your computer with everything connected, Windows runs the Add New Hardware Wizard. (A *wizard* is a series of screens that lead you step by step through the process of performing a task.)

The Add New Hardware Wizard steps you through the process of installing the software (called a *device driver*) that tells Windows how to communicate with a particular device. If a device came with its own device driver (on a floppy disk or CD), use that driver instead of the driver included with Windows. The Add New Hardware dialog box displays a **Have Disk** button, which you can click to install a driver from a disk or CD. Otherwise, you must install the driver from the Windows CD, which may be included with your system. Follow the onscreen instructions, as shown in Figure 1.5, and use your mouse as described in Chapter 2.

Figure 1.5

The Add New Hardware Wizard or Add Printer Wizard leads you through the process of installing a device driver.

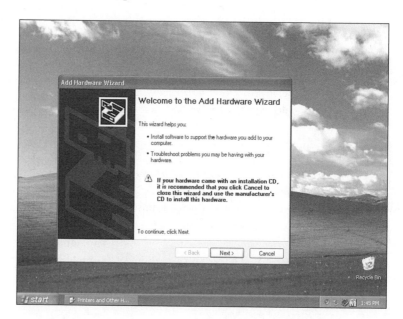

Now What?

You've arranged everything to your liking, turned everything on, and responded to any startup messages. Now what?

At this point, you're ready to start working (or playing). If the Windows desktop is displayed, as shown in Figure 1.3, you can click the **Start** button in the lower-left corner and point to **All Programs** to check out which games and programs are installed on your computer. The chapters in Part 2 show you how to move around in Windows and navigate the Windows desktop.

Shutting It Down or Leaving It On?

You might be wondering if it's better to leave your computer on or turn it off when you're not using it. In most cases, leaving the computer on is a good idea. Newer system units and monitors have built-in power-saving features that automatically shut down the devices that use the most power (disk drives and monitors) or place them in standby mode.

Turning your computer on and off places additional strain on the power switches and sensitive electrical components. Each time you turn the computer off and back on, the components cool down and heat up, which, over a long period of time, can cause components or solder joints to crack.

When your computer goes into power-saving mode, the screen might go blank. Don't panic. Your computer is just taking a snooze. The best way to wake it up is to press and release the **Shift** key. Sometimes you can wake your computer by rolling the mouse around, but the **Shift** key is more reliable—and because the **Shift** key doesn't type any characters or enter any commands, it's a safe way to snap your computer out of hibernation. On some computers, you have to tap the power button to wake up the computer.

> **Inside Tip**
>
> If you decide to leave your computer on all the time, consider purchasing an uninterruptible power supply to keep a steady flow of current running to your computer during short power outages or brownouts (those fluctuations that cause your lights to flicker and that might force your computer to restart).

If you decide to leave your computer on, be sure you save any documents you're working on before you step away from your computer. (You learn how to save documents in Chapter 12.) Saving a document records the document to a permanent storage medium, such as a hard drive, recordable CD, or flash drive, so that if the power goes out, you don't lose your work.

The Least You Need to Know

◆ Place your computer in an environment that is clean, dry, and cool.

◆ Plug all your computer components into a high-quality surge suppressor or uninterruptible power supply to prevent damage from lightning and power fluctuations.

◆ When inserting a connector into a port, be sure the pins align with the holes, and never force the connection.

◆ Turn on all the components that are connected to the central unit before you turn on the central unit so that your computer can identify the components during startup and you can view the startup messages.

◆ The first time you run your computer, you might need to install hardware drivers (software that tells Windows how to use specific devices).

◆ It's okay to leave your computer on when you're not using it, but be sure you save your work before you step away.

Taking the Wheel with Your Keyboard and Mouse

In This Chapter

- ◆ Ctrl, Alt, F1, and other bizarre keys
- ◆ Go beyond typing with a programmable keyboard
- ◆ Pointing, clicking, dragging, and other manic mouse moves
- ◆ Pointing devices for alternative types

If you're brave (and extremely patient), you can strap on a headset and microphone and train your computer to interpret commands and take dictation. However, most people still prefer using the more traditional, low-tech input devices—the mouse and keyboard. But even these tools require a little bit of technological know-how and manual dexterity to master. In this chapter you learn how to use these standard input devices along with a few other technologies to "talk" to your computer and enter text and other data.

Pecking Away at the Keyboard

The old, manual typewriter keyboard was fairly basic. It had letter keys, number keys, a shift key, a backspace key, and a spacebar. When you needed to start a new paragraph, you reached up and took a swipe at the carriage return. Newfangled computer keyboards are much more complex, as you can see in Figure 2.1. They still have the letter and number keys, but they also have several keys that you might not recognize:

- **Function keys.** The 10 or 12 F keys at the top or left side of the keyboard (F1, F2, F3, and so on) were frequently used in older programs to quickly enter commands. F1 is still used to display help in Windows and most Windows programs, and you can assign function keys to perform specialized tasks in most programs.

- **Arrow keys, Page Up, Page Down, Home, and End.** Also known as cursor-movement keys, these keys move the cursor (the blinking line or box) around onscreen. Wherever the cursor (also known as the insertion point) ends up is where your text will appear as you type.

- **Numeric keypad.** A group of number keys positioned like the keys on an adding machine. You use these keys to type numbers or to move around onscreen. Press the NumLock key to use the keys for entering numbers. With NumLock off, the keys act as arrow or cursor-movement keys. Most computers turn on NumLock on startup.

- **Ctrl and Alt keys.** The Ctrl (Control) and Alt (Alternate) keys make the other keys on the keyboard act differently from the way they normally act. For example, in Windows you can press Ctrl+A (hold down the Ctrl key then press A) to select all of the text or objects displayed in the current document. Some programs allow you to assign commonly used commands to short-cut keystrokes consisting of Ctrl, Alt, and Shift in combination with other keys.

- **Esc key.** You can use the Esc (Escape) key in most programs to back out of or quit whatever you are currently doing.

- **Print Screen/SysRq.** This sends the screen image to the Windows Clipboard, a temporary storage area for data. To learn more about the Clipboard, see Chapter 12.

◆ **Scroll Lock.** Another fairly useless key, in some programs Scroll Lock makes the arrow keys push text up and down on the screen one line at a time instead of moving the insertion point.

◆ **Pause/Break.** The king of all useless keys, Pause/Break is used to stop your computer from performing the same task over and over again—something that old programs seemed to enjoy doing. I have pressed this key only a few times, usually by mistake.

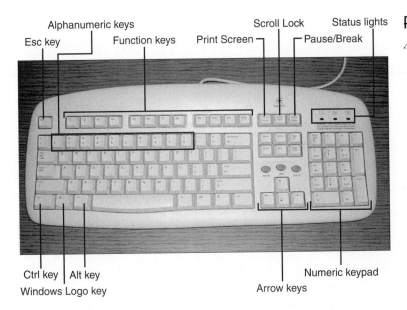

Figure 2.1

A typical keyboard.

Cutting Corners with the Windows Logo Key

Inspect your keyboard carefully to find the Windows Logo key. This key has a picture of a four-paned window that looks as though it is flying through the sky. The key is typically located near the lower-left corner of the keyboard—to the left of the spacebar. Keyboards with this key are called "Windows keyboards." Besides acting as a decorative addition to your keyboard, the Windows Logo key provides quick access to commonly entered Windows commands, as presented in Table 2.1.

Table 2.1   Windows Logo Key Shortcuts

Press	To
Windows	Open the Start menu.
Windows+Tab	Cycle through running programs in the taskbar.
Windows+F	Find a file.
Ctrl+Windows+F	Find a computer on a network.
Windows+F1	Display the Windows Help window.
Windows+R	Display the Run dialog box (for running programs).
Windows+Break	Display the System Properties dialog box.
Windows+E	Run Windows Explorer for managing folders and files.
Windows+D	Minimize or restore all program windows.
Shift+Windows+M	Undo minimize all program windows.

Dual-Function Keys on Notebook PCs

Portable computers, including notebook and laptop PCs, typically lack the space for a full set of keys plus buttons to turn on the computer, adjust the display, and move the mouse pointer. To fit all the keys and buttons in this limited amount of space, many keys are assigned double-duty. For example, some of the keys can be used to adjust the brightness and contrast of the display.

In most cases, the keyboard includes a key labeled Fn that is a different color (typically blue). Keys that perform double-duty have their primary functions displayed in black or white, and their secondary functions displayed in the same color used for the Fn key. To take advantage of the secondary function of the key, hold down the Fn key while pressing the key that is labeled with the desired secondary function.

Keyboards with Buttons (Programmable Keyboards)

Most keyboards include special buttons that enable you to quickly open your Internet home page, navigate the Internet, check e-mail, and put your computer in sleep mode. In addition, if you don't use one of the buttons for its designated function, you can reprogram it to perform some other time-saving shortcut. Figure 2.2 shows one of the more popular programmable keyboard models from Logitech.

Programmable buttons

Figure 2.2

An Internet keyboard contains buttons you can assign to your favorite web pages and programs.

(Photo courtesy of Logitech, Inc.)

Mastering Basic Mouse Moves

If you're the type of person who orders from the menu by pointing at the item of your choice rather than speaking to the waiter, you're going to love your computer's mouse. The mouse provides a more intuitive way for you to enter commands—you simply slide the mouse across your desk until the mouse pointer (on the monitor) is over the desired menu or object, and then you click (press and release) the left mouse button. Figure 2.3 shows a typical mouse. To use a mouse you must master the following basic moves:

- **Point.** Slide the mouse around until the tip of the onscreen arrow is over the item you want. Easy stuff.

- **Click.** Point to something (usually an icon or menu command), and then press and release the left mouse button. You can also click in a document to move the insertion point to where you want to type. When you click, be careful not to move the mouse when you click, or you might click the wrong thing or move an object unintentionally.

Inside Tip

A typical mouse has a ball inside it that turns rollers inside the mouse to move the mouse pointer on screen. The ball tends to pick up a lot of dust and hair, which eventually makes the mouse pointer move erratically. The newer, optical mouse, uses laser technology to sense the mouse movement, making the mouse much more reliable. You can clean a standard mouse, as explained in Chapter 28. An optical mouse usually requires no cleaning.

♦ **Right-click.** Same as a click but with the right mouse button. The right mouse button is used mainly to display context menus, which contain commands that apply only to the currently selected object.

♦ **Double-click.** Same as a click but you press and release the mouse button twice quickly without moving the mouse. Mastering this move takes some practice.

♦ **Drag.** Point to an object and then hold down the left mouse button while moving the mouse. You typically drag to move an object, select text (in a word processing program), or draw (in a drawing or paint program). In some cases, you can drag with the right mouse button; when you release the mouse button, a context menu typically appears asking what you want to do.

Figure 2.3

A typical mouse.

Mouse buttons

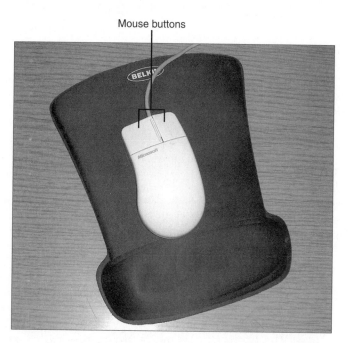

Mouse on Wheels

Computer designers have never been satisfied with the standard, two-button mouse. They've tried adding a third button, adding shortcut buttons (like those on a programmable keyboard), and modifying the shape of the mouse. I have even seen a new mouse that includes an FM radio tuner, so you can listen to the radio while you work! Finally, designers have come up with a relatively stable design called the IntelliMouse as shown in Figure 2.4. Similar in shape to the standard two-button Microsoft mouse, the IntelliMouse has a small, gray wheel between the left and right buttons. Although it feels like a growth on an otherwise smooth mouse, the wheel gives you more control over scrolling and entering commands and is fairly easy to use.

The left and right mouse buttons work as they always have; however, in applications that support the IntelliMouse (including most Microsoft applications), you can do two things with the wheel: spin it and click it. What spinning and clicking do depends on the application. For example, in Microsoft Word you can use the wheel to scroll more accurately, as described here:

◆ Rotate the wheel away from yourself to scroll text up; rotate toward yourself to scroll down.

◆ To pan up or down, click and hold the wheel while moving the mouse pointer in the direction of the text you want to bring into view. (Panning is sort of like scrolling, but it's smoother.)

◆ To autoscroll up or down, click the wheel and then move the mouse pointer up (to scroll up) or down (to scroll down). Autoscrolling remains on until you click the wheel again.

◆ To zoom in or out, hold down the **Ctrl** key and rotate the wheel. Rotate away from yourself to zoom in or toward yourself to zoom out.

Wheel

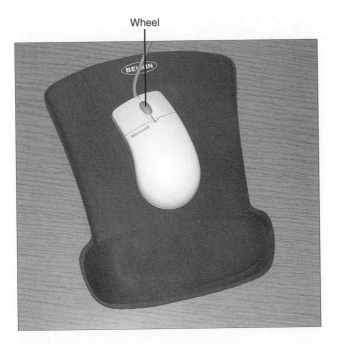

Figure 2.4

The IntelliMouse sports a wheel between its two buttons.

Customizing Your Mouse

If you're a lefty or if you have trouble clicking fast enough to execute a double-click, you will be happy to know that you can customize your mouse to accommodate the way you work. In Windows XP, click the **Start** button (in the lower-left corner of the screen) and click **Control Panel.** Click or double-click **Printers and Other Hardware** and then click or double-click **Mouse.** This opens the Mouse Properties dialog box, shown in Figure 2.5. You can use this dialog box to specify the function of each mouse button and the appearance of the mouse pointers.

Figure 2.5

The Mouse Properties dialog box enables you to customize the mouse and mouse pointer.

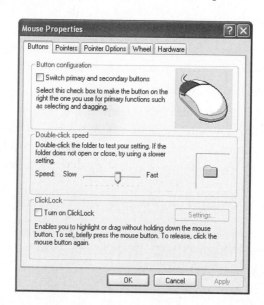

If you have a different version of Windows, such as Windows Me, display the Control Panel by clicking the **Start** button, pointing to **Settings,** and clicking **Control Panel.** When the Control Panel appears, double-click the **Mouse** button and use the resulting dialog box to enter your settings. The chapters in Part 2 provide additional instructions on how to customize Windows for the way you work.

Panic Attack

Click or double-click? Your version of Windows may enable you to click the Mouse icon once to open the Mouse Properties dialog box or it may require you to double-click the icon. In Chapter 6, you learn how to adjust the setting in Windows that controls this option. For now, you should know that if the icon's name appears underlined when the mouse pointer is resting on it, you can single-click; otherwise, you must double-click.

Pointing Devices for the Alternative Crowd

In search of the perfect pointing device, computer manufacturers have toyed with other ideas: trackballs, joysticks, touchpads, light-sensitive pens, and little gear shifts stuck in the middle of keyboards. I've even seen two-foot pedals set up to act like a mouse! The following list describes the more standard fare:

- **Trackball.** A trackball is an upside-down mouse (sort of). Instead of sliding the mouse to roll the ball inside the mouse, you roll the ball itself. The good thing about a trackball is that it doesn't require much desk space and it doesn't get gunked up from dust and hair on your desk. The bad thing about trackballs is that manufacturers haven't figured out a good place to put the buttons. You almost need two hands to drag with a trackball: one to hold down the button and the other to roll the ball. Stick with a mouse.

- **Touchpad.** A touchpad is a pressure-sensitive square that you slide your finger across to move the pointer. A typical touchpad has two buttons next to it that act like mouse buttons. You click or double-click the buttons or hold down a button to drag. With most touchpads you can also tap the touchpad itself to click or double-click. Touchpads are the pointing devices of choice on most notebook computers, but they can be temperamental, especially if your fingers are a little sweaty.

> **Inside Tip**
>
> Laptops typically come equipped with a touchpad or a pointer or both. Try out the different controls before purchasing a laptop computer, to see which you prefer. You can always add an external mouse to the laptop.

- **TrackPoint or AccuPoint pointers.** You've probably seen portable computers with a little red lever smack dab in the middle of the keyboard. The lever acts sort of like a joystick; you push the lever in the direction you want to move the mouse pointer. You use buttons next to the keyboard to click and drag.

- **Joystick.** A joystick is a must-have for most computer games. A standard joystick looks like a flight stick or one of those controls you've seen on video arcade games. It has a base with a lever sticking out of it, which you push or pull in the direction you want to move. The lever usually has a few buttons for blasting away at opponents and making a speedy getaway.

◆ **Voice activation.** For no-hands control over your computer, you can purchase voice activation software and bark commands into a microphone. With speech-recognition software, such as IBM's Via Voice, you can even type without touching your keyboard. Microsoft Office XP and later versions include voice activation features that enable you to enter commands and text in the Office applications: Microsoft Word, Excel, Access, Outlook, and PowerPoint.

The Least You Need to Know

◆ The 12 function keys on your keyboard are positioned across the top or along one edge of your keyboard.

◆ The Ctrl and Alt keys augment the standard keyboard keys to provide extra functions.

◆ The cursor keys move the cursor or insertion point around onscreen.

◆ The five basic mouse moves are point, click, right-click, double-click, and drag.

◆ The center wheel on an IntelliMouse can be used to make scrolling through documents and web pages easier.

◆ Other devices for poking around on your computer include a trackball, touch-pad, TrackPoint or AccuPoint pointer, joystick, and voice-recognition software.

Part 2

Navigating Microsoft Windows

A computer is like a newborn baby. It's packed with potential, but until it has operating system software that provides it with the instructions it needs to function, it's relatively unproductive. Fortunately, your computer comes equipped with an operating system called Windows that enables the computer to communicate with its various components and run application software that you can use to perform specific tasks and play games.

The chapters in this part show you how to use Windows and customize it to look and behave the way you want it to. By mastering the Windows basics, you're well on your way to mastering your computer as well as all of your applications.

Meeting Windows: Up Close and Personal

In This Chapter

- First encounters with your new electronic desktop
- Conversing with menus and dialog boxes
- Checking out a few choice Windows programs
- Moving, resizing, and hiding windows on your desktop
- Dumping stuff in the Recycle Bin and digging it out later

When you start a PC-compatible computer, it automatically runs some version of Windows: Windows XP, Windows Me (Millennium edition), Windows 98, Windows 95, or Windows 2000 (or Windows NT for networked computers). But what is Windows?

If you pry off the top of your desk and hang it on the wall, you have Windows ... well, sort of. Although its initial appearance might be deceiving, Windows is little more than an electronic desktop that's displayed on a two-dimensional vertical surface—your computer's monitor. It even comes complete with its own *desktop utilities*, including a calculator, a notepad, and a blank canvas that you can doodle on during your breaks.

This chapter teaches you the basics of how to work on your new computerized desktop.

Checking Out the Windows Desktop

When you first start your computer, your new desktop appears, very neat and tidy. Several *icons* (small pictures) dot the surface of the Windows desktop, and a gray or blue strip called the *taskbar* appears at the bottom of the screen, as shown in Figure 3.1 (unless you or someone else moved it). On the left end of the taskbar is the all-important **Start** button, which opens a menu containing the names of all the programs installed on your computer.

Figure 3.1

Initially, the Windows desktop is sparsely populated.

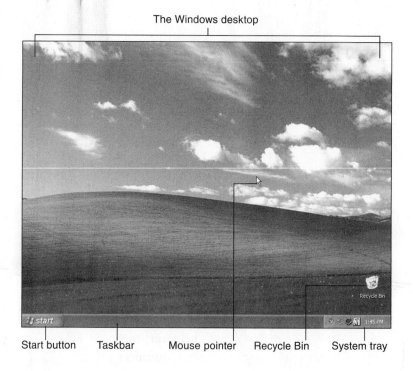

The Windows desktop

Start button · Taskbar · Mouse pointer · Recycle Bin · System tray

Before we start exploring the Windows desktop, find out which version of Windows you have. This book assumes you are using a relatively new computer that is running Windows XP—the most popular version of Windows for both home and business users. To find out which version of Windows you're running, right-click **My Computer** on the desktop (or click the **Start** button and right-click **My Computer),** and then click **Properties.** The System Properties dialog box appears, as shown in Figure 3.2, displaying the version of Windows installed on your computer along with some additional interesting tidbits about your computer.

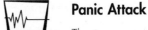

Panic Attack

The icons you see on your desktop might differ depending on how you or the manufacturer installed Windows and on whether you have additional programs.

Windows version

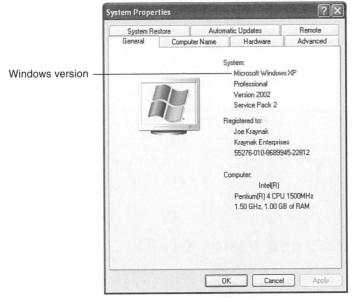

Figure 3.2

The System Properties dialog box.

If the icon names are underlined, you click an icon once to run its corresponding program. If the icon names are not underlined, you must double-click the icon to run the program. To enable the single-click option, take the following steps:

1. Double-click the **My Computer** icon on the Windows desktop, or click the **Start** button and click **My Computer.**

2. Click **Tools** in the menu bar near the top of the window and click **Folder Options.** (If **Folder Options** is not on your **Tools** menu, open the **View** menu by clicking it, and then click **Folder Options.)**

3. Click **Single-click to Open Item (Point to Select)** and then click **OK,** as shown in Figure 3.3.

4. Click **File** in the menu bar, and then click **Close.**

Figure 3.3

In Windows XP, turn on the Single-Click to Open Item option.

With the single-click option enabled, you simply point to icons to select them and single-click icons to activate them. With the single-click option disabled, you click to select and double-click to activate.

Ordering from Menus and Dialog Boxes

Computer technology hasn't quite reached the point of *2001: A Space Odyssey* (you know, that 1968 Stanley Kubrick flick in which the astronauts actually converse with Hal, the computer that runs the spaceship). However, Windows provides several ways for you to "talk" to your computer by clicking buttons, selecting menu commands, and responding to *dialog boxes* (onscreen fill-in-the-blank forms).

Clicking Menu Options

The Windows interactive tool of preference is the *menu*. You'll find menus everywhere: on the left end of the taskbar (the Windows **Start** menu), in menu bars near the top of most program windows, in toolbars, and even hidden inside objects. To open a menu, you simply click its name, and it drops down or pops up on the screen, as shown in Figure 3.4. Then you click the desired menu option. (To display a hidden—*context*—menu, right-click the desired object or the selected text or image.)

Click the menu's name to open it

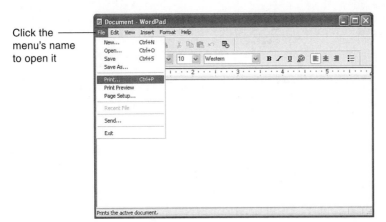

Figure 3.4

Menus are available in the menu bar at the top of most program windows.

Computer Cheat

To quickly open a menu without lifting your fingers from the keyboard, hold down the **Alt** key and press the key that corresponds to the underlined letter in the menu's name. For example, press **Alt+F** to open the **File** menu. Press **Shift+F10** to display a context menu for the currently selected text or object. To open the Windows **Start** menu, press **Ctrl+Esc**. Use the arrow keys to highlight the desired command and then press **Enter**.

As you flip through any menu system, you might notice that some of the menu options look a little strange. One option might appear pale. Another might be followed by a series of dots. And still others have arrows next to them. Their appearances tell you how these options behave:

◆ Light gray options are unavailable for what you are currently doing. For example, if you want to copy a chunk of text but you have not yet selected the text, the **Copy** command is not available; it appears light gray.

◆ An option with an arrow next to it opens a submenu that requires you to select another option. Point to the option to open the submenu.

◆ An option with a check mark indicates that an option is currently active. To turn the option off, click it. This removes the check mark; however, you won't know it, because selecting the option also closes the menu.

◆ An option followed by a series of dots (...) opens a dialog box that requests additional information. You learn how to talk to dialog boxes in the next section.

Whoa!

To further confuse new users, Microsoft has come up with something called the "smart" menu, featured in its Office applications, which lists only the most commonly selected options. To view additional options, you must point to a double-headed arrow at the bottom of the menu. In addition, the menu is designed to customize itself, so options automatically move up on the menu the more often you use them. In other words, you never know where they'll be. In case you can't tell, I think smart menus are pretty dumb.

Talking with a Dialog Box

If you choose a menu command that's followed by a series of dots (…), the program displays a *dialog box*, as shown in Figure 3.5, requesting additional information. You must then navigate the dialog box, select the desired options, type any required text entries, and give your okay—all using the following controls:

- **Tabs.** If a dialog box has two or more "pages" of options, tabs appear near the top of the pages. Use your mouse to click the tab for the desired options.

- **Text boxes.** A text box is a "fill in the blank"; it allows you to type text, such as the name of a file.

- **Option buttons.** Option buttons (also known as *radio buttons*) allow you to select only one option in a group. Click the desired option to turn it on and to turn any other selected option in the group off.

- **Check boxes.** Check boxes allow you to turn an option on or off. Click in a check box to turn it on if it's off or off if it's on. You can select more than one check box in a group.

- **List box.** A list box presents two or more options. Click the desired option. If the list is long, you'll see a scrollbar. Click the scrollbar arrows to move up or down in the list.

- **Drop-down list box.** You will see only one item when you first view this kind of list box. The rest of the items are hidden initially. Click the arrow to the right of the box to display the rest of the list, and then click the desired item.

Inside Tip

In the upper-right corner of most dialog boxes is a button with a question mark on it. Click the button, and a question mark attaches itself to the mouse pointer. Then you can click an option in the dialog box to display information about it. You can also right-click the option and choose **What's This?**

◆ **Spin box.** A spin box is a text box with controls. You can usually type a setting in the text box or click the up or down arrow to change the setting in predetermined increments. For example, you might click the up arrow to increase a margin setting by .1 inch.

◆ **Slider.** A slider is a control you can drag up, down, or from side to side to increase or decrease a setting. Sliders are commonly used to adjust speaker volume, hardware performance, and similar settings.

◆ **Command buttons.** Most dialog boxes have at least three buttons: **OK** to confirm your selections, **Cancel** to quit, and **Help** to get help.

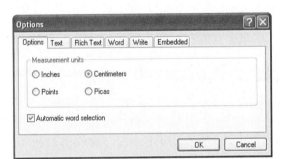

Figure 3.5

A dialog box asks you to enter additional information and settings.

Bypassing Menus by Using Toolbar Buttons

Although menus contain a comprehensive list of available options, they can be a bit clunky. To perform a task using a menu, you must click the menu name, hunt for the desired command, and then select it. To help you bypass the menu system, most programs include *toolbars* that contain buttons for the most frequently used commands. To perform a task, you simply click the desired button, as shown in Figure 3.6.

Inside Tip _____

Some of the pictures used to identify buttons are no more helpful than Egyptian hieroglyphics. To view the name of a button, rest the mouse pointer on it. A little yellow box, called a ScreenTip, pops up, showing the button's name.

Figure 3.6

Toolbars provide quick access to commonly used commands.

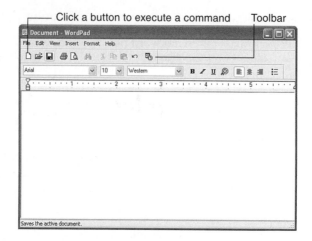

Checking Out Some Windows Programs

Chances are your computer came loaded with all sorts of software. If you purchased a home PC, it probably came with Microsoft Works or some other program suite (package) and a couple of computer games. But even if your computer wasn't garnished with additional programs, Windows has several programs you can use to write letters, draw pictures, play games, and perform other tasks.

To run any of these programs, click **Start,** point to **Programs** or **All Programs,** point to **Accessories,** and then click the program you want to run:

- ◆ **Games** is a group of simple computer games, including Solitaire. (You might find the Games submenu on the Programs or All Programs menu, rather than on the Accessories submenu.)

- ◆ **Entertainment** is a group of programs enabling you to play audio CDs and video, and adjust the speaker volume.

- ◆ **System Tools** is a collection of programs that help you maintain your system. These tools include a backup program, a program for fixing your hard disk, and a hard disk *defragmenter,* which can increase the speed of your disk. See Chapter 30 for details.

- ◆ **Calculator** displays an onscreen calculator to perform addition, subtraction, division, and multiplication.

- ◆ **Notepad** is a text editing program useful for typing notes and other brief documents.

- **Paint** is a graphics program for creating and printing pictures.

- **WordPad** is a more advanced word processing program that enables you to create fancier, longer documents.

Rearranging the Windows Inside Windows

Each time you run a program or open a document in Windows, a new window opens on your desktop. After several hours of work, your desktop can become as cluttered as a real desktop, making it difficult to locate your desktop utilities and documents. To switch to a window or reorganize the windows on the desktop, use any of the following tricks:

- To quickly change to a window, click its button in the taskbar. (To hide the window later, click its taskbar button again, or click the **Minimize** button in the upper-right corner of the window; it's the button with the small horizontal line on it.)

- If you can see any part of a window, click it to move it to the front of the stack.

- To quickly arrange the windows, right-click a blank area of the taskbar and, from the shortcut menu that appears, choose one of the following options: **Tile Windows Horizontally, Tile Windows Vertically,** or **Cascade Windows.**

- To close a window (and exit the program), click the **Close** button (the one with the *X* on it) that's located in the upper-right corner of the window, as shown in Figure 3.7.

- To increase the size of a window so that it takes up the whole screen, click the **Maximize** button (just to the left of the **Close** button). The **Maximize** button then turns into a **Restore** button, which you can click to return the window to its previous size.

Inside Tip _____

You can also double-click a window's title bar to maximize the window or restore it to its previous size.

- To shrink a window, click the **Minimize** button (two buttons to the left of the **Close** button). The minimized window appears as a button on the taskbar. Click the button on the taskbar to reopen the window.

♦ To resize or reshape a window that is not at its maximum size, place your mouse pointer in the lower-right corner of the window and, when the pointer turns to a double-headed arrow, drag the corner of the window. (You can't resize a maximized window.)

♦ To move a window, drag its title bar. (You can't move a maximized window, because it takes up the whole screen.)

Figure 3.7

You can close, maximize, and resize windows.

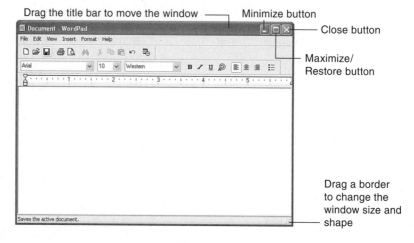

Drag the title bar to move the window — Minimize button — Close button — Maximize/ Restore button — Drag a border to change the window size and shape

You can also control your windows from the taskbar. Whenever you run a program, a button for it appears in the taskbar. The button acts like a toggle switch; click the program's button to open the program's window, and click again to hide the program's window. Right-click a program's button to display options for minimizing, maximizing, restoring, moving, resizing, or closing the program's window.

Try this trick: click a program's button in the taskbar, and then **Ctrl+click** all other program buttons. Right-click one of the buttons and click **Minimize.** All program windows are minimized, returning you to the Windows desktop. Pretty cool, huh? Well, there's actually an easier way. To the right of the **Start** button is a tiny toolbar called the Quick Launch toolbar, which contains buttons for Internet Explorer (Microsoft's web browser), Outlook Express (an e-mail program), Windows Media Player, and the desktop. Click the **Show Desktop** button or hold down the **Windows** key and press **D** to quickly return to the Windows desktop. Click the button again to return to your programs.

Seeing More with Scrollbars

If a window cannot display everything it contains, a scrollbar appears along the right side or bottom of the window. The scrollbar on the right enables you to scroll up and down; the scrollbar at the bottom lets you scroll left and right. You can use the scrollbar to bring the hidden contents of the window into view, as follows (see Figure 3.8):

- **Scrollbar.** Click once inside the scrollbar, on either side of the scroll box, to move the view one window at a time. For example, if you click once below the scroll box, you will see the next window of information.

- **Scroll box.** Move the mouse pointer over the scroll box, hold down the mouse button, and then drag the box to the area of the window you want to view. For example, to move to the middle of the window's contents, drag the scroll box to the middle of the bar.

- **Scroll arrow.** With the mouse pointer over the up or down scroll button, hold down the mouse button to scroll continuously in that direction. The insertion point remains in place when you scroll, so you can press the right or left arrow key to return to where you were.

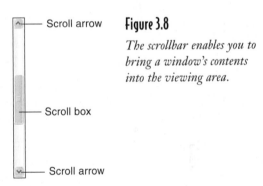

Scroll arrow

Scroll box

Scroll arrow

Figure 3.8

The scrollbar enables you to bring a window's contents into the viewing area.

Moving On Up to Windows Vista

During the writing of this book, Microsoft was wrapping up development and testing of its new version of Windows: Windows Vista. By the time you read this, Vista may be on the shelves, and if you just bought a new computer, it may come with Vista installed. So what can you expect from this new, improved version of Windows? The following list describes the most significant improvements:

◆ **Enhanced performance.** Vista makes smarter use of the latest technology in computer hardware to make your computer run faster and more reliably.

◆ **Renovated desktop.** You'll recognize most of the items on the desktop, including the **Start** button, taskbar, and Recycle Bin, but the overall appearance of Windows Vista is slicker, more transparent, and more three-dimensional. When you have multiple application windows open in Vista, you can flip through the stack in 3D, using the scroll button on your mouse. When you rest the mouse pointer on a taskbar button in Vista, a thumbnail view of the application's window pops up, so you can preview the window's contents before switching to it.

◆ **Powerful tools for finding files, folders, and programs.** Vista makes browsing and finding your files, folders, and programs much easier. When you open a disk or folder, the window that appears provides a Search option you can use to have Windows help you track down a misplaced file or folder. You can also search your desktop by typing a description of what you're looking for in the **Search** box on the **Start** menu. Preview options enable you to view the contents of a document before opening it.

◆ **Beefed-up media features.** Windows Vista supports the latest trends in media, enabling you to use your PC as a media center as well as a computer. With Windows Vista and the necessary hardware, you can watch TV on your computer, download and edit digital photos, and store and play all your favorite tunes.

◆ **Tightened security.** Vista has several built-in security features designed to automatically block unauthorized access to your computer over the Internet, prevent infection from computer viruses, and block Internet adware and spyware—two types of very intrusive software that you can learn more about in Chapter 25.

◆ **New Internet Explorer web browser.** In Chapter 19, you learn how to use a web browser to explore interactive, multimedia "pages" on the Internet. Vista features a new Internet Explorer window that enables you to explore the Internet more securely and flip through several open pages by clicking tabs.

◆ **New sidebar and gadgets.** The new sidebar in Windows Vista provides quick access to customizable mini-applications (called *gadgets*), which include weather updates, news headlines, late-breaking sports scores, your personal calendar, a calculator, and other often-used features and tools.

◆ **New backup utility.** Everyone tells you to back up the files on your computer, but Windows XP offers a shoddy backup utility. Vista improves the backup capabilities of Windows, enabling you to back up your files to recordable CDs or DVDs, external hard drives, and other backup media.

- **Speech recognition.** If you'd rather bark out commands than point and click with a mouse, Windows Vista can accommodate your preference. Equip your computer with a microphone, train Vista to tune its ear to your voice, and you're ready to enter commands and type without touching your keyboard or mouse. The more you use the feature, the better it works!

- **Windows SideShow.** Designed for notebook computers, Windows SideShow enables notebook computers to display critical information on a secondary or auxiliary screen whether the notebook is on, off, or in sleep mode. In other words, you don't have to power up your computer to view meeting schedules, phone numbers, addresses, and recent e-mail messages. This saves you gobs of time and conserves battery power at the same time. Of course, your notebook computer must be equipped with a secondary or auxiliary screen.

Whoa!

Windows Vista is a powerful operating system that requires powerful hardware to fully exploit all of its features. Computer manufacturers are marketing their new computers as "Vista capable" to help consumers choose computers that can run Vista more effectively. However, Vista is **scalable**; that is, it automatically takes an inventory of your system hardware and then scales its fancy graphics features and other advanced features to the capabilities of the available hardware.

The Least You Need to Know

- When you start your computer, Windows presents you with an electronic desktop on which you do all your work.

- When you choose an option that's followed by three dots, Windows displays a dialog box asking for additional information.

- Three buttons appear in the upper-right corner of every window. Use these buttons to open, close, or quickly hide (minimize) or restore the window.

- To manually resize a window, drag its lower-right corner.

- To scroll up or down in a window, click the scroll arrows at the top or bottom of the scrollbar, drag the scroll box, or click inside the scrollbar above or below the scroll box.

Chapter 4

Managing Disks, Folders, and Files

In This Chapter

◆ Identify your computer's disk drive (if it has one)

◆ Find drive A, C, D, and sometimes B

◆ Insert a disk into a disk drive and pull it out

◆ Explore your computer's disks, folders, and files in Windows

◆ Cut, copy, move, and dump files and folders

Your computer comes complete with a well-stocked library of instructions and data that it uses to function, to help you do your job, and to play games. This library is stored on various disks inside the computer. The hard disk (or *fixed disk*), which you never see, is hidden inside the system unit. Other disks, called *removable disks*, reside outside the computer. These are the disks or "floppy disks," CDs (compact discs), DVDs (digital video discs), and other disks (and discs) that you load into your computer's disk drives to install programs or copy files to your computer.

In this chapter, you learn everything you need to know about disks and drives, including how to insert and remove various types of disks; recognize a drive by its letter; keep your disks, CDs, and DVDs in good condition; and explore and manipulate the files and folders stored on your disks.

Disk Drives: Easy as A-B-C

Most computers have at least three disk drives, as shown in Figure 4.1. Your computer refers to the drives as A, C, and D. If you're wondering what happened to B, it's typically used only if the computer has a second floppy drive.

Figure 4.1

Your computer uses letters from the alphabet to name its disk drives.

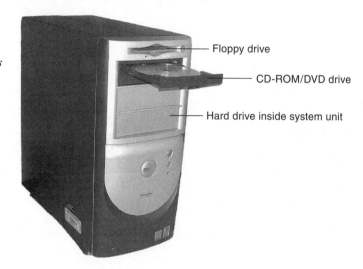

— Floppy drive

— CD-ROM/DVD drive

— Hard drive inside system unit

The Floppy Drives: A (and Sometimes B)

Your computer's system unit disk may have one or more slits or openings on the front, into which you can insert a disk. The slit may be horizontal or vertical, depending on how your system is set up. This is your computer's "floppy disk" drive. Your computer typically refers to this drive as drive A. If your computer has two floppy drives, the computer refers to the second drive as drive B; otherwise, the letter B is not applied to any of your computer's drives.

Panic Attack

If your computer has no floppy drive, don't panic—you might not need it. Many manufacturers exclude floppy drives from their PCs, because most programs are distributed on CDs.

The Hard Disk Drive: C

The drive inside the computer is the internal hard disk drive, usually called drive C. With hard drives you don't handle the disk; it's hermetically sealed inside the drive.

Inside Tip

A hard disk drive can be partitioned (or divided) into one or more drives, which the computer refers to as drive C, drive D, drive E, and so on. The actual hard disk drive is called the physical drive; each partition is called a logical drive. If you encounter a computer that displays letters for more than one hard drive, the computer might have multiple hard drives or a single drive partitioned into several logical drives. In some cases, the manufacturer places a copy of all the original software, including Windows, on a small partition instead of supplying the software on CDs.

The CD-ROM, CD-RW, or DVD Drive: D

A CD-ROM (Compact Disc-Read Only Memory) is standard equipment on every new computer. It typically is located on the front of the system unit above or below the floppy drive, and the computer typically refers to it as drive D. A standard CD-ROM drive can only read data from discs—it cannot write data to discs. However, most computers feature disc drives with more advanced functions. Following is a list of fairly common disc drives:

- **CD-R** drives can read data from CDs and can write data to special CD-R discs. These drives write data only once; they cannot erase data from a CD-R disc or record over it.

- **CD-RW** (CD-ReWritable) drives can read data from CDs and write data to CD-R or CD-RW discs. With CD-RW discs, the drive can record over data, erase data, and write data to the disc many times. This makes CD-RW drives an excellent choice for backing up the data files you create.

- **DVD** (Digital Video Disc) drives can play DVD videos and read data from DVDs. DVDs can store more than seven times as much data as can be stored on a CD, which is why they are used for full-length feature films.

- **CD/DVD, CD-R/DVD, or CD-RW/DVD** drives are combination drives that can read both CDs and DVDs. The CD-R/DVD and CD-RW/DVD drives can record data to CDs, but cannot record data to DVDs.

- ◆ **DVD-R** drives can record data to special DVD-R discs. These drives are excellent for storing home videos (which take up a great deal of storage space).

- ◆ **DVD-RW or DVD+RW** drives can record data to special DVD-RW discs, erase or record data over existing data, and write to a disc several times.

Serving Information to the Computer on Floppy Disks

A floppy disk is like a skinny cassette. To get information that's stored on the floppy disk into your computer, you must load the disk into your computer's floppy drive. Likewise, if there is something in your computer that you want to store for safekeeping or share with another user, you can copy the information from the computer to a floppy disk.

Two characteristics describe floppy disks: *size* and *capacity*. You can measure size with a ruler. All new computers use 3½-inch disks. Capacity is the amount of information the disk can hold; it's sort of like pints, quarts, and gallons. A 3½-inch high-density disk (typically labeled HD) can store 1.44MB (*megabytes*). A 3½-inch, double-density disk (typically labeled DD) can store 720KB (*kilobytes*).

def•i•ni•tion

> Capacity is measured in **kilobytes** (KB) and **megabytes** (MB). Each *byte* consists of 8 bits and is used to store a single character—A, B, C, 1, 2, 3, and so on. (For example, 01000001 is a byte that represents an uppercase *A*; each 1 or 0 is a bit.) A kilobyte is 1,024 bytes (1,024 characters). A megabyte is a little more than a million bytes. A gigabyte is just more than 1,000 megabytes. A terabyte is more than a thousand gigabytes!

Floppy disks are fairly sturdy. You can fling a disk across the room, and it probably will survive the flight. However, you should be somewhat gentle with your disks, especially if they contain data that you don't want to lose. To avoid damaging the sensitive magnetic media inside the disk case, don't slide open the metal piece that covers the disk, don't store it next to magnets or devices that generate strong magnetic fields (such as speakers or fans), don't carry the disk around in your pocket or purse, don't eject the disk when the drive light is on, and never use a disk as a drink coaster. When you're not using a disk, keep it in a pouch or envelope to prevent it from collecting dust.

To load a floppy disk in your computer's floppy drive, insert the disk, label side up, into the drive and push it all the way in. (If the disk slot is vertical, hold the disk so the label faces away from the eject button.) To eject a floppy disk, make sure the drive light is off, press the eject button on the drive, and then pull out the disk.

Loading and Unloading CDs and DVDs

If you ever have loaded a compact disc into your audio CD player or a DVD into your DVD player, you have all the technical expertise required to load discs into your computer's CD or DVD drive. Just be sure to handle the disc only by its edges so that you don't scratch the surface or get any dirt or fingerprints on it. The technique for loading a disc in a CD or DVD drive differs depending on the drive. The following list covers the three most common ways to load a disc:

- ◆ If the drive has an open slot on the front, slide the disk, shiny side down, into the slot, just as you would insert a coin in a Coke machine.

- ◆ If the drive has a drive tray, press the load/eject button on the front of the drive to open it, and then lay the disc in the tray and press the load/eject button to load the disc.

- ◆ If the drive has a removable carriage, which is rare, press the load/eject button to eject the carriage, remove the carriage from the drive, place the disc inside the carriage, and insert the carriage into the drive.

Panic Attack

If you ever have trouble playing a CD or DVD, the disc might be dirty. To clean the disc, wipe it off with a soft, lint-free cloth from the center of the disc out to its edges. (Wipe the side without the picture or printing on it, because this is the side that the drive reads.) If something sticky gets on the disc, dampen the cloth with a little distilled water and wipe. Let the disc dry thoroughly before inserting it into the drive.

Whoa!

Windows should start to play the audio CD as soon as you insert it. If you're using Windows XP, and Windows does not start to play the CD, hold down the **Alt** key while double-clicking the **My Computer** icon and then click the **Device Manager** tab. Click the plus sign next to CD-ROM, and then double-click the name of your CD-ROM. Click the **Settings** tab and make sure there is a check mark in the **Auto Insert Notification** box. Click **OK** to save your changes and click **OK** again to close the System Settings dialog box.

Inside the Belly of Your Computer: The Hard Disk

The hard disk drive is like a big floppy drive complete with a non-floppy disk. (You don't take the disk out; it stays in the drive forever.) A small hard disk drive can store more than 20 gigabytes (GB), the equivalent of about 15,000 3½-inch, high-density floppy disks. Many new computers come with hard drives that can store more than 100 gigabytes! Sound excessive? Well, 100 gigabytes is excessive if you plan on using your computer to play games and do a little work; if you plan on editing video and storing photo albums on your computer, however, your computer can gobble up a gigabyte in a hurry. A 20 to 30GB hard drive is plenty for most users.

> **Inside Tip** _____
>
> If your computer is part of a network, it might not have a disk drive. If that's the case, forget all this babble about floppy disks, CDs, and hard drives. Your network probably has a central network server with a disk drive as big as a building that stores all the information and programs you and everyone else in the company will ever need.

To get information to the hard disk, you copy information to it from floppy disks, CDs, DVDs, or Internet sites, or you save the files you create directly to the hard disk. The information stays on the hard disk until you erase the information. When the computer needs information it goes directly to the hard disk, reads the information into memory, and continues working.

The Outsiders: External Drives and Other Anomalies

Although the hard disk, CD-ROM, and floppy disk drives round out the team lineup for standard drives, other types of disk drives have been and continue to be popular additions to computer systems. Some of these drives are installed in the drive bays inside the system unit and appear next to the floppy and CD-ROM drives, whereas others sit outside the system unit, like your printer, and connect to the system unit with a USB cable or other type of cable. The following list describes some of these more popular add-on drives:

◆ **Iomega Zip drives** store data on 100MB, 250MB, or 750MB removable disks. These drives are excellent for doing small backups and for storing presentations that you need to take on the road.

◆ **External hard drives** sit outside the computer and are connected to the system unit by a data cable; the extra drive typically is assigned a letter that comes later in the alphabet, such as E or F.

◆ **USB flash drives** are small enough to fit on a keychain and plug right into your computer's USB port. They typically store between 64MB and 1GB per card and are great for carrying around audio clips, digital images, and other files. Before removing a flash drive from a USB port, click the **Safely remove hardware** icon in the lower right corner of the screen, so you won't lose information stored on the flash drive.

◆ **Compact Flash drives** are used primarily in digital cameras and printers designed to print digital photos. The cards are smaller but a little fatter than a credit card and generally store anywhere from 256MB to several gigabytes of data.

◆ **Tape drives** are more similar to audio cassettes than they are to disks. Tape drives are primarily used to back up data. They're too slow for most other purposes.

What's on a Disk? Files and Folders

Your computer uses two types of files: *data files* and *program files*. Data files are the files you create and save—your business letters, reports, the pictures you draw, the results of any games you save. Program files are the files you get when you purchase a program. These files contain the instructions that tell your computer how to run the program. A program can consist of hundreds of interrelated files.

To manage all of these files, your computer stores the files in separate folders (also called *directories*). Whenever you install a program, the installation utility (which places the program on your hard disk) automatically creates a folder for the program.

Before you lay your fingers on any folders or files, you should understand how the folders are structured. Think of your disk as an oversized filing cabinet stuffed with manila folders. Each folder represents a directory that stores files or additional folders. The structure of the folders comprises what is called a *directory tree*, which looks a little like a family tree, as shown in Figure 4.2. The drive letter always sits atop the directory tree; the drive letter is considered to be the *root directory*. Folders then branch off from the root directory. Programs often display the location of a file as a *path* to the directory or folder in which the file is saved. For example, if Tom's My Documents folder contains a file named taxes.doc, the path to the file would be as follows:

```
c:\documents and settings\tom\my documents\taxes.doc
```

The path begins at the root (drive C), proceeds through the first folder to the second folder, through the third folder, and then specifies the file name. Paths can be much longer, of course.

Figure 4.2

Directory tree.

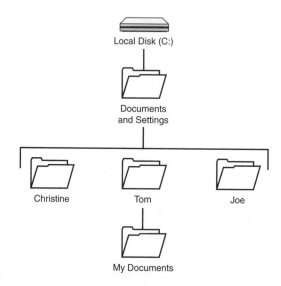

Exploring Your Disks and Folders

Windows gives you two ways to poke around on your computer and find out what's on your disks and what's in your folders. You can double-click the **My Computer** icon on the Windows desktop (or click the **Start** menu and click **My Computer**), or you can run Windows Explorer by taking the following steps:

1. Click Start.

2. Point to **All Programs.**

3. Point to **Accessories.**

4. Click **Windows Explorer.**

To find out what's on a disk or in a folder, double-click its icon. (Remember, if your icons are underlined, click once; double-clicking these icons might perform the action twice.) In Windows XP, My Computer displays icons for all disks plus a bar on the left that contains icons for system tasks, network resources, and other items, as shown in Figure 4.3.

Navigation bar

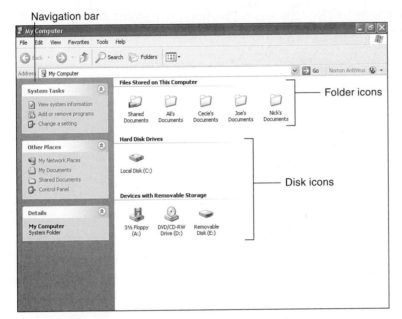

Figure 4.3

My Computer enables you to explore the contents of your computer's disk drives.

Windows Explorer is My Computer's older, more capable sibling. It allows you to perform the same basic tasks you can perform in My Computer, but it provides a two-pane window that displays a folder list on the left and a file list on the right. This two-paned layout lets you easily copy and move files and folders from one disk or folder to another by dragging them from one pane to the other, as shown in Figure 4.4.

Computer Cheat

You can make Windows Explorer or any other program more accessible by placing an icon for it on the Windows desktop. Open the **Start** menu and display the icon for Windows Explorer or whichever program you want to add to the desktop. Right-click the icon, point to **Send To,** and click **Desktop (Create Shortcut).**

Figure 4.4

Windows Explorer is a useful tool for copying and moving files.

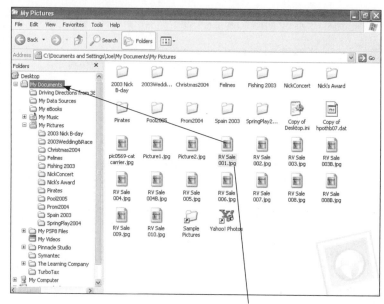

You can drag files from one pane to the other to copy or move them to other disks and folders

Copying, Moving, and Dumping Files and Folders

Using My Computer or Windows Explorer, you can copy files from any disk. On hard disk drives, floppy disks, and other rewritable storage media, you have complete control over the folders and files on the disks. You can copy files, move files from one disk or folder to another, or even delete files or folders to completely remove them from a disk. The following sections show you how to perform these essential disk-management tasks.

Selecting Folders and Files

If you're copying, deleting, or moving a single file or folder, selecting it is about as easy as picking a lemon off a used car lot. If the file or folder name is underlined, simply rest the tip of the mouse pointer on the icon for the file or folder you want to select. If the file or folder name is not underlined, click the file or folder. You would think that if you clicked another file or folder you'd select that one, too, but it doesn't work that way. Selecting another file deselects the first one. This can be maddening to anyone who doesn't know the tricks for selecting multiple files or folders; here's how you do it:

◆ To select neighboring (*contiguous*) files and folders, click the first file or folder and hold down the **Shift** key while pointing to or clicking the last file or folder in the group (see Figure 4.5).

◆ To select non-neighboring (*noncontiguous*) items, hold down the **Ctrl** key while pointing to or clicking the name of each item.

◆ To deselect an item, hold down the **Ctrl** key while pointing to or clicking its name.

◆ You also can select a group of items by dragging a box around them. When you release the mouse button, all the items within the box's borders are highlighted.

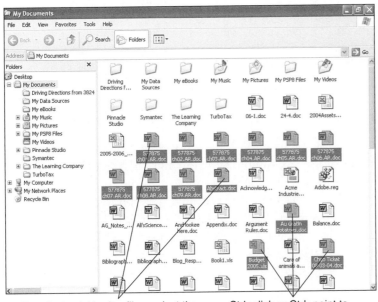

Figure 4.5

You can use the Shift and Control keys to select neighboring or non-neighboring files.

To select neighboring files, select the first file and then hold down the Shift key while selecting the last file

Ctrl+click or Ctrl+point to select non-neighboring files

When you're selecting groups of files, it often helps to change the way the files are sorted or arranged. Open the **View** menu and choose to sort files by name, by type (using their file name extensions), by size, or by date. For example, you can sort files by type to list all the document files that end in .DOC. You also can arrange the icons by opening the **View** menu and selecting one of the following options.

- **Large Icons.** Good if you want to select only a few files or folders.

- **Small Icons.** Displays tiny icons. Folders appear at the top, files at the bottom. In this display you can drag a box around items down and to the right.

- **List.** Displays tiny icons (just like Small Icons view), but folders (directories) are listed on the left; files are listed on the right.

- **Details.** Displays additional information such as the date and time at which files were created. (This view makes it tough to manage large numbers of files.)

Inside Tip

In Small Icons view, if you click an item in one column and Shift+click an item in another column, you select a rectangular block of items, just as if you had dragged a box around them. In List view, items snake up and down a page like newspaper columns. If you click an item in one column and Shift+click an item in another column, you select the two items you clicked and all the items in between.

Making Your Own Folders

You rarely need to create your own folders. When you install a program it usually makes the folders it requires or uses existing folders. In addition, Windows creates a folder for you called My Documents, in which you can save all the files you create. However, if you want to store your files in a different folder or you want to store files in a subfolder inside the My Documents folder, you need to know how to create a folder. Give it a shot; create a new folder on drive C. You can always delete the folder later if you don't need it. Follow these steps:

1. Run **My Computer.**

2. Double-click the icon for drive **C.** A window opens showing all the folders on drive C.

3. Right-click a blank area inside the window to display a shortcut menu.

4. Rest the mouse pointer on **New** and then click **Folder.** Windows creates a folder on drive C, cleverly called New Folder.

5. Type a name for the folder (255 characters or fewer). As you start typing, the **New Folder** name is deleted and is replaced by what you type. You can use almost any character or number, but you cannot use any of the following characters: \ / : * ? " < > |.

6. Press **Enter.**

Long names (255 characters for folders and files) are great for programs that support them, but some older programs cannot display them. In such cases the program displays a portion of the name, such as letter~1.doc. This does not affect the contents of the file, and you can still open it.

Dumping Files in the Recycle Bin

Windows comes complete with its own trash compactor. Whenever a file or icon has outlived its usefulness, either drag it over the trash can icon (the **Recycle Bin**) and release the mouse button, or click the file in My Computer or Windows Explorer to select it and then click the **Delete** button (the button with the *X* on it just below the menu bar) or press the **Del** key. Windows displays a dialog box asking you to confirm the deletion or cancel it; respond accordingly. If you confirm the deletion, Windows moves the file to the Recycle Bin without permanently deleting it, so you can recover it later should the need arise.

Pulling things out of the **Recycle Bin** is as easy as dragging them into it. Double-click the **Recycle Bin** icon to display its contents. If the icon names are underlined, rest the mouse pointer on the icon you want to restore to highlight it. If the icon names are not underlined, click the item you want to restore to select it. **Ctrl+point** or **Ctrl+click** to select additional items. Open the **File** menu and click **Restore.**

Whoa!

Never delete program files, because doing so may incapacitate your program. If you want to remove a program, use the Windows Add/Remove Program utility, which is explained in Chapter 5.

Inside Tip

To change the properties of the **Recycle Bin,** including the maximum amount of disk space it can use, right-click the **Recycle Bin** icon and click **Properties.** To empty the Recycle Bin, first make sure it contains only those files and folders you will never ever need. Then right-click the **Recycle Bin** icon and click **Empty Recycle Bin.**

Renaming Folders and Files

Managing your folders and files is an exercise in on-the-job training. As you create and use folders, you find yourself slapping any old name on them. Later you find that the name doesn't accurately describe the folder's contents or is too long, or you are just plain sick of seeing it snake across your screen. Fortunately, renaming a folder or file is easy:

◆ If you click files and folders to select them, click the icon for the file or folder you want to rename. The name appears highlighted, as shown in Figure 4.6. Click the name of the file or folder and type the new name. Click a blank area of the screen to make the name change official.

Whoa!

Windows uses the names of program folders to find the program files it needs to run the programs. If you rename a program folder or file, Windows usually throws a fit and won't run the program for you.

◆ If you point to files and folders to select them, right-click the file or folder you want to rename and click **Rename.** Type the new name and press **Enter** or click a blank area in the window.

◆ Whether you point to or click files or folders to select them, highlight the file or folder name by pointing at it or clicking it, press the **F2** key, and type the new name. Press **Enter.**

Figure 4.6

You can easily rename files and folders.

Type a new name

Moving and Copying Folders and Files

You can quickly move files and folders to reorganize them. To move an item, simply drag it over the folder or disk icon to which you want to move it. When moving or copying files and folders, keep the following in mind:

◆ To copy or move multiple files or folders, select the items as explained earlier in this chapter. When you copy or move one of the selected items, all the other items follow it.

◆ If you drag a folder or file to a different disk (or a folder on a different disk), Windows assumes that you want to *copy* the item to that disk. To move the item, hold down the **Shift** key while dragging.

◆ If you drag a folder or file to a different folder on the same disk, Windows assumes that you want to *move* the item into the destination folder. To copy the item, hold down the **Ctrl** key while dragging.

◆ To move a file or folder to the Windows desktop, drag it from My Computer or Windows Explorer onto a blank area on the desktop and release the mouse button.

◆ If you're not sure what you want to do, drag the folder or file with the right mouse button. When you release the button a context menu appears, presenting options for moving or copying the item.

Sometimes the easiest way to move a file or folder is to cut and paste it. Right-click the icon for the item you want to move and click **Cut.** Now change to the disk or folder in which you want the cut item placed. Right-click the disk or folder icon (or right-click a blank area in its contents window), and then click **Paste.** You also can copy and move items in Windows Explorer by dragging items from the Contents list (right pane) over a disk or folder icon displayed in the left pane. You also can drag items from one My Computer window to another.

The Least You Need to Know

◆ Your computer identifies your disk drives using letters: A and B for floppy disk drives; typically C for your hard drive; and D, E, F, and so on for additional drives, such as CD-ROM drives.

◆ Be gentle with floppy disks, CDs, and DVDs.

◆ When inserting floppy disks, CDs, and DVDs, never force the disk or disc into the drive. This can damage the disks and the drive's read/write head.

◆ When you create and save a document, it is stored as a named file on your computer's hard disk.

◆ Folders hold a group of related files on a disk.

◆ Use My Computer or Windows Explorer to see what's on your disks and to move, copy, rename, or delete files and folders.

Installing, Running, and Uninstalling Programs

In This Chapter

- ◆ Picking programs your computer can run

- ◆ Installing a program in 10 minutes or less

- ◆ Running programs from the Start menu

- ◆ Making your favorite programs more accessible

- ◆ Getting rid of the programs you don't use

Without programs, a computer is just a fancy box packed with electronic circuitry. Programs enable you to harness the power of that circuitry and use it to perform specific tasks, such as typing a letter, keeping your checkbook balanced, surfing the Internet, and playing video games.

This chapter shows you how to take control of programs. Here you learn how to buy and install programs, run programs installed on your computer, and uninstall programs you no longer use.

def•i•ni•tion

Throughout this book, I use the terms **program** and **software** interchangeably. These terms refer to the instructions that control the operation of the computer. Your computer uses two types of software: **operating system** software (Windows), which controls the overall operation of the computer; and **application** software, which enables you to perform specific tasks, such as typing a letter.

Buying Software Your Hardware Can Run

Even the most experienced computer user occasionally slips up and buys a program that his or her computer can't run. The person might own a PC running Windows and pick up the Macintosh version of the program by mistake. Or maybe the program requires special audio or video equipment that the person doesn't have.

Before you purchase any program, read the minimum hardware requirements printed on the outside of the package to determine if your computer has what it takes to run the program:

- ◆ **Computer type.** Typically, you can't run a Macintosh program on a Windows-compatible computer (a PC or *personal computer* that runs Windows). If you have a PC, be sure the program is for Windows. (Some programs include both the Macintosh and Windows PC versions.)

- ◆ **Operating system.** Try to find programs that are designed specifically for the operating system you use. If your computer is running Windows XP, don't buy a program developed exclusively for Windows 2000. (Although Windows XP can run most applications designed for Windows 2000, Windows XP might have problems running some Windows 2000 programs.)

- ◆ **Free hard disk space.** When you install a program, the installation routine copies files from the installation floppy disks or CDs to the hard disk. Be sure your hard disk has enough free disk space, as explained in the next section.

- ◆ **CPU requirements.** CPU stands for *central processing unit*. This is the brain of the computer. If the program requires at least a Pentium 4 processor, and you have a Pentium III, your computer won't be able to run the application effectively.

- ◆ **Type of monitor.** All newer monitors are SVGA (Super Video Graphics Array) or better, and most programs don't require anything better than SVGA.

◆ **Graphics card.** Some games and graphics programs require a specific type of graphics card (display adapter), such as a 3D card or an advanced video card.

◆ **Mouse.** If you use Windows, you need a mouse (or some other pointing device). A standard two-button Microsoft mouse is sufficient. Some programs have special features you can use only with an IntelliMouse.

◆ **Joystick.** Although most computer games allow you to use your keyboard, games are usually more fun if you have a joystick.

◆ **CD-ROM or DVD-ROM drive.** If you have a CD-ROM or DVD-ROM drive, it usually pays to get the CD-ROM or DVD-ROM version of the application instead of using a floppy disk version. This simplifies the program installation, and the CD or DVD version might come with a few extras. Check for the required speed of the drive, too.

◆ **Sound card.** Most new applications require sound cards. If you plan on running any cool games, using a multimedia encyclopedia, or even exploring the Internet, you need a sound card, which most computers already have installed. Some applications can use an old 8-bit sound card, but newer applications require a 16-bit or better sound card, which enables stereo output.

◆ **Amount of memory (RAM).** If your computer does not have the required memory (also known as *RAM*, short for *random access memory*), it might not be able to run the program, or the program might cause the computer to crash (freeze up).

def•i•ni•tion

Your computer has two types of storage—disk storage (permanent) and RAM or ran-dom access memory (temporary). Memory provides the computer with fast access to data and instructions, but when you turn off your computer, whatever is stored in memory is erased. Disk storage, on the other hand, stores data and instructions permanently (until you choose to delete them). When your computer needs data or instructions, it reads from the disk and stores the information in memory, where it can process it.

You can find out most of what you need to know about your computer from the System Properties dialog box. Click **Start**, right-click **My Computer,** and then click **Properties** to display the System Properties dialog box, as shown in Figure 5.1. The **General** tab displays the operating system type and version number, the type of processor, and the amount of RAM. Click the **Device Manager** tab and click the plus sign next to a device type to view its make and model number. For instance, click the plus sign next to **Display Adapters** to determine the type of video card that's installed.

Figure 5.1

The System Properties dialog box can tell you a lot about your computer.

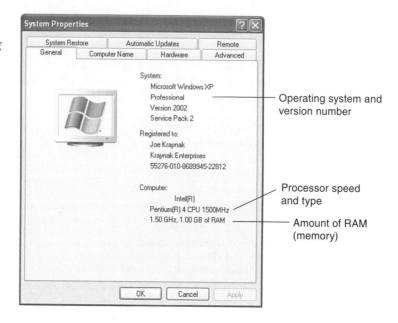

Operating system and version number

Processor speed and type

Amount of RAM (memory)

For more detailed system information, check out the Windows System Information tool. Open the **Start** menu, point to **Programs** or **All Programs, Accessories, System Tools,** and click **System Information.**

Do You Have Enough Disk Space?

Most new computers sport a multi-gigabyte hard drive that has enough free space to last you well into the next decade. However, you should be sure that your new program will fit on the disk before you start the installation. If you try to stuff a program on a hard disk that's nearly full, you'll have some serious warning messages to deal with, and you can count on your system locking up sometime during the installation.

Checking the available disk space is easy. Right-click the icon for your hard disk drive in My Computer or Windows Explorer, and then click **Properties.** The Properties dialog box displays the total disk space, the amount in use, and the amount that's free, as shown in Figure 5.2.

If your hard disk does not have sufficient free space for installing the program, you can free up some disk space using the Windows Maintenance Wizard, as described in Chapter 30.

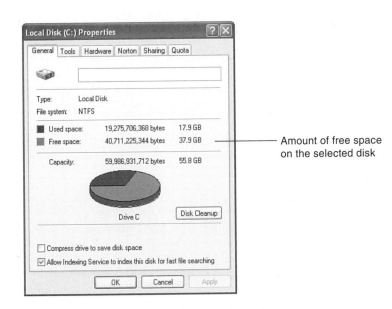

Figure 5.2

Windows displays the available space remaining on the disk.

Amount of free space
on the selected disk

Installing Your New Program

Nearly every program on the market comes with an installation component (called Setup or Install) that does everything for you. If the program is on CD-ROM, you can usually pop the disc into your CD-ROM drive, click a few options to tell the program that it can install the program according to the default settings, and then kick back and watch the installation routine do its thing.

If the program comes on floppy disks, or if the setup component on the CD doesn't start automatically when you insert the disc, take the following steps to kick start the setup routine:

1. If you haven't inserted the program CD or the first floppy disk into the drive, insert the CD or disk now.

2. Double-click **My Computer** on the Windows desktop or click the **Start** button and click **My Computer.**

3. Double-click the icon for your CD-ROM or floppy drive. This displays a list of files and folders on the disk or CD.

4. Double-click the file named **Setup, Install,** or its equivalent (refer to the program's installation instructions if necessary). This starts the installation utility.

5. Follow the onscreen instructions to complete the installation.

Panic Attack

If you cannot find the Setup or Install file, Windows can help you locate the file that initiates the installation routine. Open the **Start** menu and click **Control Panel** (in Windows XP) or choose **Start, Settings, Control Panel** (in earlier Windows versions). Double-click the **Add/Remove Programs** or **Add or Remove Programs** icon. Click the **Install** button or **Add New Programs** link, and follow the onscreen instructions.

Running Your Programs

An empty desktop might be a rare and beautiful sight, but it's useless. To get something done, have some fun, or at least make your boss think you're productive, you need a little clutter. You need to run a program or two.

The standard (albeit slow) method of running a program is to open the **Start** menu and click the name of the desired program. However, Windows provides several more creative and much faster ways to run programs with a single click of the mouse. The following sections reveal various ways to run programs in Windows.

Picking a Program from the Start Menu

Whenever you install a program, the installation utility places the program's name on the **Start, All Programs** menu or one of the All Programs menu's submenus. To run the program, you simply click the **Start** button, point to **All Programs,** point to the desired program group (the name of the program's submenu), and click the program's name, as shown in Figure 5.3.

Computer Cheat

For some programs, the installation utility places a shortcut icon on the Windows desktop or at the top of the **Start** menu so that you don't have to poke around on the **Start** menu to find the program.

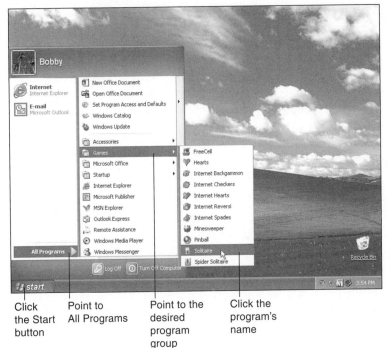

Figure 5.3

You can find all installed programs on the Start, All Programs menu.

Click the Start button | Point to All Programs | Point to the desired program group | Click the program's name

Making Your Own Program Shortcut

The Windows desktop displays a few icons, called *shortcuts*, that let you run commonly used programs. Unlike bona fide icons that represent files, these "dummy" icons merely point to the original files. Windows displays a small arrow in the lower-left corner of each shortcut icon to indicate that the icon doesn't represent an actual file.

If you frequently run a program, you can create your own shortcut for that program and place it on the Windows desktop by performing the following steps:

1. Open the **Start** menu, point to **All Programs,** and point to the submenu that contains the desired program.

2. Right-click the name of the program you want to add to the desktop.

3. Point to **Send To** and then click **Desktop (Create Shortcut).**

Inside Tip

Deleting a shortcut does not delete the original file it points to. However, deleting an actual file or program icon does delete the corresponding document or program file. Be careful whenever you choose to delete any icon.

You can create desktop shortcuts for just about any object in Windows: a disk, folder, file, or program. Simply right-click the icon and choose **Create Shortcut.** This places the shortcut inside the same window or on the same menu as the original. You must then drag the icon to a blank area of the desktop.

Running Programs from Your Keyboard

You don't need a fancy programmable keyboard to have quick keyboard access to your programs. Windows lets you program any standard keyboard to run programs with a single key press. First, however, you must assign a keystroke to the desired program. To do so, follow these steps:

1. Right-click the program's icon and choose **Properties.** (The icon might be on the **Start, All Programs** menu, on the Windows desktop, or in My Computer or Windows Explorer.)

2. Click in the **Shortcut Key** text box.

3. Press the key that you want to use to run this program. You can use any key except **Esc, Enter, Tab, Spacebar, Backspace, Print Screen,** or any function key or key combination used by Windows. If you press a number or character key, Windows automatically adds **Ctrl+Alt+** to create a *key combination.* For example, if you press **A,** Windows creates the **Ctrl+Alt+A** key combination, and you will press **Ctrl+Alt+A** (hold down **Ctrl** and **Alt,** and then press **A**) to run the program.

4. Click **OK.**

Running Programs When Windows Starts

Here's another trick for running programs. If you always run a particular program right after starting your computer, you can make Windows run the program for you on startup. In Windows XP, you can simply drag the icon for the desired program over the Start button, over All Programs, and over the Startup folder icon and drop it in place. The next time Windows starts, it automatically runs all programs in the Startup menu.

Running Programs with a Single Click

Windows XP includes a nifty little program launch pad called the Quick Launch toolbar. This toolbar roosts just to the right of the **Start** button and provides single-click access to commonly used programs. If the Quick Launch toolbar is not displayed, right-click the taskbar, point to **Toolbars,** and click **Quick Launch.** Initially, the Quick Launch toolbar contains the following four buttons:

Launch Internet Explorer Browser runs Microsoft's Internet Explorer, a program for navigating the World Wide Web.

Launch Outlook Express runs Microsoft's e-mail program to allow you to send and receive electronic mail over an Internet connection.

Show Desktop minimizes all open program windows to take you immediately to the Windows desktop.

Media Player runs the Windows Media Player, which allows you to listen to CDs and online radio stations, watch music videos and movie trailers, and experience other types of media.

To add your own buttons to the Quick Launch toolbar, simply drag the desired program icon (using the right mouse button) to a blank spot on the toolbar, release the mouse button, and click **Copy Here.** (If you use the left mouse button, you move the item rather than copying it.) If the new button does not immediately appear, drag the vertical bar located just to the right of the Quick Launch toolbar to the right to make the toolbar bigger. You can also turn on other similar toolbars or create your own toolbar; right-click a blank area of the taskbar and point to **Toolbars** to check out your options.

> **Computer Cheat**
>
> Trick 1: Drag the top edge of the taskbar up to make the taskbar taller. Trick 2: Drag the taskbar to the top, left, or right side of the desktop and see what happens. Trick 3: Right-click a blank area of the taskbar and click **Properties** to view additional options.

Removing a Program You Never Use

Your hard disk isn't an ever-expanding universe on which you can install an unlimited number of programs. As you install programs, create documents, send and receive e-mail messages, and view web pages, your disk can quickly become overpopulated.

One of the best ways to reclaim a hefty chunk of disk space is to remove (uninstall) programs that you don't use. Unfortunately, you can't just nuke the program's main folder to purge it from your system. When you install a Windows program, it commonly installs files not only to the program's folder but also to the Windows folder, Windows\System folder, and other folders. It also edits a complicated system file called the Windows Registry. If you remove files without removing the lines in the Registry that refer to those files, you might encounter some serious problems. In short, you can't remove a program from your computer simply by deleting the program's files.

To remove the program safely and completely, you should use the Windows Add/ Remove Programs utility. In Windows XP, click the **Start** button, click **Control Panel,** and click the **Add or Remove Programs** icon. This displays the Add or Remove Programs window, as shown in Figure 5.4. Click the name of the program you want to remove and then click the **Change/Remove** button. In most cases, a dialog box pops up on the screen asking if you want to completely remove the program from your computer. To confirm the removal, click **Yes.** In other cases, the program runs a custom setup routine, which provides instructions on removing the program entirely or removing only certain components. Follow the onscreen instructions.

> **Inside Tip**
>
> If the name of the program you want to remove does not appear in the Add/Remove Programs list, use the program's own setup utility to remove the program. Search the program's submenu on the **Start, Programs** menu or in the program's folder for a Setup or Install option.

Click the program you want to remove   Click the Remove button

Figure 5.4

Let Windows remove the program for you.

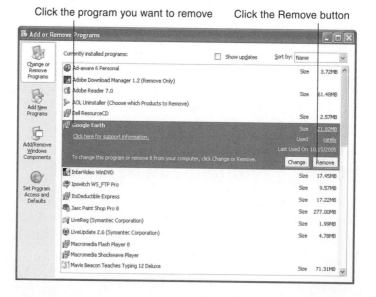

The Least You Need to Know

◆ Software provides the instructions your computer needs in order to perform a task.

◆ Not all programs run on all computers. Before buying a program, be sure your computer meets the requirements that are printed on the program's box.

◆ Hold down the **Alt** key while double-clicking **My Computer** to view important information about your computer.

◆ To install a program, use My Computer to change to the CD-ROM or floppy drive in which the program floppy disk or CD is loaded, and double-click the **Setup** or **Install** icon.

◆ To run a program, click **Start**, point to **All Programs,** point to the desired program group, and click the program's icon.

◆ To remove a program that you no longer use, open the Windows **Control Panel** and click **Add or Remove Programs** or double-click the **Add/Remove Programs** icon.

Chapter **6**

Customizing Windows for the Way You Work

In This Chapter

- ◆ Spreading out on your desktop
- ◆ Decorating the Windows desktop with themes and wallpaper
- ◆ Animating your screen and protecting your privacy with a screen saver
- ◆ Tweaking the Windows sound system
- ◆ Adjusting the date and time

If you're like most people, you enjoy decorating your home or office to add your own personal touch. You might paint the walls a different color, hang a few photos of friends or family members, or populate your shelves with knickknacks and family photos.

In similar ways, you can customize and decorate the Windows desktop. Windows provides the tools you need to change the color of your desktop, pick a theme for icons and mouse pointers, turn on an animated screen saver, build your own icons and menus, and reset the date and time. This chapter shows you how to completely renovate your computerized desktop.

Maximizing Your Desktop Space

Wouldn't it be great if you could grab the edges of your monitor and stretch it? Maybe turn your 17-inch monitor into a big-screen, 21-inch version? Well, you can't, but you can do the next best thing—shrink everything on the desktop to give yourself a little more real estate. Here's what you do:

1. Right-click a blank area of the desktop and click **Properties.**

2. Click the **Settings** tab.

3. Drag the **Screen Resolution** slider to the right one or more notches, as shown in Figure 6.1. As you drag, watch the preview area to see how the new setting affects the display.

Figure 6.1

You can't make your display bigger, but you can make everything on it smaller.

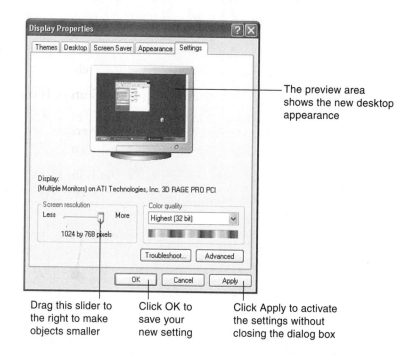

The preview area shows the new desktop appearance

Drag this slider to the right to make objects smaller

Click OK to save your new setting

Click Apply to activate the settings without closing the dialog box

4. When the preview area shows the desired desktop appearance (or the slider won't budge), click **Apply.**

5. Click **OK** to save your settings.

Panic Attack

If the icons have become too small to see, don't worry. You can make some adjustments. Open the Display Properties dialog box again. To make the icons and their labels bigger, click the **Settings** tab, click the **Advanced** button, open the drop-down list near the top of the General tab, and select **Large size**. If icons overlap, return to the Display Properties dialog box, click the **Appearance** tab, click **Advanced**, choose one of the **Icon spacing** options (**Vertical** or **Horizontal**) from the **Item** list, and increase the spacing.

Rearranging Your Desktop Icons

Although the icons on the desktop provide convenient access to all of your programs and files, you can get a little carried away with them. In about 15 minutes, you can completely cover the surface of the desktop with shortcuts, making it nearly impossible to find anything. Fortunately, Windows has several tools to help you reorganize the icons on your desktop. Try the following techniques:

♦ To move an icon, drag it to the desired location. If you try to move an icon and it jumps to a different location, Auto Arrange is on. To turn it off, right-click the desktop, point to **Arrange Icons** or **Arrange Icons By,** and click **Auto Arrange** to remove the check mark and turn off the option.

♦ To have Windows XP rearrange the icons for you, right-click the desktop, point to **Arrange Icons By,** and click **Name, Size, Type,** or **Modified** (date on which the icon was created or changed).

♦ To have Windows XP line up the icons without rearranging them by name, size, type, or date, right-click the desktop, point to **Arrange Icons By,** and click **Align to Grid.**

♦ To have Windows automatically line up icons when you move them, right-click the desktop, point to **Arrange Icons** or **Arrange Icons By,** and click **Auto Arrange.**

Computer Cheat

Windows XP can automatically remove unused shortcut icons from your desktop. Right-click the desktop, point to **Arrange Icons By,** click **Run Desktop Cleanup Wizard,** and follow the onscreen instructions to move unused shortcut icons to the Unused Desktop Shortcuts folder.

Hiding the Taskbar

The taskbar is a great tool to have around, but when you're working on a document, playing a game, or viewing a web page, you need that extra half-inch of screen space where the taskbar resides. To reclaim the space, make the taskbar hide itself when you're doing other stuff:

1. Right-click a blank area of the taskbar and click **Properties.**

2. Click **Auto-hide the taskbar,** as shown in Figure 6.2.

3. Click **OK.**

Figure 6.2

Give yourself some elbow-room.

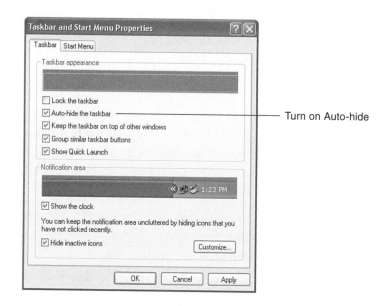

Turn on Auto-hide

As you work, the taskbar hides below the bottom of the screen (unless you moved the taskbar to a different edge of the screen, which you can do by dragging it). To bring the taskbar back into view, simply move the mouse pointer to the edge of the screen where the taskbar normally appears.

To make your taskbar larger, move the mouse pointer over the taskbar's top edge, so that the pointer appears as a two-headed arrow, and then drag up. With Auto hide on, you don't have to worry about the taskbar taking up too much screen space because it hides itself when you're not using it.

Panic Attack

It's possible to make your taskbar so skinny that it becomes virtually invisible. If you can't find your taskbar, roll your mouse pointer around the edge of the screen to see if the taskbar pops up. If it does not appear, roll the mouse pointer around the edge of the screen and see if the mouse pointer turns into a two-headed arrow, meaning that it is over the edge of the taskbar. Hold down the mouse button and drag the pointer toward the center of the screen to make the taskbar wider. This should bring it back into view.

Renovating the Start Menu

If Windows buries your favorite program five levels down on the Start menu, you don't have to live with it. You can move your programs to place them right at your fingertips. Simply click **Start,** open the menu on which the program appears, and then, using the right mouse button, drag the program to the desired location—to the **All Programs** submenu, the top of the **Start** menu, another submenu, or a blank area on the desktop. When you release the mouse button, a menu pops up, and you can click **Copy Here** or **Move Here.** If you drag the program to a different location on the **Start** menu, a horizontal bar appears as you drag the program, showing where it will be placed (see Figure 6.3). When the bar shows the desired location, release the mouse button.

This bar shows where the program will be placed

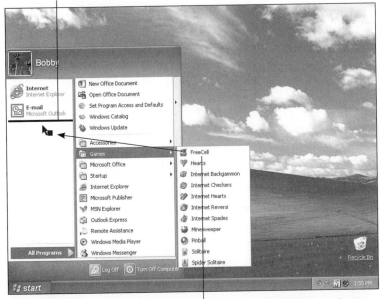

Figure 6.3

You can rearrange items on the Start menu and its sub-menus.

Drag the program to the desired location using the right mouse button

Computer Cheat

To place a program at the top of the Start menu in Windows XP, open the **Start** menu, point to **All Programs**, right-click the desired program name or icon, and click **Pin to Start Menu.**

To further customize the Start menu, right-click the **Start** button and click **Properties.** The Taskbar and Start Menu Properties dialog box appears with the Start Menu tab in front. You can choose to use the new **Start Menu** or the older **Classic Start Menu** or click **Customize** to customize either menu. If you choose Customize and have questions about a particular customization option, right-click the option and click **What's This?**

Animating Windows with Themes

Spreading your work out on the standard Windows desktop is about as exciting as spending an eight-hour day in a gray cubicle. Fortunately, Windows provides a selection of *desktop themes* to revitalize your working environment. Each desktop theme contains a graphical desktop background and specialized icons, mouse pointers, and sounds. For example, the Jungle theme places a jungle scene on the Windows background and plays animal sounds when certain events occur, such as Windows startup. To check out the available desktop themes and pick your favorite theme in Windows XP,

Whoa!

Windows XP comes with only a handful of desktop themes, none of which is very exciting. To obtain additional desktop themes, you must purchase Microsoft Plus! for Windows. (If you upgraded from an older version of Windows that had Desktop Themes installed on it, those themes will be available in Windows XP.)

right-click a blank area of the Windows desktop, and then click **Properties.** This calls up the Display Properties dialog box, as shown in Figure 6.4. Click the **Themes** tab. Open the **Theme** list and click the desired theme. (The **Browse** option enables you to poke around in the folders on your computer's hard disk to look in vain for more themes. The **More Themes Online** option opens an advertisement page for Microsoft Plus!)

If your computer seems a bit sluggish after you turn on a desktop theme, you might want to disable it. Desktop themes require disk space and memory that some computers just can't spare.

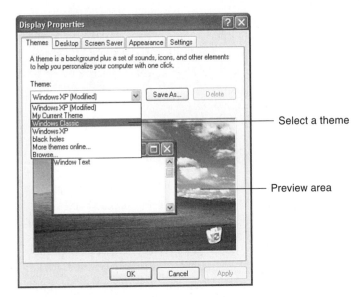

Figure 6.4

Windows XP features a couple of desktop themes.

Tweaking the Screen Colors

A desktop theme makes a nice novelty item, but the color combinations and fonts used in some of the themes can make it almost impossible to decipher the text and get any work done. If you're looking for a more subtle change in the desktop appearance, try tweaking the color scheme yourself as shown in Figure 6.5.

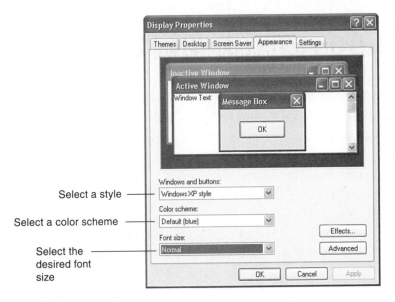

Figure 6.5

Pick a prefab color scheme and style.

To try out various color combinations, right-click a blank area of the desktop, and click **Properties.** The Display Properties dialog box appears. Click the **Appearance** tab to access the color schemes, as shown in the previous figure. In Windows XP, you can use the options on the Appearance tab to choose a prefab design, color scheme, and font size that control all your windows. To make more specific adjustments, click the **Advanced** button.

Hanging Wallpaper in the Background

Have you ever decorated your desk with wallpaper? Of course not! Maybe a new coat of varnish, some paint, or even contact paper, but never wallpaper. Well that's about to change. In Windows, you can use wallpaper to add a more graphic background to your desktop.

Inside Tip

To use an image from the web as your desktop background, right-click the image and choose **Set as Background.** Refer to Chapter 19 for details on cruising the web.

To hang wallpaper in Windows, first right-click a blank area of the desktop and click **Properties.** Click the **Desktop** tab to bring it to the front. In the list of backgrounds, near the bottom of the dialog box, click the name of the desired wallpaper. If the preview area shows a dinky icon in the middle of the screen, open the **Display** drop-down list and click **Tile** (to use the image as a pattern to fill the screen) or **Stretch** (to make the image cover the desktop). Click **OK.**

Controlling the Desktop Icons and Visual Effects

A quick glance at the desktop icons might give you the impression that they're immutable. However, Windows provides a set of options for controlling the appearance and behavior of these icons and other visual elements that make up the desktop.

To take control of your desktop icons in Windows XP, right-click a blank area of the Windows desktop and click **Properties.** Click the **Desktop** tab and click the **Customize Desktop** button. This displays the Desktop Items dialog box, as shown in Figure 6.6.

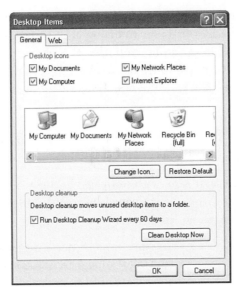

Figure 6.6

The Desktop Items dialog box lets you change the appearance of icons and other desktop effects.

Using the Desktop Items dialog box, you can customize the desktop icons in any of the following ways:

- To display additional system icons on the desktop, including icons for My Computer, Internet Explorer, My Network Places, and My Documents, click the check box next to each icon you want placed on the desktop.

- To change the appearance of one of the desktop icons, click the icon, and then click the **Change Icon** button. Click the desired icon and click **OK.** You can return to the original icon by clicking it and clicking the **Restore Default** button.

- To have Windows automatically remove unused shortcut icons from the desktop after 60 days, click **Run Desktop Cleanup Wizard Every 60 Days** to place a check mark next to the option.

Panic Attack

I've seen many a desktop with icons that overlap. If your desktop seems overly cluttered, try respacing the icons. In the **Item** list, choose **Icon Spacing (Horizontal)** or **Icon Spacing (Vertical)** and increase the **Size** setting.

Click **OK** to save your settings and return to the Display Properties dialog box. To access additional preferences that control the overall appearance of the icons, click the **Appearance** tab and click the **Effects** button, and enter your preferences. When you're done, click **OK** to return to the Display Properties dialog box, and then click **OK** to save your settings and return to the Windows desktop.

Securing Some Privacy with a Screen Saver

Have you ever seen a school of fish swimming across a computer screen? How 'bout a flock of flying toasters? A shower of meteors? A pack of creepy crawling cockroaches? If you've seen any of these animated patterns scurrying about a monitor, you have already witnessed screen savers in action.

Inside Tip

The best screen savers that are included with Windows are part of the desktop themes. If you selected a theme earlier in this chapter, you have already selected a screen saver. The following sections show you how to change the screen saver's properties.

In addition to functioning as an interesting conversation piece, screen savers serve a useful purpose: they deter passersby from snooping at your screen while you're away from your desk. For example, if you play Solitaire all day at work and you don't want your boss to know about it, you can activate a screen saver whenever you step away from your desk. You can even set up the screen saver with password protection so that nobody can turn it off without knowing the password.

Checking Out the Windows Screen Savers

Windows comes with several of its own screen savers. To check out the selection, right-click a blank area of the Windows desktop, click **Properties,** and click the **Screen Saver** tab. Open the **Screen Saver** drop-down list and click the name of a screen saver that appeals to you, as shown in Figure 6.7. To view the screen saver in action, click the **Preview** button. To deactivate the screen saver (and return to the Display Properties dialog box), roll the mouse or press the **Shift** key.

The Scrolling Marquee is great for keeping family members and coworkers informed when you're away from your desk. Open the **Screen Saver** list and click **Marquee.** Click the **Settings** button. Drag over the text in the **Text** box, type the desired message, and click **OK.** Click **OK** to save your changes and close the Display Properties dialog box. When the Scrolling Marquee screen saver kicks in, it displays your message, scrolling across the screen.

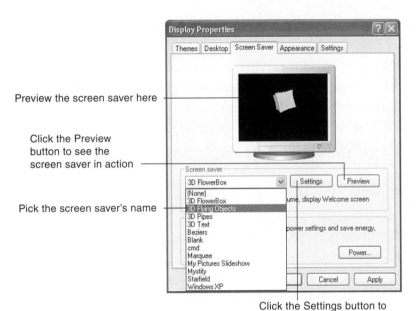

Preview the screen saver here

Click the Preview button to see the screen saver in action

Pick the screen saver's name

Click the Settings button to customize the screen saver

Figure 6.7

Check out the screen savers included with Windows.

Turning a Screen Saver On and Off

To turn on a screen saver, first select the desired screen saver, as explained in the preceding section. Click the arrows to the right of the **Wait__Minutes** spin box to specify how long your system must remain inactive (no typing and no mouse movement) before the screen saver kicks in. To specify how the screen saver operates (for example, the number of flying windows), click the **Settings** button, enter your preferences, and click **OK** to return to the Display Properties dialog box. To save your settings, click **OK.**

When your computer has been inactive for the specified period of time, the screen saver kicks in. To turn off the screen saver, simply move the mouse or press the **Shift** key.

Using a Password for Weak Security

Unlike earlier versions of Windows, Windows XP offers no password setting for the screen saver, because Windows handles the password through user accounts. To add password protection to the screen saver, first set up your user account to require a password, as explained in Chapter 7. Then, right-click a blank area of the Windows desktop, click **Display Properties,** and make sure there is a check mark next to **On resume display Welcome screen.** Click **OK.**

Whenever your screen saver kicks in and you return to your computer and press the **Shift** key or roll the mouse around, instead of returning to the Windows desktop, Windows displays the Welcome screen, prompting you to choose your user name and enter your password.

Making Your Computer Play Cool Sounds

In addition to the beeps and grunts your computer emits at startup, it can produce more refined tones. When you start Windows, for instance, it ushers itself in with heavenly harp music or some other short audio clip. When you open a menu, close a window, or exit a program, Windows plays a unique audio clip for each of these actions or *events*. If you listen closely as you work in Windows, you'll be able to link each sound with its event.

If you keep listening closely (over several weeks), these sounds might start to annoy you and inspire an overwhelming desire to smash your speakers. Before you take such drastic action, read through the following sections. Here you learn how to pick a different sound scheme, assign different sounds to various Windows events, and even mute your system altogether.

Checking Your Audio Equipment

If you've ever prepared for a speech or presentation, you know how important it is to test your equipment before show time. After setting up and turning on the microphone, you hold it a few inches from your mouth and do the standard "Testing ... one ... two ... testing ..." thing. Well, before you start messing with audio clips in Windows, you should test your sound card and speakers by taking the following steps:

1. Click the **Start** button, click **Control Panel,** and click **Sounds, Speech, and Audio Devices.**

2. Click **Change the Sound Scheme.**

3. Click an event that has a speaker next to it under **Program Events** and click the **Play** button, as shown in Figure 6.8.

Figure 6.8

Use the Sounds and Audio Devices Properties dialog box to test your computer's audio output.

Click a Windows event that has a speaker icon next to it

Click the Play button

At this point, Windows should play the audio clip that's assigned to the selected event. If you can't hear the clip, try adjusting the volume (as explained in the next section), or skip ahead to Chapter 32 to track down less obvious causes.

Adjusting the Volume

The big problem with computer audio is that computers have too many volume controls. You might find a volume control on the sound card (where the speakers plug in), on the speakers, and in Windows. In addition, if you're playing a computer game that has audio clips (most do), it might have its own volume control!

The trick to adjusting the volume is to start with the obvious controls first: the volume dials on the sound card and speakers. Set these controls to the desired level. If you're not sure which way to turn them, set them at the halfway point.

Next, check the volume control in Windows. Click **Start**, click **Control Panel,** and click **Sounds, Speech, and Audio Devices.** Click **Adjust the Speaker Volume.** Under Device Volume, drag the slider to the right to crank up the volume or to the left to decrease it. Be sure the **Mute** option is *not* checked. (Mute silences the device.) (You can click the **Speaker Volume** button to adjust the volume of the left and right speakers individually.) Click **OK** to save your settings.

Choosing a Different Sound Scheme

When you're certain that your audio system is working properly, you can try out various sound schemes included with Windows. A sound scheme is a collection of audio clips assigned to various Windows events (such as opening or exiting a program).

To check out different sound schemes, double-click the **Sounds, Speech, and Audio Devices** icon in the Windows Control Panel and click **Change the Sound Scheme.** Open the **Sound Scheme** list and click the name of the sound scheme you want to try. Click the **OK** button.

> **Panic Attack**
>
> If the **Scheme** list provides only the **Windows Default** and **No Sounds** options, the schemes are not installed. Run **Add/Remove Programs** from the Control Panel, click the **Windows Setup** tab, double-click **Multimedia,** and be sure **Multimedia Sound Schemes** is selected. Pop in the Windows CD, click **OK** to close the Multimedia dialog box, and click **OK** again to start the installation. To add sound schemes to Windows XP, you must purchase and install Microsoft Plus! for Windows.

Assigning Specific Sounds to Events

Picking a sound scheme is like choosing a vacation package. Each scheme provides all the settings you need for a consistent, thematic sound. If you want more control over which sounds Windows plays for the various events, you can assign a specific audio clip to each event.

To assign audio clips to events, display the Sounds and Multimedia Properties or Sounds and Audio Devices Properties dialog box as explained in the previous section. In the **Program Events** list, click the event whose sound you want to change. Open the **Name** or **Sounds** list and click the name of the desired audio clip. To preview the sound, click the **Play** button. To save your settings, click **OK.**

> **Inside Tip**
>
> When you start poking around on the Internet, you might stumble upon some cool audio files. If the file name ends in .WAV, you can assign the audio file to a Windows event. Save the file to the Windows\Media folder on your hard drive, and it will appear in the **Sounds** list. See Part 4 of this book for more information.

Adjusting the Date and Time

At the right end of the taskbar, Windows displays the current time. Rest the mouse pointer on the time, and a ScreenTip pops up, displaying the day and date. If the date or time is incorrect, you can adjust either setting:

1. Double-click the time display in the taskbar. The Date and Time Properties dialog box appears.

2. Click the desired date. (You can choose a month or year from the boxes above the calendar.)

3. Click the hour, minute, or second display and use the spin buttons (the up and down arrow buttons) to adjust the selected setting. You can also double-click the hour, minute, or second and then type the desired setting.

4. Click **OK.**

The Least You Need to Know

- Use the Display Properties dialog box to shrink everything on the desktop and increase your work area.

- To hide the taskbar, right-click it, choose **Properties,** and turn on **Auto hide.**

- To move an item on the Start menu, drag the item to the desired location and drop it in place.

- To select a desktop theme, right-click the desktop, click **Properties,** click the **Themes** tab, open the **Theme** drop-down list, and click the desired theme.

- To use a screen saver, right-click the desktop, click **Properties,** click the **Screen Saver** tab, open the **Screen Saver** drop-down list, and click the desired screen saver.

- You can adjust the date and time in Windows by double-clicking the time display in the taskbar and modifying the settings.

- To have Windows automatically arrange the icons on the desktop, right-click the desktop, point to **Arrange Icons** or **Arrange Icons By,** and click **Auto Arrange.**

- If you don't use a particular shortcut icon, drag it to the Recycle Bin.

Chapter **7**

Creating and Managing User Accounts

In This Chapter

- ◆ Creating a user account for each person who uses your computer

- ◆ Requiring a password to log on

- ◆ Logging off Windows so that someone else can log on

- ◆ Acquiring a .Net passport to access valuable Microsoft services

Sharing a computer with other users is like sharing a car with other drivers. When you share a car, each driver adjusts the seat and steering wheel for his or her own comfort, adjusts the mirrors so that the driver can see out the back, and stores the garage door opener in a unique hiding place. Likewise, some computer users prefer to clutter the Windows desktop with an assortment of icons, decorate their desktop with colorful images, and keep several programs running at the same time. Other users might prefer a cleaner, well-organized desktop with fewer bells and whistles.

Fortunately, Windows XP enables you to set up a separate user account for each person, so each person can customize Windows without affecting the appearance and function of Windows for other users. In addition, user accounts enable each user to keep a separate e-mail account, which means the messages for all users do not get mixed up in the same mailbox. User account passwords also provide privacy in a shared environment.

This chapter shows you how to create a user account for each person who plans to share the computer, how to log on and log off Windows XP, how to add a password to the accounts, and how to perform some other tricks with user accounts.

Adding a New User to Your Computer

When you or your computer's manufacturer installed Windows, the setup program automatically created a user account so that Windows could greet you on startup. The user account that Windows created is an *administrator account*, which gives you the authority to create additional accounts, assign passwords to users, and limit other users' access to system settings and computer resources. To add a user account for another user, follow these steps:

1. Click the **Start** button, in the lower left corner of your screen, and then click **Control Panel.** The Control Panel appears, as shown in Figure 7.1.

Figure 7.1

The Control Panel provides access to User Accounts.

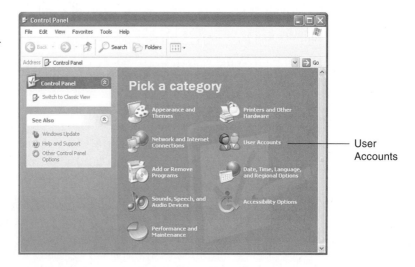

User Accounts

2. Click the **User Accounts** icon shown in 7.1. The User Accounts window appears, as shown in Figure 7.2.

3. Under **Pick a task,** click **Create a New Account.** The User Accounts feature prompts you to type a name for the account.

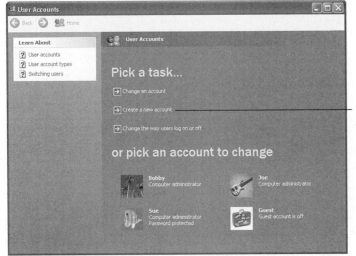

Figure 7.2

You can create a new user account.

Click Create a New Account

4. Type the user's name as you want it to appear on the Windows Welcome screen and on the Start menu.

5. Click the **Next** button. The User Accounts feature prompts you to pick an account type.

6. Click the desired account type:

   ◆ **Computer Administrator** allows the user to create, edit, and delete accounts; change system settings; install programs; and access all folders and files on the computer.

   ◆ **Limited** allows the user to change his or her own password, change the picture used to identify the user, change Windows desktop settings, view files that the user created, and view any files in the Shared Documents folder.

7. Click the **Create Account** button. Windows returns to the User Accounts window and displays the icon and name of the new user account, as shown in Figure 7.3.

Whoa!

If you're using a networked computer at your place of business, your business should have a network administrator who is in charge of adding user accounts. The process is much different for setting up user accounts on a corporation's network. Ask the network administrator for help.

Figure 7.3

Windows displays the name of the new user account and its icon.

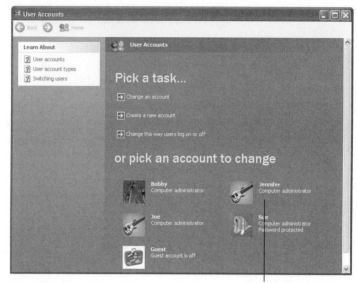

New User Account

Requiring a Secret Password to Log On

When you first create a user account, the account has no password. When the Windows log on screen appears, the user can simply click the account icon to freely access that account. If you're looking for privacy, you need to lock the account by adding a password. Windows then requires the password before allowing the user to log on.

 Whoa!

Choose a password that's easy for you to remember but difficult for anyone else to guess. In addition, write down your password and store it in a secure location, so that if you do forget it, you won't be locked out of your account permanently.

To add a password to an account, take the following steps:

1. Click the **Start** button, and then click **Control Panel.** The Control Panel appears.

2. Click the **User Accounts** icon. The User Accounts window appears.

3. Click the icon for the account you want to password-protect. The User Accounts feature prompts you to choose the aspect of the account you want to change.

4. Click **Create a Password.** The User Accounts feature prompts you to enter your password, as shown in Figure 7.4.

5. In the **Type a New Password** text box, type the desired password.

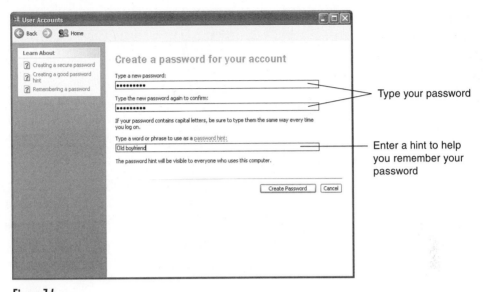

Figure 7.4

A password deters other users from logging on in your name.

6. Click in the **Type the New Password Again to Confirm** text box, and type your password again, exactly the same way you typed it in Step 5.

7. *(Optional)* Click in the **Type a Word or Phrase to Use as a Password Hint** text box and type a hint to help remind you of the password. (This hint will appear on the Windows log on screen, so don't use a hint that can help other users guess your password.)

8. Click the **Create Password** button.

You can change your password at any time or remove it. To remove a password, log on, repeat Steps 1 to 4, and then click **Remove the Password.**

Giving Your Account Icon a Makeover

Every account has its own picture to help identify each account and add a little personality to the log on screen. To personalize your account, consider choosing a picture that represents your personality and interests using the following steps.

Inside Tip

You can use nearly any graphic image on your computer as your picture. When selecting a picture, click **Browse** and then use the resulting dialog box to locate the desired image. You can navigate drives and folders just as you do in My Computer. When you find the picture you want, click the picture and click the **Open** button.

1. Click the **Start** button, and then click **Control Panel.** The Control Panel appears.

2. Click the **User Accounts** icon. The User Accounts window appears.

3. Click the icon for the account whose picture you want to change. The User Accounts feature prompts you to choose the aspect of the account you want to change.

4. Click **Change the Picture.** The User Accounts feature displays a collection of available images, as shown in Figure 7.5.

5. Click the desired picture and click the **Change Picture** button.

Figure 7.5

Personalize your account with a unique image.

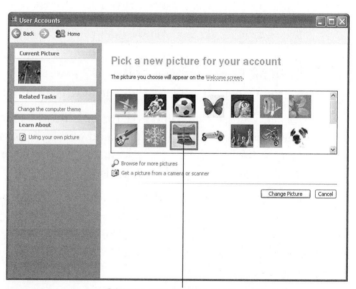

Click the picture you want to represent you

Wiping Out a User Account

When you customize Windows, as discussed in Chapter 6, Windows saves your settings in your user account. In addition, Windows saves all files in your My Documents folder, your e-mail messages, any websites you add to your Favorites menu, and any passwords to websites that you choose to save on the computer. Some of the settings and information Windows saves might be private; so if you stop using the computer, you might want to delete your user account.

To delete an account, open the **Start** menu and click **Control Panel.** Click the **User Accounts** icon, and then click the icon for the account you want to delete. Click **Delete the Account.** Windows asks whether you want to save the desktop settings and the contents of the My Documents folder for this account. To save the desktop settings and the contents of My Documents, click the **Keep Files** button.

Whoa!

Don't delete an account unless you're absolutely sure you will never again use it. Deleting an account permanently removes any passwords you've chosen to save and any e-mail messages.

To completely remove the account and any files and settings saved for this account, click the **Delete Files** button. The User Accounts feature asks you to confirm that you want to delete this user account. If you are absolutely sure you want to delete this account, click the **Delete Account** button; otherwise, click the **Cancel** button.

Letting Guest Users Log On

If you have guests who occasionally use your computer to check their e-mail, browse the web, or play games, you can enable the Guest Accounts feature so that others can log on as guests without having to enter a password. They can run programs, check their e-mail, browse the web, and perform other tasks; but they cannot install new software or change any account settings. In short, guest users can use your computer without messing it up.

To enable the guest account, click the **Start** button and click **Control Panel.** Click the **User Accounts** icon and then click the **Guest** icon. The User Accounts feature displays a message asking whether you want to turn on the guest account. Click **Turn On the Guest Account.**

Inside Tip

To find out who's currently logged on to Windows, click the **Start** button and look at the top of the Start menu for the name of the current user.

Logging On and Logging Off Windows

On weekends, when my kids and their friends are hanging out, they circle my computer like vultures, just waiting for me to step away from the keyboard. Then they descend to play games, chat with friends, and do other things that don't require them to work or play outside. When I return to the computer, I usually find a couple new programs installed on "my" account and several changes to my desktop. The moral of the story is: always log off when you step away from the computer. When you log off, Windows shuts down your desktop and user account and displays the log on screen so that another user can log on. This prevents other users from changing your settings, snooping in your e-mail account, and performing other sinister or careless acts. The following sections show you how to log on, log off, and switch users when sharing your computer.

Logging On at Startup

When you turn on your computer, the Windows Welcome screen appears, as you saw in Chapter 1. To log on, click your user account icon. If your user account is password protected, Windows prompts you to type your password, as shown in Figure 7.6. Type your password and then click the green arrow button to log on to Windows. Windows displays the Windows desktop, and you can start working.

Figure 7.6

Enter your log on password if prompted.

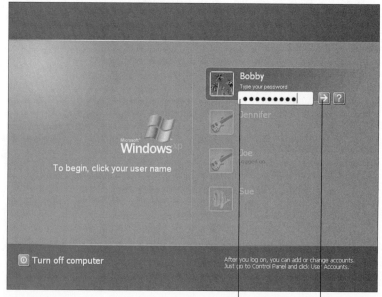

Type your password   Click the green arrow button

Inside Tip

To make it more difficult for unauthorized users to log on, disable the Welcome screen. With the Welcome screen disabled, a log on dialog box appears on startup, requiring the user to type both a user name and password. Click **Start, Control Panel, User Accounts.** Click **Change the Way Users Log On or Off** and then click **Use the Welcome Screen** to remove the check mark from its check box. Click the **Apply Options** button.

Logging Off Windows

As explained earlier in this section, you should log off whenever you have finished using your computer to prevent other users from changing your Windows settings. Before logging off, you should save any files you have been working on to avoid losing any of your work. When you're ready to log off, just open the **Start** menu and click **Log Off.** The Log Off Windows dialog box appears.

At this point, you have two choices. You can click **Log Off** to log off completely, which shuts down any programs that might be running and returns you to the Windows Welcome screen. The other option is to use *fast user switching*, which keeps you logged on to your account but allows another user to log on, too. When the other user is done working, you can then quickly switch back to whatever you were in the process of doing. To remain logged on, click **Switch User.** Whichever option you choose, Windows displays its Welcome screen so that another user can log on.

def•i•ni•tion

Fast user switching allows a second user to log on without shutting down the first user's programs. For instance, if you're in the middle of writing the great American novel and your son wants to check his e-mail, he can use fast user switching to quickly log on, check his mail, and log off. After he logs off, you can log on and immediately return to work, because your document comes back onscreen.

If you have programs running and Windows locks up when the other user is working, you are at a greater risk of losing data. To ensure that Windows safely shuts down any running applications when you log off, you can disable fast user switching. Click **Start, Control Panel, User Accounts.** Click **Change the Way Users Log On or Off** and then click **Use Fast User Switching** to remove the check mark from its check box. Click the **Apply Options** button.

Setting Up Your Account to Use a .Net Passport

Microsoft encourages all users to register for a .Net passport, which acts as an online identification tag, providing access to any .Net-enabled sites and services on the Internet. .Net passports are designed to simplify your ability to access various Internet sites and services. Instead of having to use a different user name and password for each site, Microsoft wants you to be able to use your .Net passport as your universal ID badge so that you have only one user name and password to remember. (To register for a .Net passport, you must be connected to the Internet. See Chapter 18 for details.)

def•i•ni•tion

.Net (pronounced *dot-net*) is an operating system technology designed to expand the capabilities of personal computers through the Internet. With .Net, your computer will be able to run *rented* programs from the Internet. .Net also provides a central storage location for your data, enabling you to access your work from any computer or computerized device that's connected to the Internet from anywhere in the world. The .Net initiative is also designed to integrate communications services, including phone, fax, and e-mail services. Most Microsoft sites and services require a .Net passport, including MSN Messenger for instant messaging.

To obtain a .Net passport and add it to your user account, follow these steps:

1. Log on to the Windows user account for which you want to obtain a .Net passport. See "Logging On and Logging Off Windows" earlier in this chapter for instructions.

2. Click the **Start** button and then click **Control Panel.** The Control Panel appears.

3. Click the **User Accounts** icon. The User Accounts window appears.

4. Click the icon for the user account for which you want to obtain a .Net passport. The User Accounts feature prompts you to select the aspect of the account you want to change.

5. Click **Set Up My Account To Use a .Net Passport.** The .Net Passport Wizard appears, as shown in Figure 7.7, displaying a brief introduction.

6. Read and follow the wizard's instructions to obtain your .Net passport and enter your preferences.

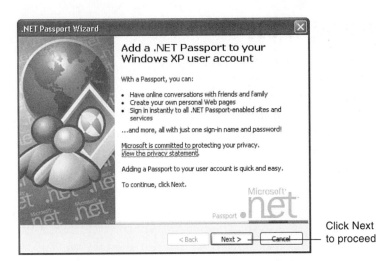

Figure 7.7

The .Net Passport Wizard can lead you through the process of obtaining and setting up your passport.

Click Next to proceed

Your passport initially contains your e-mail address and your geographical location (your country, state, and ZIP code). To make additional information available to other .Net Passport users whom you might bump into online, you can edit your Passport profile. You can, for instance, enter your real name, birthday, and occupation.

To edit your profile, first log on to Windows with the user account whose .Net Passport information you want to change. Choose **Start, Control Panel,** and click **User Accounts.** Click the icon for your user account, and then click **Change My .Net Passport.** Click the **Change Passport Attributes** button, enter or edit the passport details, and then click the **Update** button.

Whoa!

Don't enter your real last name, especially if it's unique. Anyone on the Internet could use your last name and other details in your profile to track you down.

The Least You Need to Know

◆ To access most user account settings, display the Control Panel and click the **User Accounts** icon.

◆ To prevent others from logging on to your Windows account, add a password to your account.

◆ To enable guest users to log on to Windows and prevent them from making any changes to Windows, enable the Guest Accounts feature.

◆ Fast user switching enables two or more users to remain logged on at the same time and switch accounts without logging off.

◆ To gain access to some valuable Microsoft online services, register for a .Net passport and add it to your user account.

Chapter 8

Finding Lost or Misplaced Files and Other Stuff

In This Chapter

◆ Finding lost files and folders

◆ Tracking down your printer

◆ Obtaining information about your computer

◆ Locating a computer on your network

With all your letters, resumés, photos, records, financial data, and other documents stored on your computer, you might think that you'd never lose anything ever again. After all, everything is stored in one place. It's not as though you have stacks of papers scattered in different rooms throughout the house, right?

Wrong. Unfortunately, computer storage is a lot like having stacks of papers scattered in different rooms throughout the house. Although Windows tries to steer you to your My Documents folder or one of its submenus whenever you attempt to save or open a document, some applications insist on saving documents elsewhere. Or you may choose to keep your documents organized in separate folders and then later forget the name and location of the folder in which you saved the document.

Fortunately, you can learn a few tricks to harness the power of your computer's search tools. In this chapter, you learn to use various search tools and techniques to track down everything from files and folders to printers, networked computers, and information about your computer.

Searching for Missing Files and Folders

I get calls all the time from friends, relatives, and colleagues who claim that a file they were working on mysteriously vanished. In about 1 percent of those cases, they're right—whatever file they were working on did vanish. Perhaps they didn't save it when the program asked them to or a power outage simply wiped the file off the map. In 99 percent of these cases, however, the person simply misplaced the file.

Tracking down misplaced files requires a certain amount of patience and the confidence that the file still exists. It also helps to know the following file hunting tips:

◆ Click the **Start** button and point to **My Recent Documents** to view a list of the last 15 documents you opened. Click the name of the desired document.

◆ Run the program you used to create or edit the document and open the **File** menu. Most programs list the last four or five documents you opened at the bottom of the File menu.

◆ Run the program you used to create or edit the document and then click **File, Open.** This usually displays the contents of the folder in which the program normally saves documents.

Inside Tip

If My Recent Documents is not on the Start menu, the feature may be turned off. To turn it back on, right-click the **Start** button, click **Properties**, click the **Start Menu** tab, click **Customize**, click the **Advanced** tab, and click **List My Most Recently Opened Documents** to check the check box. Click **OK** and then click **OK** again to save your changes. (You may want to turn this option off to prevent other users from snooping around to see what you've been recently working on. You can also click **Clear List** to remove all documents from the list.)

If none of those quick search tricks turns up the document, you can use the Windows Search utility to hunt for the file by name or by a specific phrase or string of characters that you're sure are included in the document. Take the following steps to search for a file in Windows:

1. Click the **Start** button.

2. Click **Search.** The Search Results dialog box appears.

3. Click **All Files and Folders.** Windows prompts you to enter search criteria—any information that uniquely describes the file or folder, such as its name or a portion of its name, a word or phrase in the file, and the general location of the item (if you know it). See Figure 8.1.

Inside Tip

In Step 3, you can choose **Documents** rather than **All Files and Folders,** but I prefer using the All Files and Folders option because it enables you to enter more focused search criteria. If you choose Documents, you can click **Use Advanced Search Options** to enter additional criteria.

4. Click in the **All or Part of the Filename** box and type as much of the file name as you can remember. If you can't remember any part of the file name, leave this blank.

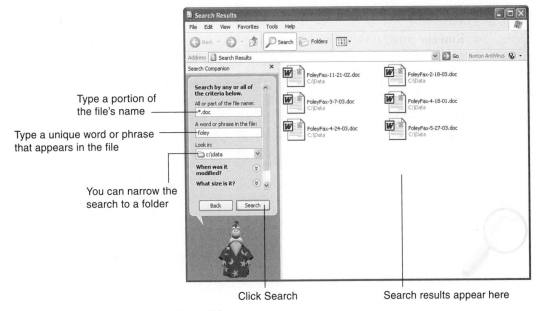

Type a portion of the file's name

Type a unique word or phrase that appears in the file

You can narrow the search to a folder

Click Search   Search results appear here

Figure 8.1

The Windows Search utility can help you find misplaced files and folders.

Computer Cheat

Most documents you create in a word processor, such as Microsoft Word, have names that end with the .DOC filename extension. You can type ***.doc** in the **All or Part of the Filename** box to find all documents that have the .DOC file name extension. The asterisk is a *wildcard character* that stands in for any and all characters that come before the .DOC file name extension. If the program uses a different file name extension, replace the .doc with the extension the program uses.

5. Click in the **A Word or Phrase in the File** box, and type a word, phrase, or unique string of characters that are included in the document. What you type must match exactly the way the word, phrase, or character string appears in the document.

6. To limit the search to a specific drive, open the **Look in** drop-down list and click the drive letter. To limit the search to a specific folder and its subfolders, click in the **Look in** box and type a path to the folder; for example, **C:\data\ personal.**

Inside Tip

When Windows locates a file or folder, it displays the complete path to it in the In Folder column of the list of files and folders it found. Jot down the path so that you can more easily locate the file or folder later.

7. For more options, click the button next to **When Was It Modified?, What Size Is It?,** or **More Advanced Options,** and enter your preferences. (More Advanced Options provides an option for searching all the subfolders of the selected folder.)

8. Click the **Search** button. Windows begins searching for the file or folder and displays a list of any files or folders that match the search criteria you specified. (The search can take several minutes, depending on how focused the search is, how much stuff is stored on your computer, and the speed of your computer.)

9. To open a found file or folder, double-click it.

Hunting for Your Printer

When you print a document, as explained in Chapter 17, if all goes right and your printer begins printing, you don't need to worry about where your printer happens to be hanging out. If something goes wrong, however, you may need to locate your printer and determine the cause of the problem.

To track down your printer, click the **Start** button and click **Printers and Faxes.** The Printers and Faxes window appears, as shown in Figure 8.2.

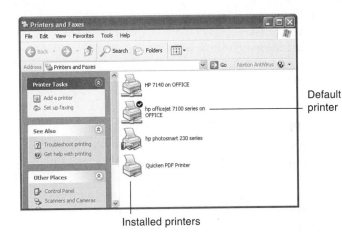

Figure 8.2

The Printers and Faxes window displays icons for all installed printers and fax machines.

The printer with the check mark next to it is the default printer—the printer your computer uses unless you specify otherwise. If you have more than one printer installed, you can make another printer the default printer by right-clicking its icon and clicking **Set As Default.**

Double-click the printer's icon to call up a window that displays any documents currently being printed or waiting to be printed. The list of documents often includes information indicating whether a print job has failed to print or is paused. See Chapter 17 for more information.

Panic Attack

If no printers are installed and you know that your computer is connected to a printer, you can install a printer, as explained in Chapter 17. In the Printers and Faxes window, you can click the **Add Printer** icon (on the left) to run a wizard that leads you step by step through the process of locating and installing your printer. If your computer is on a network and uses a shared printer that's connected to a different computer on the network, printer setup is a little different; see Chapter 10 for more information.

Exploring Your Computer's Vital Statistics

When you first purchase a computer, you usually know what you're getting. You know the amount of memory installed, the type and speed of the processor, and the version of Windows that's installed. Over time, however, you might have trouble remembering, and this system information can come in handy when you're buying new software or trying to troubleshoot problems with your computer. Technical support personnel often request such information to help you solve a problem.

The best place to gather specific information about your computer is to consult the Windows System Information utility. Take the following steps:

1. Click the **Start** button.

2. Point to **All Programs, Accessories, System Tools.**

3. Click **System Information.** The System Information window appears, as shown in Figure 8.3, displaying your computer's vital signs.

Figure 8.3

The System Information utility reveals important information about your computer.

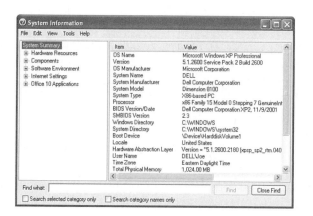

You can poke around in the System Summary tree on the left to discover more information about your computer. Of particular interest are the items listed under Components. Click the plus sign next to Components, and explore some of the items it contains. Here you can find out about your computer's hard drives, CD-ROM drives, audio devices, modem, and other hardware components.

Computer Cheat

The Windows Help system, described in Chapter 11, offers another way to obtain information about your computer. Click **Start, Help and Support** to call up the Help and Support window. Click **Windows Basics, Searching for Information, Get Information About Your Computer.** The help system displays four links that enable you to access general information about your computer, the status of system hardware and software, hardware information, and Microsoft software installed on the computer.

Scanning the Network for a Specific Computer

If your computer is part of a home network or you're using a networked computer at work, you may need to locate another computer on the network to access its files, folders, and other resources. (Chapter 10 discusses basic networking in greater detail.) When you don't know the specific location of a networked computer, the Windows Search utility can help you track it down.

Take the following steps to search for a computer on your network:

1. Click **Start, Search.** The Search Results window appears, as shown in Figure 8.4.

2. Click **Computers or people.**

3. Click **A Computer on the Network.**

4. In the **Computer Name** text box, type the name of the computer you're looking for. (To find all computers on your network, leave the Computer Name text box empty, as shown in Figure 8.4.)

> **Inside Tip**
>
> When you search for all computers on your network by leaving the Computer Name text box blank, the name of your computer also appears in the list of networked computers.

You can type a computer's name here or leave it blank to display the names of all computers on the network

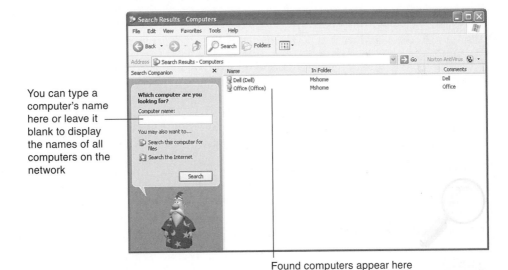

Found computers appear here

Figure 8.4

The Windows Search utility can help you track down computers on your network.

5. Click **Search.** If the search utility locates any computers that match the name you typed, it displays their names in the Search Results window.

6. To see a list of shared resources (folders, printers, and so on) on a networked computer, double-click the computer's name.

The Least You Need to Know

◆ To quickly locate a misplaced document you worked on recently, click **Start** and point to **My Recent Documents.**

◆ Most programs keep a list of recently opened documents at the bottom of their File menu.

◆ To have Windows fetch a misplaced file, click **Start, Search,** and use the Search Results window to enter your search criteria.

◆ To view all printers installed on your computer, click **Start, Printers and Faxes.** The printer with the check mark is the one Windows is set up to use.

◆ To view technical information about your computer, click **Start, All Programs, Accessories, System Tools, System Information.**

◆ To locate a computer on your network, click Start, **Search, Computers or People,** and then type the name of the computer and click **Search.**

Protecting Files and Folders from Snoops

In This Chapter

♦ Tightening security with private folders

♦ Making files invisible to other users

♦ Locking a file so others can view it without changing it

♦ Encrypting a file to prevent unauthorized access

People can be quite snoopy, so if you have any sensitive documents on your computer (love letters, a diary, financial information, and so on), consider implementing some security measures to prevent other users who share your computer from peeking at those documents or changing them without your permission.

Windows features several tools you can use to hide documents, encrypt them, or lock them so that others can look at the documents without modifying them in any way. This chapter shows you how to use the Windows security features to protect your documents and your privacy on a computer that you share with others.

Making Your Own Private Folder

Before we get into the step-by-step instructions for blocking access to a folder, you need to understand a little about how Windows treats the My Documents folder. Each user has a My Documents folder, but it appears as My Documents only for that user. When Bob logs on to the computer, Bob's folder appears as My Documents, but Susan's folder appears to Bob as Susan's Documents. When Susan logs on, Bob's folder appears to her as Bob's Documents.

Whoa!

You cannot hide your My Documents folder unless your account is set up to require a password when you log on. See Chapter 7 for details on creating and modifying your user account to require a password.

To lock your My Documents folder, you designate the folder to be a private folder. This keeps the folder hidden when other users log on to Windows. To make your My Documents folder private, follow these steps:

1. Run **My Computer** by selecting it on the desktop or on the **Start** menu. The My Computer window opens, displaying icons for the available drives.

2. Double-click the icon for the drive on which Windows is installed, typically drive C. My Computer displays the contents of drive C.

3. Right-click your **Documents** folder and click **Sharing and Security.** (Your Documents folder appears as My Documents or appears with your user name followed by "Documents," such as "Pat's Documents.") The My Documents Properties dialog box pops up with the Sharing tab in front, as shown in Figure 9.1.

4. Click **Make This Folder Private,** and then click **OK.**

Can't Make Your Folder Private?

If the Make This Folder Private option is grayed out, indicating that it is unavailable, your computer's hard drive may be formatted as a FAT32 drive. FAT32, short for File Allocation Table 32, is a system that controls the way data is stored on the disk. To make a folder private, the disk must be converted to the NTFS (New Technology Filing System) format, which is the preferred format for computers running Windows XP.

Windows XP comes with its own conversion utility that converts your hard drive to the NTFS format in a matter of minutes. To run the conversion utility, take the following steps:

1. Close all programs that are currently running.

2. Open the **Start** menu, point to **All Programs** and then **Accessories,** and click **Command Prompt.**

3. Type `convert c: /fs:ntfs` and press **Enter.** (If Windows is installed on a drive other than C, replace *c* with the drive's letter.)

4. Follow the onscreen instructions.

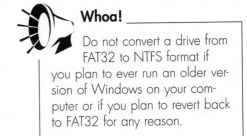

Whoa! _____

Do not convert a drive from FAT32 to NTFS format if you plan to ever run an older version of Windows on your computer or if you plan to revert back to FAT32 for any reason.

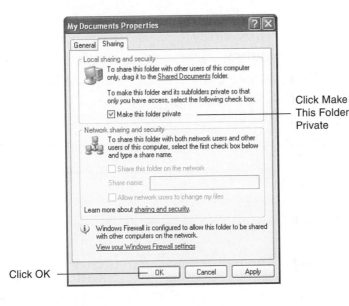

Click Make This Folder Private

Click OK

Figure 9.1

Make your My Documents folder private.

Sharing Your Documents with Other Users

Now that you locked your confidential files in a safe place, how do you provide access to those files you want to share with your fellow users? Simply copy or move the files you want to share to the Shared Documents folder. The Shared Documents folder also contains a Shared Pictures folder and a Shared Music folder, so you can share digital images and music clips with your fellow users. The Shared Documents folder is accessible to all users on the computer. See Chapter 4 to learn how to copy files from one folder to another.

Hiding a File from Other Users

The Klingons on Star Trek used a cloaking device to hide their spaceship when threatened by enemies. Windows has a similar tool that can hide files from other users. To hide a file, follow these steps:

1. Right-click the file you want to hide.

2. Click **Properties.** The file's Properties dialog box appears, as shown in Figure 9.2.

3. Click **Hidden** to place a check in its box.

4. Click **OK.** The file now remains hidden whenever you or anyone else views a list of files in this folder.

Figure 9.2

You can mark a file as Hidden to conceal it.

Click Hidden

Click OK

To view hidden files, take the following steps:

1. Run My Computer.

2. Click **Tools, Folder Options.** The Folder Options dialog box appears.

3. Click the **View** tab.

4. Under Advanced Settings, click **Show Hidden Files and Folders.**

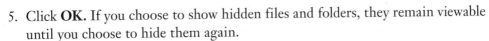

Panic Attack

When you hide files, they remain hidden from you as well as from other users. If you search for the file, as explained in Chapter 8, Windows won't display it in the Search Results window, so you need to remember which files you've chosen to hide.

5. Click **OK.** If you choose to show hidden files and folders, they remain viewable until you choose to hide them again.

When you're ready to hide the files, simply repeat Steps 2 and 3 and then click **Do Not Show Hidden Files and Folders** and click **OK** to hide files marked as Hidden.

Write-Protecting a File to Prevent Changes

Other users have complete access to your documents, so they can open, view, and edit your documents. To provide limited access to a document so that users can view it but not modify it in any way, you can write-protect the document file. Here's what you do to write-protect a file:

1. Right-click the file you want to protect.

2. Click **Properties.** The file's Properties dialog box appears, as shown in Figure 9.3.

3. Click **Read-only** to place a check in its box.

4. Click **OK.** You and other users can now open the document to look at it and edit it; but to save your changes to the edited document, you must save it under another name. This prevents the original document from being modified.

To remove write protection, repeat the steps.

Figure 9.3

You can mark a file as Read-only to prevent changes to it.

Click OK

Click
Read-only

Encrypting a File for Added Security

On a shared computer, other users may be able to slip past whatever security features you have in place and snatch your files. To prevent them from seeing what's inside a file, you can have Windows *encrypt* the file. Encryption scrambles a file's contents and then automatically unscrambles it only when you log on using your account and choose to open the file. Otherwise, the contents of the file remain inaccessible to other users and other computers. To encrypt a file, follow these steps:

1. Right-click the file or folder you want to encrypt.

2. Click **Properties.**

3. On the **General** tab, click **Advanced.** The Advanced Attributes dialog box appears, as shown in Figure 9.4.

4. Click **Encrypt Contents to Secure Data** to place a check in its box.

5. Click **OK.** The Encryption Warning dialog box appears, asking whether you want to encrypt only the file or also the folder that contains the file (the file's *parent folder*).

6. Select one of the following options:

   Encrypt the File and the Parent Folder to have Windows encrypt all files in the folder and in any subfolders it contains.

   Encrypt the File Only to encrypt only the selected file.

7. Click **OK.** Windows encrypts the specified file or folder.

Click
Encrypt
Contents
to Secure
Data

Click OK

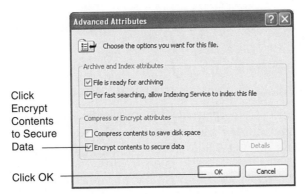

Figure 9.4

Encrypting a file prevents other users from opening it.

Whenever you pull up a list of files or folders, the names of encrypted files appear green. You can open the file; but if another user logs on to this computer on another user account, the person receives an error message when he tries to open the file, indicating that he doesn't have privileges to access the file's contents.

You can decrypt a file at any time as follows:

1. Log on under the same user account that you used to encrypt the file.

2. Right-click the file or folder you want to encrypt.

3. Click **Properties.**

4. On the **General** tab, click **Advanced.**

5. Click **Encrypt the Contents to Secure Data** to remove the check in its box.

6. Click **OK.**

The Least You Need to Know

♦ To privatize your My Documents folder, open My Computer, right-click your folder, click **Sharing and Security,** click **Make This Folder Private,** and click **OK.**

♦ To make files accessible to all users on your computer, store them in the Shared Documents folder.

♦ You can hide a file by right-clicking it and clicking **Properties** and then clicking **Hidden** and **OK.**

♦ To prevent modifications to a file, right-click it, click **Properties,** click **Read-only,** and click **OK.**

♦ To prevent other users from opening a file, right-click the file and click **Properties.** Click the **General** tab, click **Advanced,** click **Encrypt the Contents to Secure Data,** click **OK,** and follow the instructions to encrypt the selected file or all files in the folder.

Chapter 10

Networking Windows to Other Computers

In This Chapter

◆ Pick a relatively easy way to network two or more computers in your home or small business

◆ Log on to a network so that you can use stuff that's not on your computer

◆ Share folders, files, printers, and high-speed Internet service between two or more networked computers

◆ Print a document from your computer to a printer that's not even connected to your computer

You have mastered the basics of using your computer. You can run programs, make documents, copy and move files, and even dazzle colleagues with the Windows tricks you've learned. Now you find you need to deal with a network. Maybe your boss at work decided to install a network or you have two or more computers in your home and you want to connect them to share a printer or an Internet connection or to swap files and other resources between the computers. Whatever the case, you're now facing the network challenge.

Perhaps you've heard about networks, and maybe you even have a general understanding of the concept behind them but you've never actually worked on a network and you don't know what to expect. In this chapter, you learn how to use several Windows features designed especially for networks so that you can get up to speed in a hurry.

Understanding the Two Main Network Types

The two basic types of networks are *client-server* and *peer-to-peer*. On a client-server network, all computers (the clients) are wired to a central computer (the network server), as shown in Figure 10.1. Whenever you need to access a network resource, you connect to the server, which then processes your commands and requests, links you to the other computers, and provides access to shared equipment and other resources. Although somewhat expensive and difficult to set up, a client-server network offers two big advantages: it is easy to maintain centrally through the network server and it ensures reliable data transfers.

Figure 10.1

On a client-server network, clients are connected to a central server.

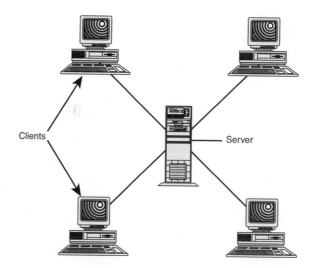

Clients

Server

def•i•ni•tion

Client-server networks typically have a **network administrator** who is in charge of assigning access privileges to each computer on the network. For example, some users might only be able to open data files on the server and might not be able to run certain programs. The administrator assigns each user a user name and password. You then must enter your user name and password to log on to the network.

On a peer-to-peer network, computers are linked directly to each other without the use of a central computer, as shown in Figure 10.2. Each computer has a network card that is connected through a network cable to another computer or to a central hub (a connection box). Many home users and small businesses use this peer-to-peer configuration because it doesn't require an expensive network server and it is relatively easy to set up. However, a peer-to-peer network does have a few drawbacks: it is more difficult to manage, more susceptible to *packet collisions* (which occur when two computers request the same data at the same time), and is not very secure because no central computer is in charge of validating user identities.

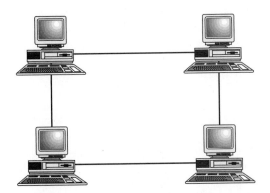

Figure 10.2

On a peer-to-peer network, each computer acts both as a client and a server.

Exploring Your Networking Options

If you're looking to set up a large network for a business or school, consult a networking specialist to install, manage, and secure your network. This chapter can help you navigate a large network, but one chapter can't possibly cover the complexities of setting up large, corporate networks.

If, on the other hand, you need to set up a network for your home or small business, the project is well within the realm of do-it-yourselfers. Your first step is to decide which type of networking hardware you want to use. You have three main choices:

♦ **Ethernet.** Fast, reliable, and secure, Ethernet networks are an excellent choice if you don't mind running network cables throughout your home or business. Building Ethernet capability into a new home or office building is the way to go, but if you have an older home and modest networking needs, consider a less-intensive, less-intrusive approach.

- **Wireless Ethernet.** Relatively fast and reliable, wireless Ethernet networks allow you to set up a network without having to run cables, and you can move the computer anywhere in your home or office without losing your connection. The only drawback is that the radio frequency signals that most wireless networking devices use to communicate occasionally run into interference from radios, microwave ovens, and other electronic devices. This can slow or interrupt the connections.

- **Phone line.** Much slower than Ethernet or wireless, phone line networks enable you to use the phone cables already installed in your home or business to communicate between computers. You can use your phone and network at the same time. Because wireless technology has become so reliable and affordable, networking over the phone lines isn't the best option.

- **Power line.** You can connect computers through the electrical system in a building, but again, wireless offers many more benefits.

Inside Tip

I've networked the three computers in my home twice in the past 5 years. The first time, I bought the standard Ethernet cards and cables and struggled an entire weekend running network cable and getting the darn thing up and running. The second time, I purchased a wireless router for one computer and two wireless networking cards for the other two computers. I connected the wireless devices, installed the software that was included, and spent the weekend with my wife and kids. The installation took about an hour. If you're considering networking the computers in your home, I strongly recommend that you go wireless.

Installing Your Networking Hardware

The best way to build your own small network is to visit your local computer store and ask one of the technical wizards working behind the counter to put together all the hardware you need. Go with one of the top brands and ask which product seems to be the most trouble-free. Your hardware needs depend on how you want the computers to communicate:

- **Ethernet.** You need an Ethernet hub with enough ports to connect all the computers on the network. Each computer must have an Ethernet card (often called an *NIC* or *network interface card*), and you need enough Ethernet cable to connect each computer to the hub.

◆ **Wireless Ethernet.** To connect computers in a wireless network, each computer must be equipped with a compatible wireless networking adapter. If you plan to share a high-speed Internet connection, one of the computers must be connected to a router, as shown in Figure 10.3. The router controls the data flow between the Internet and your networked computers, and it secures the network from unauthorized access.

Whoa!

Read the hardware installation instructions thoroughly before installing any hardware or networking software. In some cases, you need to install the software before installing the hardware or you run into problems.

Figure 10.3

A wireless network requires each computer to have a wireless network adapter installed.

Router

To Internet

Cable modem

Desktop computer

Desktop computer with wireless adapter

Notebook computer with wireless adapter

◆ **Phone line.** To build a phone line network, you install special modems in each computer and plug them into your existing phone jacks.

◆ **Power line.** Some companies offer devices that enable you to connect two or more computers and printers to the power outlets in your home or business. You plug a special networking device into the outlet and then connect your computer to the device using a parallel (printer) cable, Ethernet cable, or USB cable.

When choosing networking hardware, look for networking speeds in the 100Mbps range for Ethernet and 54Mbps for wireless Ethernet connections (the 802.11g standard). You can expect much slower connections over phone or power line networks. Also if you plan to use *VoIP* (*Voice over Internet Protocol*), which enables you to place phone calls over a high-speed Internet connection, such as a cable modem, make sure your networking equipment supports VoIP.

Running the Network Setup Wizard

Home networking kits and most wireless routers include the software you need to set up and configure the network. If you install an Ethernet network (with Ethernet cards, cables, and a hub), you can use the Windows Network Setup Wizard to get your network up and running.

Whoa!

Although Windows can lead you through the process of setting up the network, you must first install the drivers for any networking hardware you installed. Refer to the instructions included with your networking hardware for details.

To set up a standard or wireless network, take the following steps to run the applicable Network Wizard:

1. Click **Start.**

2. Click **Control Panel.**

3. Click **Network and Internet Connections.** The Network and Internet Connections window appears.

4. Click the option for the type of network you want to set up:

   Set up or change your home or small office network runs the Network Setup Wizard, which enables you to set up, configure, and secure a standard Ethernet network.

   Set up a wireless network for your home or small office runs the Wireless Network Setup Wizard, which enables you to set up, configure, and secure a wireless network, as shown in Figure 10.4.

5. Follow the wizard's instructions.

6. Repeat the steps on each computer you want to include in the network.

Each computer on the network must have a unique name that identifies it, but you must assign all computers to the same *workgroup*. The workgroup defines which computers can be part of the network. Computers in different workgroups cannot identify one another on the network.

Figure 10.4

The Wireless Network Setup Wizard leads you step by step through the process of getting your network up and running.

After a wireless device is installed on your computer, Windows automatically searches for networks that are within range of the device and displays a list of found networks. It then prompts you to choose which network you want to belong to. If you have a close neighbor who has a wireless network, that network may appear on the list. Likewise, if you take your wireless notebook computer into a business that has wireless Internet service (often called *WiFi* or *wireless fidelity*), Windows will identify the network and prompt you to connect to it. However, the network typically is set up to block unauthorized access, so you usually need to enter a special number or password (and pay something) to access the wireless Internet.

Sharing Folders and Files Across the Network

Before you can work with disks, folders, files, and printers on another networked computer, those resources must be flagged as shared. To mark a disk or folder as shared, take the following steps:

1. Right-click the icon for the disk or folder you want to share and click **Sharing.** The Properties dialog box for the selected disk or folder appears with the Sharing tab in front, as shown in Figure 10.5.

2. Click **Share this folder on the network.**

3. The Share Name text box automatically displays the drive's letter or the folder's name as it will appear to users who access your computer. You can type a different entry in this text box, if desired.

Figure 10.5

You can mark disks or folders as shared.

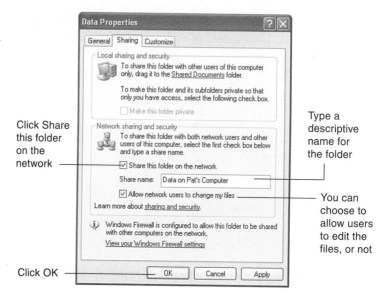

Click Share this folder on the network

Type a descriptive name for the folder

You can choose to allow users to edit the files, or not

Click OK

4. To enable other users to edit the files in this shared folder, click the check box next to **Allow network users to change my files.**

5. Click **OK.** You are returned to My Computer or Windows Explorer, and a hand appears below the icon for the shared disk or folder.

Computer Cheat

To provide access to a disk or folder without prompting the person for a password, leave the Password text boxes blank. This saves time on a small network on which you fully trust the other users.

You also can enable other users to share your printer. Open the **Start** menu, point to **Settings,** and click **Printers.** Right-click your printer icon and choose **Sharing.** Enter the requested information and click **OK.**

To terminate sharing, right-click the icon for the disk, folder, or printer and choose **Sharing.** Select the option to stop sharing the item and click **OK.**

Checking Out the Network Neighborhood

When you connect to the network, you can access any shared disks, folders, and printers on other computers that are connected to the network, assuming you have the right password (if a password is required). However, locating shared resources can be difficult, especially on a large network.

Fortunately, Windows has tools to help you track down network resources and manage them. The most basic tool is My Network Places. When you click **My Network Places** on the Start menu or Windows desktop, a window displays icons for all the computers that are on the network. You then can browse the shared resources on that computer, just as if they were on your computer.

Whoa!

If the computer you want to access is not displayed in My Network Places, try clicking the workgroup icon. Sometimes the icon for a computer doesn't pop up in the first window. If the computer is still unavailable, it might be turned off or the network settings could be wrong. Open the **Start** menu, click **Help**, click the **Troubleshooting** link, choose the option for troubleshooting network connections, and follow the onscreen instructions.

Mapping a Network Drive to Your Computer

If you frequently access a particular disk or folder on the network, you can *map* the disk or folder to a drive on your computer or create an icon for it in My Network Places. Your computer then displays the disk or folder as a folder in My Computer and in the Save As or Open dialog box in any Windows program you use. This enables you to access the disk or folder just as easily as if it were on your computer.

To map a drive or folder to your computer in Windows XP, take the following steps:

1. Click **Start, My Network Places.**

2. Click **Add a Network Place.** The Add Network Place Wizard appears.

3. Click **Next.** The wizard prompts you to select the type of network place you want to add.

4. Click **Choose another network location** and click **Next.** The Wizard prompts you to specify an Internet or network location.

5. Click **Browse.** The Browse For Folder dialog box appears, prompting you to select a computer, drive, and folder you want to add to your network places, as shown in Figure 10.6.

6. Click the plus sign next to **Entire Network,** click the plus sign next to your workgroup name, click the plus sign next to the desired computer, and continue clicking plus signs until you see the disk or folder you want to add as a network place.

Figure 10.6

You can map a disk or folder on another networked computer to the computer you're using.

Click the plus sign next to Entire Network

Click the plus sign next to the computer that has the disk or folder you want to add

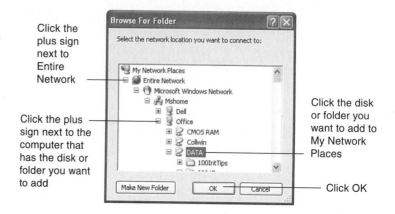

Click the disk or folder you want to add to My Network Places

Click OK

7. Click the icon for the disk or folder you want to add as a network place.

8. Click the **OK** button. You're returned to the wizard, where the path to the new network place is displayed.

9. Click **Next.** The wizard prompts you to type a more descriptive name for the drive or folder.

10. Type a brief but descriptive name of the drive or folder and click the **Finish** button.

Installing a Network Printer

To use a network printer, you must add the printer to your Printers folder. However, before you can add a network printer you must set printer sharing options on the computer that is connected to the printer, as explained earlier in this chapter. You then can run the Add Printer Wizard and select the network printer from a list of available printers. Take the following steps:

1. Click the **Start** button, point to **Settings,** and click **Printers and Faxes.** The contents of the Printers folder appears.

2. Click **Add a Printer.** The Add Printer Wizard appears.

3. Click **Next**. The wizard asks if you want to install a local or network printer.

4. Click **A network printer** or **A printer attached to another computer** and click **Next.** The wizard prompts you to specify the path to the printer.

5. Click **Browse for a printer** and click **Next.** The Browse for Printer dialog box displays a list of all shared printers on the network, as shown in Figure 10.7.

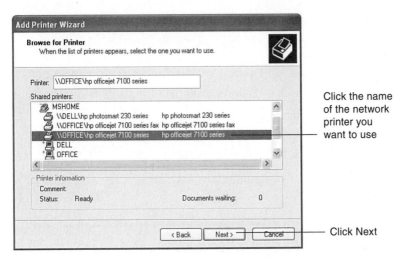

Click the name
of the network
printer you
want to use

Click Next

6. Click the icon for the printer you want to use and click **Next.** The wizard displays a warning indicating that if you continue the wizard will install a printer driver on your computer and asks whether you want to proceed.

7. Click **Yes.** The wizard asks if you want to make this the default printer. As the default printer, this is the printer Windows will use whenever you print a document.

8. Choose the desired option and click **Next.**

9. Click **Finished.** The wizard displays an icon for the newly installed network printer in the Printers and Faxes window.

After the network printer is set up, you can use it to print documents just as if the printer were connected to your computer. However, if you did not set up the network printer as your default printer, you must select the printer when you choose to print your document.

Sharing a Broadband Internet Connection

Through a feature called Internet Connection Sharing (ICS), Windows enables networked computers to share a broadband Internet connection, such as a cable modem, DSL (digital subscriber line), or satellite connection. With a shared connection, while you're working on the Internet, your significant other can be surfing the web, chatting online with friends, or checking e-mail on another computer.

To share a connection, your network requires a router. You plug your Internet modem into the router, and connect the router to one of the computers on the network or to the network hub. The router manages the data transfers between the Internet and the various computers on the network. The router typically includes its own security software to prevent unauthorized access to your network from the Internet.

Internet Connection Sharing is fairly transparent. When you install the router, Windows enables all computers on the network to use the Internet connection. The following section shows you how to implement security through Windows.

Securing Your Network

A broadband Internet connection is typically an *always-on* connection. That is, as long as you leave your computer on, you're connected to the Internet. This makes your computer and network more vulnerable to attacks from snoopy people on the Internet. With the proper know-how, someone on the Internet can connect to your computer, peek at your documents, and even destroy valuable data.

You can't completely protect your computer or network from such threats, but you can significantly deter potential break-ins by implementing various security measures, as discussed in the following sections.

Whoa!

If you have a broadband connection, consider installing Internet security software, such as Norton Internet Security. Such software protects your computer from unauthorized access, blocks pop-up ads and viruses, screens out unwanted e-mail messages, and censors web content unsuitable for children.

Activating the Windows Firewall

One of the best ways to protect your computer from break-ins is to install a firewall. A firewall is security software that stands between your computer and the Internet, enabling your computer to freely exchange data with the Internet but blocking access to your computer or network from other users on the Internet.

If you're using a router to connect to the Internet, it probably has its own firewall. If it doesn't, you can activate the Windows firewall, as explained in Chapter 25.

Limiting Access to Your Network

A wireless router enables any wireless computer that's in range of the router to connect to it and use it to access the Internet or even break into your network. Your next door neighbor, for example, can get free Internet service through your router and poke around on your network!

Most wireless routers have a security protocol called WEP (Wired Equivalent Privacy) that enables you to control which computers can connect to it. This security is typically disabled by default, so you have to enable it. With WEP, you can specify an identification number that each computer must use in order to access the router. Figure 10.8 shows a router that uses a similar security system based on MAC addresses. You must enter an approved address on each computer that you want to be able to access your network.

 Whoa!

WEP and similar network security features are not foolproof. A well-trained hacker can get around these features. However, they can usually prevent the average neighbor from hacking into your system.

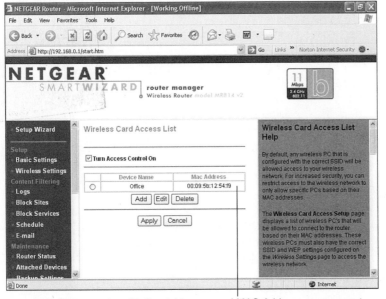

Figure 10.8

A router can limit access to only those computers that have an authorized address.

Only the computer with the right name and MAC Address can connect

The Least You Need to Know

♦ A client-server network has a central server to which all computers on the network connect. On a peer-to-peer network, every computer acts as both client and server, depending on whether it is accessing resources on another computer or sharing its resources with another computer.

♦ Before you can access the contents of a disk or folder, the disk or folder must be marked as shared.

♦ You can check out what's available on your network using My Network Places.

♦ You can map a network folder or disk to your computer to have it appear as a folder on your computer.

♦ You can use the Add Printer Wizard to set up a network printer on your computer.

♦ To prevent unauthorized access to your network, learn and implement the security features in both your networking hardware and in Windows.

Getting Free Help in Windows and Other Programs

In This Chapter

- ◆ Letting the Windows Help system guide you

- ◆ Surviving without documentation in other programs

- ◆ Poking around in a typical help system

- ◆ Getting just the help you need with context-sensitive help systems

If you plan to thrive in the world of computers, learn how to use the help system in Windows and your Windows programs. These online help systems might not provide the detailed hand-holding instructions you find in books, but they usually serve up the basic information you need to get started.

This chapter shows you how to access help in Windows and in most Windows programs and tells you where to look for additional help that might not show up in a program's help system.

Poking Around in the Windows Help System

If you get stuck in Windows, click the **Start** button, and then click **Help and Support.** The Help window appears, as shown in Figure 11.1, providing links to the most common help topics. Click a link and follow the trail of links until you find the answer you need. Or click in the **Search** text box, near the top of the window, type your question or a brief description of the desired topic, and press **Enter** to display a list of help topics that apply to the word or phrase you typed. Click the desired topic from the list that appears.

As you click topics and subtopics, you move deeper and deeper into the Help system. You may even pass up something that you want to return to later. To back up to a previous topic, just click the **Back** button near the top of the window. You can also click the **History** button to view a list of topics and subtopics you recently visited and then double-click a topic or subtopic in the list. To hide the History list, click the **History** button again.

Figure 11.1

Windows provides additional help for specific tasks.

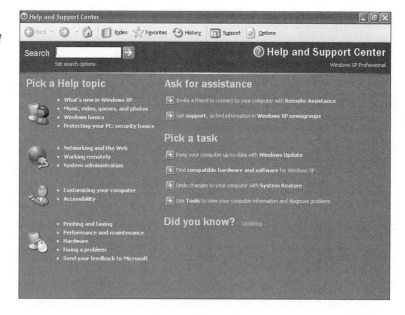

To view an index of help topics, click the **Index** button near the top of the window. The index appears in a pane on the left side of the window. You can then type a keyword or phrase in the text box above the index to quickly jump to the desired item or scroll down the list to see what it has to offer. When you find the topic of interest, double-click it. You can hide the index by clicking the **Index** button again.

Getting Help in Other Programs

Not so long ago, software developers gave you a book with your new program—some real documentation that told you how to enter commands and do something useful. Nowadays you're lucky to get a pamphlet with installation instructions. In some cases you get a CD and that's it—consider yourself lucky if you get a case for it!

More and more software companies are cutting expenses by reducing or eliminating printed documentation. As a replacement, they provide the instructions through the program's help system or on special files that you'd never think of looking at. In most cases you just open the **Help** menu, click **Contents** or **Index,** and then follow a trail of topics until you find the answer. The following sections show you how to navigate standard help systems.

Skipping Around with Hypertext Links

No matter how you get into a program's help system, you need some way to get around in the system once you're there. Most help systems contain *hypertext links,* as shown in Figure 11.2, that let you jump from one topic to another. The hypertext link is a highlighted word, phrase, or picture that, once selected, displays a definition of or additional information concerning that word or phrase. You usually have to click or double-click the hypertext link to display the additional information. Or you can tab to the link and press **Enter.**

Most help systems that allow you to jump from one topic to another also provide a way for jumping back. Look for the Back and History options. The **Back** option usually takes you back one topic at a time. The **History** option provides a list of topics you've looked at and allows you to select a topic from the list. These buttons vary from one help system to another, so remain flexible.

Figure 11.2

Hypertext links let you jump from one topic to another.

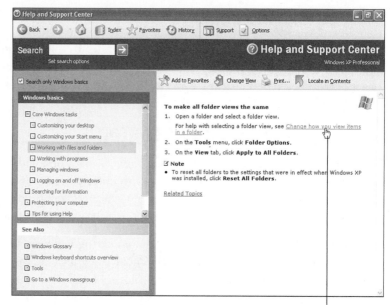

When you point to a hypertext link, the mouse pointer changes to a pointing hand

Working with the Online Librarian

Advanced help systems usually provide a way for you to search for information on a specific topic or task. For example, you might want to search for information about setting margins or printing. Here's what you do:

1. Open the **Help** menu and click **Search,** or enter the **Search** command in the help system. (The Help window might have a **Find** button, tab, or some other way of searching.)

2. Start typing the name of the term or topic, as shown in Figure 11.3. As you type, a list of available topics that match what you type scrolls into view.

3. When you see the desired topic, double-click it, or highlight it and press **Enter.** A list of subtopics appears.

4. Double-click the desired subtopic. A Help window appears, showing information that pertains to the selected subtopic.

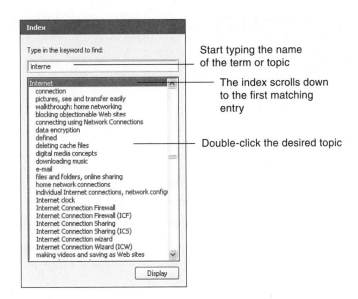

Start typing the name of the term or topic

The index scrolls down to the first matching entry

Double-click the desired topic

Figure 11.3

The Help System enables you to search for information on a specific topic.

Calling Up Context-Sensitive Help

One of the best ways to use a help system is to start performing the task and then press **F1** when you get stuck. In most programs, this displays a *context-sensitive* help screen that provides the specific information you need to continue. However, some help systems are less perceptive than others when it comes to guessing what you're trying to do.

The F1 key is the universal help key. It's sort of like dialing 411. Many programs also provide a Help button that performs the same function. Look for a button in your program's toolbar that has a question mark on it. That's usually the Help button.

Computer Cheat

Program toolbars, which typically appear near the top of a program's windows, are notorious for containing cryptic button icons; you'd never guess what some of them do. To help you sort out the buttons, most programs offer a ScreenTip or ToolTip feature. Rest the mouse on a button for a second or two, and a ScreenTip or ToolTip pops up, displaying the button's name.

Hollering for Help in a Dialog Box

Some dialog boxes contain dozens of options spread out over a half dozen tabs. Although the options are labeled, the labels might not tell you much. If you encounter a cryptic option in a dialog box, try the following to obtain additional information:

◆ **Press F1.** If you're lucky, a context-sensitive help window appears, displaying information about the dialog box and the options it contains.

◆ **Click the question mark button.** If there's a question mark button in the upper-right corner of the dialog box, click the button and then click the option about which you want more information, as shown in Figure 11.4. This typically displays a brief description of the option.

◆ **Right-click the option.** In many dialog boxes, right-clicking an option displays a menu containing a single option: What's This? Click **What's This?** to display a description of the option.

Figure 11.4

Context-sensitive help is available for most dialog box options.

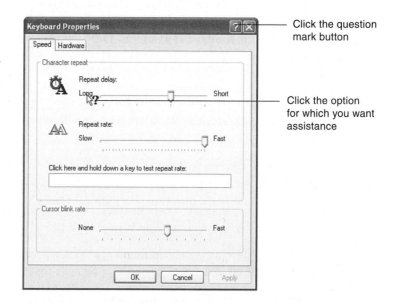

Click the question mark button

Click the option for which you want assistance

Inside Tip

In an attempt to make your computer seem more personal, some programs, including Microsoft programs, offer animated characters that pop up on your screen whenever they think you need help. For example, if you start typing a letter in some versions of Microsoft Word, a cartoon character (an Office Assistant) might pop up and ask if you need help. Just click links as you would in a standard help system or click the **Close** button to tell him to go away.

Finding Answers in ReadMe Documents

Most programs come with a help menu of some type, which is the most logical place to look for help. However, if you can't even get the program running (or running right), you won't be able to get into its help system. When that happens, the first thing you should do is look for a ReadMe file. A ReadMe file typically contains information about installing and running the program, details about how the program works, information about new features, and descriptions of known *bugs*.

def•i•ni•tion

A **bug** is a problem in a program that causes it to behave erratically, lock up your system, and make you want to smash your computer with a baseball bat.

To view a ReadMe file, use **My Computer** to display the contents of the folder in which the program's files are stored or the contents of the program's installation disk or CD-ROM. Look for a file called README.TXT or README.DOC. If you have My Computer set up to hide filename extensions, you won't see the .TXT or .DOC. Instead, Windows indicates the file type graphically. A text (.TXT) file icon looks like a small spiral notebook; a document (.DOC) file icon appears with your word processor's logo on it (W, if you have Word). Double-click the file to open it in NotePad, WordPad, or in your word processor.

In rare cases, the ReadMe file is in the form of a program. If you find a file called ReadMe with a funny looking icon next to it, double-click the file's name to run the program.

The Least You Need to Know

- You can access the Windows help system by selecting **Start, Help and Support,** to obtain assistance with various Windows tasks.

- Most programs feature a Help menu that provides a key to open the door of their Help systems.

- Pressing the **F1** key in most programs is like dialing 411 for help.

- To obtain help for an option in a dialog box, right-click the option and click **What's This?**

- If you're having trouble installing or running a program, check its folder or installation CD for a ReadMe file.

Part 3

Getting Down to Business with Office Programs

Playing Solitaire and fiddling with the Windows desktop can keep you entertained for hours, but you didn't lay down a few hundred bucks for a computer only to use it as a 99¢ deck of playing cards. You want to type letters, crunch numbers, manage data, and take control of your personal finances ... you want to use the computer to get more out of life!

In this part, you become productive with your computer as you learn how to type and format letters, add images, create automated accounting worksheets, and print your documents. Along the way, you even learn how to perform some basic tasks that apply to most applications, including saving, naming, and opening the files you create.

Chapter 12

Typing Letters and Performing Other Word Processing Chores

In This Chapter

♦ Typing on an electronic page

♦ Inserting the date and time from your computer

♦ Making your text big and pretty

♦ Shoving your paragraphs around on a page

♦ Saving the document you created

When my wife and I purchased a new computer for our home, I was dazzled by the hardware: the state-of-the-art processor, the all-in-one fax-copier-scanner-printer, the big-screen monitor, the surround sound audio system, and the super-speed cable modem. With this bad boy, we'd be cruising, rather than surfing, the Internet; building our own websites; scanning family photos; and editing videos!

As I ran down the list of all the cool things we could do with our new computer, my wife just stared at the screen. When I finished, she looked at me and said, "I just want to type a letter."

With the popularity of the Internet and other computer technologies, it's easy to forget that many people still use a computer primarily to type and print documents. In this chapter, you learn how to type, format (style), edit (cut and paste), and save a document using the most popular word processor on the planet—Microsoft Word.

Panic Attack

Although this chapter uses Microsoft Word to show you basic word processing features, don't worry if you're using a different word processor. The basic features and commands covered in this chapter differ only slightly between word processing programs. If you don't have Word or another high-end word processor installed on your computer, run WordPad, which is included with Windows. Open the **Start** menu, point to **All Programs,** point to **Accessories,** and then click **WordPad.**

Making the Transition to the Electronic Page

When you run Word (or whichever word processor is installed on your computer), it displays a blank "sheet of paper." The program also displays a vertical line called the *cursor* or *insertion point* to show you where the characters will appear when you start typing. Just below the insertion point is a horizontal line that marks the end of the document, as shown in Figure 12.1. As you type, this line moves down automatically to make room for your text. (You can't move the cursor or insertion point past this line no matter how hard you try.)

The best way to learn how to type in a word processor is to start typing. As you type, keep the following information in mind:

◆ If the text is too small to read, open the **Zoom** list, as shown in Figure 12.1, and pick **120%** or a higher percentage zoom. If the text is still too small, make it bigger, as explained in "Making the Text Bigger or Smaller" later in this chapter.

◆ Press the **Enter** key only to end a paragraph and start a new paragraph. Within a paragraph, the program automatically *wraps* the text from one line to the next as you type.

◆ Don't press the **Enter** key to insert a blank line between paragraphs. Later in this chapter, I show you a better way to add space between paragraphs.

◆ Use the mouse or the arrow keys to move the insertion point around in the document. If you're working on a long document, use the scroll bar to move more
quickly and then click in the document to move the insertion point where you
want it.

◆ Delete to the right; backspace to the left. To delete a character that's to the right
of the insertion point, press the **Delete** key. To delete characters to the left of
the insertion point, press the **Backspace** key.

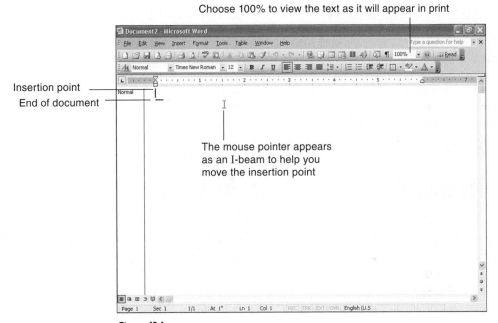

Choose 100% to view the text as it will appear in print

Insertion point

End of document

The mouse pointer appears
as an I-beam to help you
move the insertion point

Figure 12.1

Start typing!

In addition to allowing you to zoom in and out on a page, most word processing programs offer various views of a page. To change to a view, you typically open the **View**
menu and click one of the following view options (in Word, you can quickly switch to
a view by clicking a button for the desired view in the lower-left corner of the document window):

◆ **Normal** shows your document as one continuous document. In Normal view,
the word processor hides complex page formatting, headers, footers, objects with
wrapped text, floating graphics, and backgrounds. Scrolling is smooth because
this view uses the least amount of memory.

◆ **Print or Page Layout** provides a more realistic view of how your pages will appear in print. Print Layout displays graphics, wrapping text, headers, footers, margins, and drawn objects. This uses a lot of memory, however, and might make scrolling a little jerky.

Computer Cheat

If you really just want to type a letter, and you're using Microsoft Word, you can run Word's Letter Wizard to have Word format your letter for you. To run the Letter Wizard, click **Tools, Letters and Mailings, Letter Wizard.**

◆ **Web Layout** displays a document as it will appear when displayed in a web browser. In Web Layout view, a word processor displays web page backgrounds, wraps the text to fit inside a standard browser window, and positions the graphics as they will appear when viewed online.

◆ **Outline** allows you to quickly organize and reorganize your document by dragging headings from one location to another in the document.

What's with the Squiggly Red and Green Lines?

As you type, you might get a strange feeling that your sixth-grade English teacher is inside your computer, underlining your spelling mistakes. Whenever you type a string of characters that Word can't find in its dictionary, Word draws a squiggly red line under the word to flag it for you so that you can immediately correct it. If the word is misspelled, right-click the word and choose the correct spelling from the context menu. (A squiggly green line marks a questionable grammatical construction.)

If the squiggly lines annoy you, you can turn off automatic spell checking. Open the **Tools** menu and click **Options.** Click the **Spelling & Grammar** tab, and turn off both **Check spelling as you type** and **Check grammar as you type.** Click **OK.**

Inserting Today's Date

When you're typing a letter, you should include the date as part of the heading, just below your address. Of course, you could type the date, but that's too much like work. Have Word insert the date for you. Open the **Insert** menu and click **Date and Time.** Click the desired format and click **OK,** as shown in Figure 12.2.

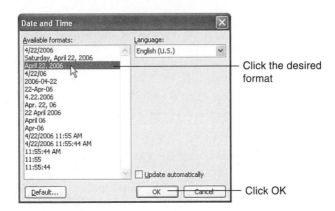

— Click the desired
format

— Click OK

Figure 12.2

*You can have your word pro-
cessor insert the date or time
for you.*

Panic Attack

If the date or time is not current, your computer has the wrong information.
Double-click the time display on the right end of the Windows taskbar and
use the resulting dialog box to reset the date or time.

Making the Text Bigger or Smaller

When you first start typing, you might notice that the text looks rather bland. Word
processors choose the dullest, dreariest-looking typestyle available. To give your text
a facelift, try choosing a different typestyle (or *font*) and varying the size (measured in
points) and attributes of the text. Fonts can be serif or sans serif. Serif fonts have short
cross lines at the end of the main stroke of
each character, which is supposed to make
them easier to read.

To change the appearance of existing text,
drag over the text to *highlight* it. Highlighting displays white text on a black
background to indicate that the text is
selected. Then choose the desired formatting options from the Formatting toolbar,
as shown in Figure 12.3. (By the way, you
can change the properties of the text before
you start typing.)

def•i•ni•tion

Technically, a **font** is a collection
of characters that share the same
typestyle and size. (Type size is
measured in **points**; a point is
approximately $1/72$ of an inch.)
Most programs use the terms *font*
and *typestyle* interchangeably.

Inside Tip

Where do you get fonts? Windows comes with dozens of fonts. Most word processors, desktop publishing programs, and other applications come with additional font sets. You can purchase font collections on CD or download (copy) fonts from the Internet, but you probably already have more fonts than you'll ever use.

Select a text size   Make the text bold, italic, or underlined

Highlighted text ——

Pick a different ——
type style

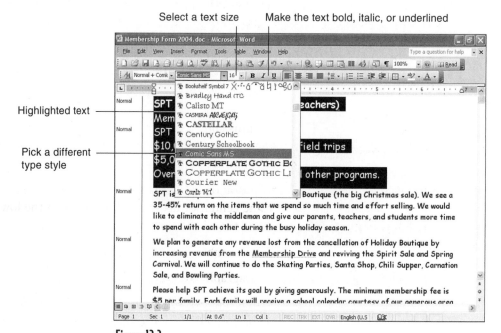

Figure 12.3

Use the Formatting toolbar to quickly change the text's appearance.

Shoving Text Left, Right, or Center

As you type a document, you might want to center a heading or push a date or address to the right side of the page to set it apart from surrounding text. To quickly change the text alignment, click anywhere inside the paragraph and then click one of the following buttons on the Formatting toolbar:

 Align Left pushes all lines of the paragraph against the left margin.

 Center positions each line of the paragraph at an equal distance from both the left and right margins.

Align Right pushes all lines of the paragraph against the right margin. This is a useful option for placing a date in the upper-right corner of a page.

 Justify inserts spaces between the words as needed to make every line of the paragraph the same length, as in newspaper columns.

 The Formatting toolbar also contains buttons for creating numbered and bulleted lists. Simply highlight the paragraphs that you want to transform into a list and then click the desired button: **Numbering** or **Bullets.**

To indent the first line of a paragraph, you can press the **Tab** key at the beginning of the paragraph or enter a setting for the first line indent. Most word processors display a ruler, as shown in Figure 12.4, that lets you quickly indent paragraphs and set *tab stops*. (Tab stops determine where the insertion point stops when you press the **Tab** key.) To indent text and change margins and tab stop settings, select the paragraph(s) you want the change to affect (to modify a single paragraph, just make sure the insertion point is inside the paragraph), and then take one of the following steps:

◆ To place a tab stop, click the button on the far left end of the ruler to select the desired tab stop type (left, right, center, or decimal). Then click in the lower half of the ruler where you want the tab stop positioned.

◆ To move a tab stop, drag it left or right. To delete it, drag it off the ruler.

◆ To indent the right side of a paragraph, drag the right indent marker to the left.

◆ To indent the left side of a paragraph, drag the left indent marker to the right. (The left indent marker is the rectangle below the upward-pointing triangle.)

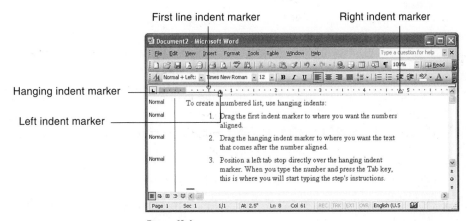

Figure 12.4

Use the ruler to quickly indent paragraphs and set tabs.

◆ To indent only the first line of a paragraph, drag the first line indent marker to the right. (This is the downward-pointing triangle on the left.)

◆ To create a hanging indent, drag the hanging indent marker to the right. (This is the upward-pointing triangle on the left.)

Changing the Line Spacing

Here's a section just for kids. If you're working on a five-page paper for school, and you have only two and a half pages of material, you can stretch this out by double-spacing:

1. Press **Ctrl+A** to select all the text.

2. Open the **Format** menu and click **Paragraph.** The Paragraph dialog box pops up on your screen.

3. Open the **Line spacing** list and click **Double.**

4. Click **OK.**

A quicker way to change line spacing is to select the text and press one of the following keystrokes: Ctrl+2 for double-spacing, Ctrl+5 for 1.5 line spacing, and Ctrl+1 for single spacing.

Computer Cheat

If your teacher wises up and issues formatting restrictions on your next assignment, bump up the text size by one or two points (barely noticeable), use the **File, Page Setup** command to increase the margins, and increase the line spacing by only a few points instead of double-spacing. An even more subtle technique is to use a larger font. Some fonts, such as Arial and Courier New, take up more space at the same point size than other fonts.

Inserting Space Between Paragraphs

Leaving space between paragraphs helps the reader easily see where one paragraph ends and another begins. Of course, you can insert blank lines between paragraphs by pressing the **Enter** key twice at the end of a paragraph, but that's a sloppy technique that limits your control over paragraph spacing later.

By specifying the exact amount of space you want inserted between paragraphs, you ensure that the amount of space between paragraphs is consistent throughout your document.

To change the space between paragraphs, drag over the paragraphs to highlight at least a portion of each paragraph. (You don't need to highlight all of the first and last paragraphs.) Open the **Format** menu and click **Paragraph.** Under **Spacing,** click the arrows to the right of **Before** or **After** to specify the amount of space (measured in points) you want to insert before or after each paragraph. In most cases, 6 points of extra spacing after each paragraph does the trick. Click **OK.**

Save It or Lose It

Unless you're the type of person who loves the thrill of risking everything for no potential gain, you should save your document soon after you type a paragraph or two. Why? Because right now, your computer is storing everything you type in RAM (random access memory). A little dip in your local electric company's power grid can send your document off to never-never land. To prevent losing your work, save it to a permanent storage area—your computer's hard disk.

The first time you save a document, your program asks for two things: a name for the document, and the name of the drive and folder where you want the document stored. Here's the standard operating procedure for saving documents in most Windows programs:

1. Click the **Save** button on the toolbar, or open the **File** menu and click **Save.** The Save As dialog box appears, asking you to name the file.

2. Click in the **File name** text box and type a name for the file, as shown in Figure 12.5. The name can be up to 255 characters long, and you can use spaces, but you cannot use any of the following taboo characters: \ / : * ? " < > |

3. Open the **Save in** list and click the letter of the disk on which you want to save the document (typically drive C).

4. In the file/folder area, double-click the folder in which you want the document saved. (To save the document in a folder that's inside another folder, repeat this step.)

5. Click the **OK** or **Save** button. The file is saved to the disk.

Panic Attack

If you pass up the folder you wanted to select, you can back up. Click the **Up One Level** button.

From now on, saving this document is easy; you don't have to name it or tell the program where to store it ever again. The program saves your changes in the document you already created and named. You should save your document every 5 to 10 minutes to avoid losing any work. In most programs, you can quickly save a document by pressing **Ctrl+S** or by clicking the **Save** button on the program's toolbar.

Figure 12.5

Use the Save As dialog box to save your document to your computer's hard disk.

Select a drive or folder here

Select a folder here

Type a filename here

![key icon] **Inside Tip**

Most new word processors are set up to save files in the My Documents folder. If you create your own folders for storing documents, you might want to set up one of these folders as the one your word processor looks to first. In Word, open the **Tools** menu and click **Options**. Click the **File Locations** tab, click **Documents** (under **File types**), and click the **Modify** button. Use the Modify Location dialog box to pick the desired drive and folder, and then click **OK** to return to the Options dialog box. Click **OK** to save your changes. Now, whenever you choose to open or save a document, Word will display the contents of the folder you selected.

Editing Your Letters and Other Documents

Is your letter perfect? Are you sure? Take a 10-minute break, come back, and read it again with fresh eyes. Chances are your letter has at least a couple of minor flaws and possibly even some major organizational problems. To perform the required fixes and purge common errors from your letter, you need to master the tools of the trade. The following sections show you how to use your word processor's editing tools to copy, move, and delete text, and how to check for and correct spelling errors and typos.

Selecting Text

Before you can do anything with the text you just typed, you must select it. You can always just drag over text to select it (as explained earlier in this chapter), but Word offers several quicker ways to select text. The following table describes these techniques.

Quick Text-Selection Techniques

To Select This	Do This
Single word	Double-click the word.
Sentence	**Ctrl+click** anywhere in the sentence.
Paragraph	Triple-click anywhere in the paragraph. Alternatively, position the pointer to the left of the paragraph until it changes to a right-pointing arrow, and then double-click.
Several paragraphs	Position the pointer to the left of the paragraphs until it changes to a right-pointing arrow. Then double-click and drag up or down.
One line of text	Position the pointer to the left of the line until it changes to a right-pointing arrow, and then click. (Click and drag to select additional lines.)
Large block of text	Click at the beginning of the text, scroll down to the end of the text, and **Shift+click.**
Entire document	Press **Ctrl+A.** Alternatively, position the pointer to the left of any text until it changes to a right-pointing arrow, and then triple-click.
Extend the selection	Hold down the **Shift** key while using the arrow keys, **Page Up, Page Down, Home,** or **End.**

Cutting and Pasting Without Scissors

Every word processor features the electronic equivalent of scissors and glue. With the cut, copy, and paste commands, you can cut or copy selected text and then insert it in a different location in your document. You can even copy or cut text from one document and paste it in another document!

To cut or copy text, first select it, and then click either the **Cut** or the **Copy** button on the toolbar. Move the insertion point to where you want the text inserted, and then click the **Paste** button. (Note that cutting a selection deletes it, whereas copying it leaves the selection in place and creates a duplicate.)

Whenever you cut or copy data in any Windows program, Windows places the data in a temporary storage area called the *Clipboard*. In the old days, the Clipboard could store only one chunk of data. If you cut one selection and then cut another selection, the second selection would bump the first selection off the Clipboard. Recent versions of Office, starting with Office 2000 and including Office XP and Office 2003, have upgraded the Clipboard to store 12 or more copied or cut items.

When you cut or copy two or more selections, the Clipboard toolbar or task pane appears, displaying an icon for each copied or cut selection. To paste the selection, click its icon. To paste all of the cut or copied selections, click the **Paste All** button. If the Clipboard toolbar does not appear in Word 2000, right-click any toolbar and click **Clipboard.** In Word 2002 and 2003, open the **Edit** menu and click **Office Clipboard.** This displays a Clipboard task pane on the right, providing a list of the 24 most recently cut or copied selections. Double-click the desired selection to paste it.

> **Inside Tip**
>
> To quickly move selected text, just drag it to the desired location in the document and release the mouse button. To copy the text, hold down the **Ctrl** key while you drag.

Oops! Undoing Changes

What if you highlight your entire document, intending to change the font size, and then press the **Delete** key by mistake? Is your entire document gone for good?

Nope.

As you cut, paste, delete, and perform similar acts of destruction, your word processor keeps track of each command and lets you recover from the occasional blunder. To undo the most recent action, open the **Edit** menu and choose **Undo,** or click the **Undo** button (the button with the counterclockwise arrow on it) in the Standard toolbar or press **Ctrl+Z**. You can continue to click the **Undo** button to undo additional actions. Click the **Redo** button (the clockwise arrow) to undo Undo (or to again perform the action you just performed). You can Redo a previous edit by pressing **Ctrl+Y**.

Whoa!

Make sure you finish using the Undo feature before closing your document. After you save your document and close it, you cannot reopen it and undo actions you performed during a previous work session.

Checking Your Spelling and Grammar

Earlier in this chapter, you learned that Word automatically checks for typos and spelling errors as you type. If you turned off that option, you can initiate a spelling check by opening the **Tools** menu and selecting **Spelling and Grammar** or by clicking the **Spelling and Grammar** button on the Standard toolbar.

Word starts checking your document and stops on the first questionable word (a word not stored in the spelling checker's dictionary or a repeated word, such as *the the*). The Spelling and Grammar dialog box displays the word in red and usually displays a list of suggested corrections, as shown in Figure 12.6. (If the word appears in green, the grammar checker is questioning the word's usage, not its spelling.) You have several options:

- If the word is misspelled and the **Suggestions** list displays the correct spelling, click the correct spelling and then click **Change** to replace only this occurrence of the word.

- Double-click the word in the **Not in Dictionary** text box, type the correction, and click **Change.**

- To replace this misspelled word and all other occurrences of the word in this document, click the correct spelling in the **Suggestions** list and then click **Change All.**

- Click **Ignore** or **Ignore Once** if the word is spelled correctly and you want to skip it just this once. Word will stop on the next occurrence of the word.

♦ Click **Ignore All** if the word is spelled correctly but is not in the dictionary and you want Word to skip all other occurrences of this word in the document.

♦ Click **Add** or **Add to Dictionary** to add the word to the dictionary so that the spelling checker never questions it again in any of your Office documents. (The dictionary is shared by all Office applications.)

Inside Tip

To check the spelling of a single word or paragraph, double-click the word or triple-click the paragraph to select it before you start the spelling checker. When Word is done checking the selection, it displays a dialog box asking if you want to check the rest of the document.

Don't place too much trust in your spell checker. It merely compares the words in its dictionary to the words in your document and highlights any string of text that's not in the dictionary. If you typed "its" when you should have typed "it's," the spelling checker won't flag the error. Likewise, if you type a scientific term correctly that is not in the spelling checker's dictionary, the spelling checker will flag the word, even if it is correct. Proofread your documents carefully before considering them final.

When Word completes the spelling check, it displays a dialog box telling you so. Click **OK**.

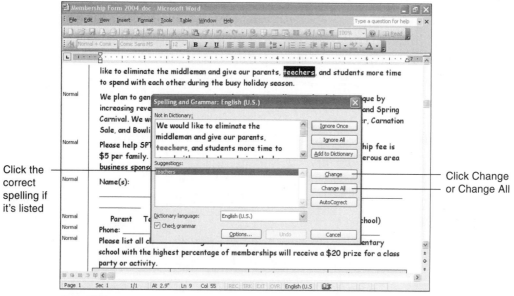

Click the correct spelling if it's listed

Click Change or Change All

Figure 12.6

If Word finds a misspelling and displays the correct spelling, your options are easy.

The Least You Need to Know

◆ Use the **Zoom** list to zoom in if the text is too small.

◆ Use the arrow keys or the mouse to move the insertion point.

◆ Drag the mouse pointer over text to highlight it.

◆ Use the buttons in the Formatting toolbar to quickly style and align your text.

◆ To avoid losing your document, press **Ctrl+S** to save it to your computer's hard disk.

◆ To undo your most recent action, open the **Edit** menu and click **Undo** or click the **Undo** button.

Chapter **13**

Crunching Numbers
with Spreadsheets

In This Chapter

◆ See the similarities between your checkbook and a spreadsheet

◆ Type text, numbers, and dates in a spreadsheet cell

◆ Add formulas to a spreadsheet to perform calculations on the values
you entered

◆ Graph the values in a spreadsheet even if you don't know how to graph

There's no mystery to spreadsheets. A checkbook is a spreadsheet. A calendar is a spreadsheet. Your 1040 tax form is a spreadsheet. Any sheet that has boxes you can fill in is a type of spreadsheet.

So what's so special about computerized spreadsheets? For one thing, they do the math for you. For example, a computerized grade book spreadsheet can add each student's grades, determine the average for each student, and even assign the correct letter grade for each average. And that's not all. The spreadsheet can also display the averages as a graph, showing how each student is doing in relation to the other students or highlighting a student's progress or decline in performance. In this chapter, you learn what it takes to create your own spreadsheets, and some of the things you can do with them.

A Computerized Ledger Sheet

A spreadsheet is a grid consisting of a series of columns and rows that intersect to form thousands of small boxes called *cells*, as shown in Figure 13.1. Most spreadsheet applications display a collection of spreadsheets (also called *worksheets*) in a workbook. You can flip the pages in the workbook by clicking the *worksheet tabs* (a.k.a. *spreadsheet tabs*).

Figure 13.1

A popular spreadsheet application with a sample file open.

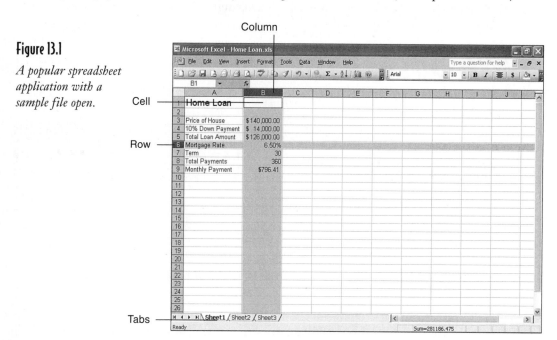

Why Did the Column Cross the Row?

Look across the top of any computer spreadsheet, and you'll see the alphabet (A, B, C, and so on). Each letter stands at the top of a *column*. Along the left side of the spreadsheet, you'll see numbers representing *rows*. The place where a column and row intersect forms a box, called a *cell*. This is the basic unit of any spreadsheet. You will type text, values, and formulas in the cells to make your spreadsheet. Some spreadsheet applications let you name individual cells or groups of cells (*ranges*). You can then use the names, instead of the cell addresses, to refer to the cells.

Knowing Where a Cell Lives

To keep track of where each cell is located and what each cell contains, the spreadsheet uses *cell addresses.* Each cell has an address made up of a column letter and row number. For example, the cell that's formed by the intersection of column B and row 3 has the address B3 (see Figure 13.2).

Cell Hopping

To select a block of cells, drag over the cells to highlight them. To select a row, click the row number that's to the left of the desired row or drag over two or more row numbers to select multiple rows. To select a column, click the letter that's above the desired column or drag over two or more column letters to select multiple columns.

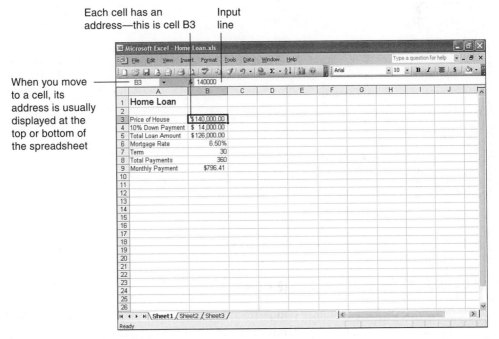

Figure 13.2

A cell's contents appear in the input line.

Building a Spreadsheet from the Ground Up

I bet you're just dying to know how you go about making a spreadsheet. The easiest way is to get a friend to set it up for you—to insert all the formulas and other complicated stuff. Then all you have to do is type in your data and watch the spreadsheet do its thing. If you're a do-it-yourselfer, however, you need to take the following steps (don't worry, I go into more detail later in this chapter):

Step 1:   Design the spreadsheet.

Step 2:   Label the columns and rows.

Step 3:   Enter your data: labels (text), values (numbers), and dates.

Step 4:   Enter the formulas and functions that the spreadsheet will use to perform calculations.

Step 5:   Format the cells (to display dollar signs, for instance).

There's no law that says you have to perform the steps in this order. Some users like to enter their formulas before entering their data, so the formulas calculate results as they work. Regardless of how you proceed, you will probably have to go back to previous steps to fine-tune your spreadsheet.

Computer Cheat

If you need a spreadsheet for a common task, such as determining a loan payment, check to see if your spreadsheet program features a template for the task you want to perform. Open the **File** menu, select **New,** and choose the option for creating a spreadsheet from a template. Excel comes with dozens of templates, and later versions of Excel enable you to copy additional templates from Microsoft's "Office on the Web" site. With a template, everything is laid out for you; you simply plug in the specific data you want to use.

Step 1: Designing the Spreadsheet

If you have a form that you want the spreadsheet to look like, lay the form down by your keyboard and use it as a model. For example, if you're going to use the spreadsheet to balance your checkbook, use your most recent bank statement or your checkbook register to model the columns and rows.

If you don't have a form, draw your spreadsheet on a piece of paper or a napkin to determine the columns and rows you need. (It doesn't have to be perfect, just something to get you started.)

Step 2: Labeling Your Columns and Rows

When you have some idea of the basic structure of your spreadsheet, you're ready to enter *labels*. Labels are commonsense names for the columns and rows.

To enter a label, click in the cell where you want it to appear, type the label, and press **Enter.** If your label starts with a number (for example, 2007 Sales), you may have to type something in front of it to tell the spreadsheet to treat it as text rather than as a value. In most applications you type an apostrophe (') or a quotation mark ("). Usually, whatever you type appears only in the input line until you press Enter. Then the label is inserted into the current cell. (If you type an apostrophe, it remains invisible in the cell, although you can see it when the entry is displayed on the input line.)

If an entry is too wide for a cell, it overlaps cells to the right of it … unless the cell to the right has its own entry. In such a case, the entry on the left appears chopped off (hidden). If you click the cell, you can view the entire entry on the input line. If you want to see the entire entry in the cell, you can widen the column, usually by dragging the right side of the column header, as shown in Figure 13.3.

Step 2½: Editing Your Entries

When you make mistakes or change your mind about what you entered, the best way to make corrections usually is to replace the entry. **Tab** to the cell that contains the entry, type the replacement, and press **Enter.** That's all there is to it.

To edit an entry, click in the cell you want to change, and then click inside the entry in the input line or press the key for editing the entry (the **F2** key in Excel). This puts you in *Edit mode*, and allows you to edit the entry on the input line. You can then use the arrow keys to move the cursor or insertion point and type your change. Press **Enter** when you're done. Newer versions of most spreadsheet applications offer something called *in-cell editing*. Instead of editing the entry on the input line, you edit it directly inside the cell. To edit an entry, you simply double-click it, and then enter your changes.

Click the check mark or press
Enter to accept the entry

Input
line

If an entry is too wide for a cell, drag the right side
of the column header to increase the column width

This button
cancels the entry

The entry is
inserted into
the cell

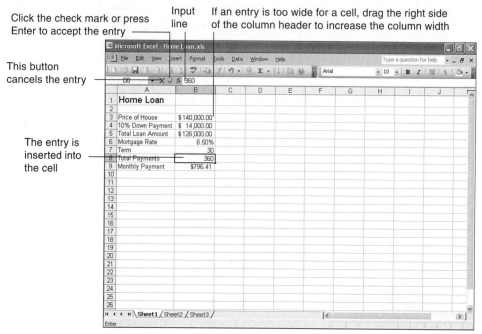

Figure 13.3

Select a cell, and then type your entry.

Step 3: Entering Values and Dates

After you have labeled your rows and columns, you're ready to enter your raw data: the values and/or dates that make up your spreadsheet. As you type your entries, keep the following in mind:

♦ **Values are numbers.** Whenever you type a number, the spreadsheet "knows" it's a value. You don't have to do anything special.

♦ **Don't enter dollar or percent signs.** You can have the spreadsheet add these symbols for you when you format the cells. Type only the number. In some spreadsheets, you must pick a number format before you start typing. For instance, you might type a date and have it appear as a number rather than as a date. See "Step 5: Making the Cells Look Pretty," later in this chapter, for more information on how to do this.

♦ **Type dates in the proper format for your spreadsheet.** In most spreadsheets, you must type the date in the format mm/dd/yy (02/25/07) or dd-mmm-yy (02-FEB-07).

◆ **Dates are handled as numbers.** Although the spreadsheet displays dates in a format that people understand, it treats a date as a numeric value (typically the number of days since January 1, 1900). You can then have the spreadsheet use the date in a formula to calculate when a payment or delivery is due.

◆ **######## Long entries.** If a value you type is too wide for a cell, the spreadsheet may display a series of number signs (#) or asterisks (*) instead of the value. Don't worry—your entry is still there. You can click the cell to see the entry in the input line, and if you widen the column, the spreadsheet will display the entire value.

To enter values or labels quickly, many spreadsheets let you copy entries into one or more cells or *fill* selected cells with a series of entries. For example, in an Excel spreadsheet, you can type **January** in one cell, and then use the **Fill** command to have Excel insert the remaining 11 months in the 11 cells to the right. Fill also allows you to duplicate entries. For example, you can type **250** in one cell, and then use the **Fill** command (or drag the Fill handle down, as shown in Figure 13.4) to enter 250 into the next 10 cells down.

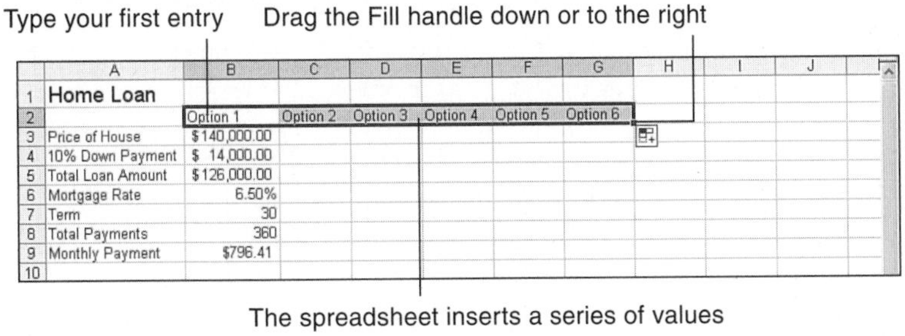

Type your first entry   Drag the Fill handle down or to the right

Figure 13.4

Excel's Fill feature in action.

The spreadsheet inserts a series of values

Step 4: Calculating with Formulas and Functions

At this point, you should have rows and columns of values. You need some way to total the values, determine an average, or perform other mathematical operations. That's where formulas and functions come in. They do all the busy work for you ... after you set them up.

What Are Formulas?

Spreadsheets use formulas to perform calculations on the data you enter. With formulas, you can perform addition, subtraction, multiplication, or division using the values contained in various cells.

Formulas typically consist of one or more cell addresses and/or values and a mathematical operator, such as + (addition), – (subtraction), * (multiplication), or / (division). For example, if you want to determine the average of the three values contained in cells A1, B1, and C1, you use the following formula:

(A1+B1+C1)/3

Entering Formulas in Your Spreadsheet

To enter a formula, move to the cell in which you want the formula to appear, type the formula, and press **Enter.** Some spreadsheets assume that you want to type a formula if you start your entry with a column letter. Other spreadsheets require you to start the formula with a mathematical operator, such as an equal sign (=) or plus sign (+). Figure 13.5 shows some basic formulas in action.

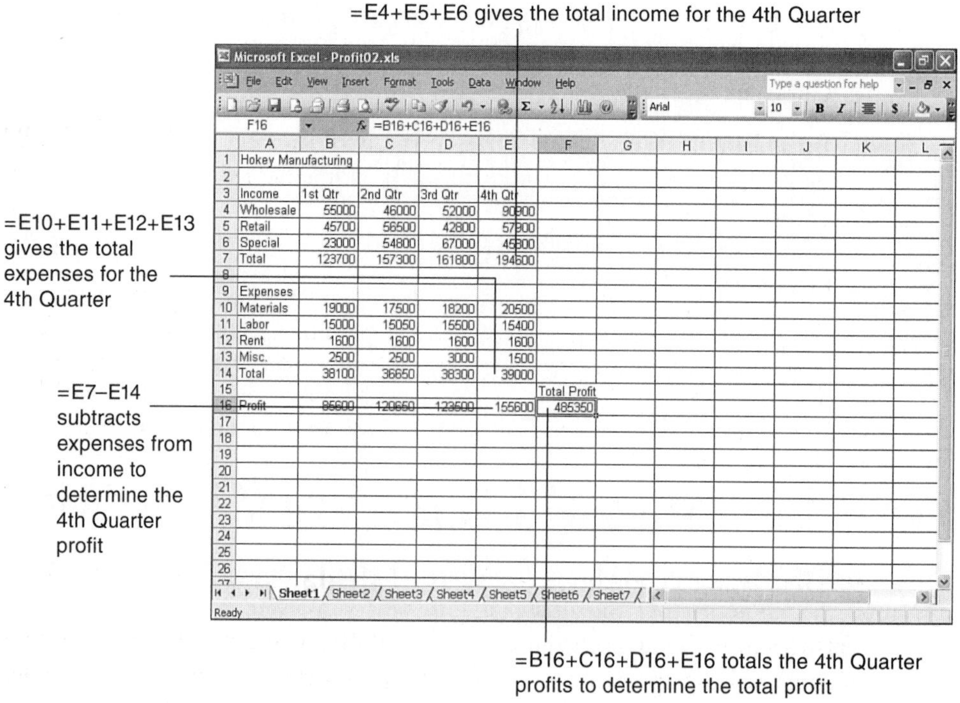

=E4+E5+E6 gives the total income for the 4th Quarter

=E10+E11+E12+E13 gives the total expenses for the 4th Quarter

=E7–E14 subtracts expenses from income to determine the 4th Quarter profit

=B16+C16+D16+E16 totals the 4th Quarter profits to determine the total profit

Figure 13.5

Some formulas at work.

Most spreadsheets let you enter formulas in either of two ways. You can type the formula directly in the cell in which you want the result inserted or you can use the mouse to point and click on the cells whose values you want inserted in the formula. To use the second method, called *pointing*, you use the keyboard and mouse together. For example, to determine the total of the values in B4, B5, and B6, you perform the following steps:

1. Click the cell in which you want to enter the formula. The formula's result will appear in this cell.

2. Type = to mark this as a formula.

3. Click cell **B4** to add the cell's address to your formula.

4. Type + to add another cell address to the formula.

5. Click cell **B5.**

6. Type + to add the final cell address to the formula.

7. Click cell **B6.**

8. Press **Enter** to accept the formula. If any of the cells in the formula (B4, B5, or B6) contains a value, the formula's result appears in the cell in which you entered the formula.

Inside Tip

If your spreadsheet application has a toolbar, it probably has a Sum button. To quickly determine a total, the cell in which you want the total inserted, click the **Sum** button, and then drag over the cells that contain the values you want to add. When you release the mouse button and press **Enter**, the spreadsheet performs the required calculations and inserts the result.

Using Ready-Made Functions for Fancy Calculations

Creating simple formulas (such as one for adding a column of numbers) is a piece of cake, but creating the formulas required for a mortgage refinance spreadsheet can pose quite a challenge. To help you in such cases, many spreadsheet applications offer predefined formulas called *functions*.

Functions are complex ready-made formulas that perform a series of operations on a specified *range* of values. For example, to determine the sum of a series of numbers in cells A1 through H1, you can enter the function =SUM(A1:H1), instead of entering =A1+B1+C1+ and so on. Every function consists of three elements:

◆ The @ or = sign indicates that what follows is a function.

◆ The **function name** (for example, SUM) indicates the operation to be performed.

◆ The **argument** (for example A1:H1) gives the cell addresses of the values the function will act on. For example, =SUM(A1:H1) determines the total of the values in cells A1 through H1.

> **Inside Tip**
>
> Use this mnemonic device to remember the order in which a spreadsheet performs mathematical operations: My (multiplication) Dear (division) Aunt (addition) Sally (subtraction). To change the order of operations, use parentheses. Any operation inside parentheses is performed first.

Although functions are fairly complicated and intimidating, many spreadsheets have tools to help. For example, Microsoft Excel offers a tool called the Function Wizard (or Insert Function tool), which leads you through the process of inserting functions. It displays a series of dialog boxes asking you to select the function you want to use, and pick the values for the argument. Figure 13.6 shows the Insert Function tool in action.

Figure 13.6

Tools such as the Insert Function tool makes it easier to work with functions.

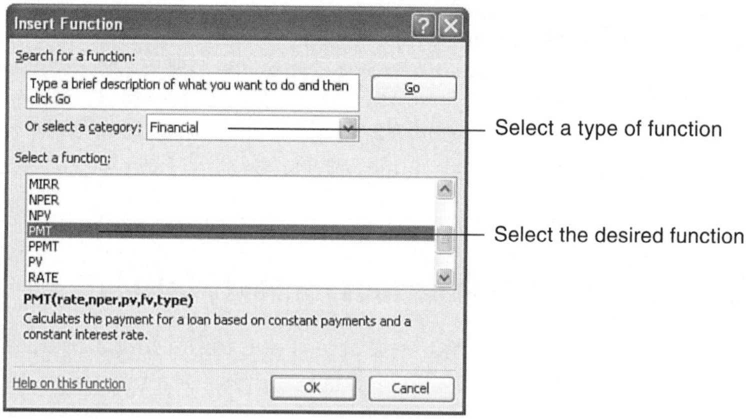

Select a type of function

Select the desired function

Step 5: Making the Cells Look Pretty

When you have the basic layout of your spreadsheet under control, you can *format* the cells, to give the spreadsheet the desired "look." The first thing you might want to do is change the column width and row height to give your entries some breathing room. You may also want to format the values—tell the application to display values as dollar amounts or to use commas to mark the thousand's place.

def•i•ni•tion

Formatting cells means to improve the look of the cells or cell entries without changing their content. Formatting usually includes changing the type style and size of type, adding borders and shading to the cells, and telling the application how to display values (for example, as currency or in scientific notation). Formatting a cell that contains a value or formula may change the appearance of the value in the cell but does not change the actual value stored in the cell.

In addition, you can change the type style and type size for your column or row headings, change the text color, and align the text in the cells. For example, you may want to center the headings or align the values in a column so that the decimal points line up. To improve the look of the cells themselves, and to distinguish one set of data from another, you can add borders around the cells and add shading and color to the cells.

To format cells, select the cells you want to format and then use the controls on the Formatting toolbar or the options on the Format menu to apply the desired formatting.

Many newer spreadsheet applications have an AutoFormat feature that enables you to select the look you want your spreadsheet to have. The application then applies the lines, shading, and fonts to give your spreadsheet a makeover, as shown in Figure 13.7.

After you've formatted your spreadsheet, you can print it. With some spreadsheet applications, such as the latest version of Excel, you can publish your spreadsheet and graphs electronically on the World Wide Web.

Figure 13.7

Some applications can format your spreadsheet for you.

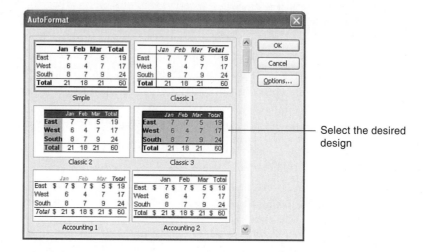

Select the desired design

Instant Graphs (Just Add Data)

People, especially management types, like to look at graphs. They don't want to have to compare a bunch of numbers; they want the bottom line. They want to see immediately how the numbers stack up. Most spreadsheet applications offer a graphing feature to transform the values you entered into any type of graph (a.k.a. *chart*) you want: bar, line, pie, area, or high-low (to analyze stock trends). The steps for creating a graph are simple:

1. Drag with the mouse over the labels and values that you want to include in the graph. (Labels are used for the *axes*.)

2. Enter the **Graph** or **Chart** command. (This command varies from application to application.)

3. Select the type of graph you want to create.

4. Select the **OK** option. The application transforms your data into a graph and inserts it into the spreadsheet, as shown in Figure 13.8.

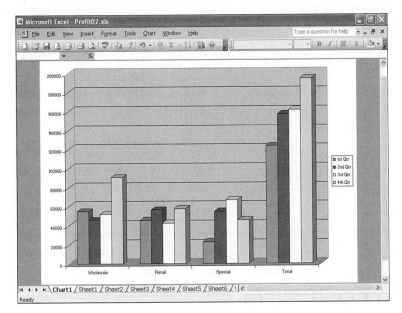

Figure 13.8

Most spreadsheet applications can quickly throw together any type of graph you need.

Special Spreadsheet Printing Considerations

When you print a letter or other document created in a word processing application, you typically don't need to worry that your paragraphs will be too wide for the pages. The word processor automatically wraps the text to make it fit. Spreadsheets, however, can be much wider than a typical 8½ × 11-inch sheet of paper. To accommodate extra wide spreadsheets, your spreadsheet application features special print options. The following sections explain some of these options in greater detail.

Previewing Your Spreadsheets Before Printing

Before you start tweaking the spreadsheet layout and adjusting print settings to make a spreadsheet fit on 8½ × 11-inch pages, check your page setup to determine how your spreadsheet application is prepared to print your spreadsheet(s). Frequently, the application inserts awkward page breaks, omits titles and column headings from some of the pages, and uses additional settings that result in an unacceptable printout.

To check your spreadsheet before printing, click the **Print Preview** button (or select **File, Print Preview**). This displays your spreadsheet in Print Preview mode, as shown in Figure 13.9.

Figure 13.9

Excel's Print Preview lets you see how a spreadsheet will print before you print it.

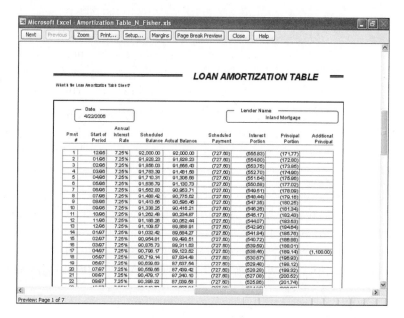

Along the top of the preview area are several buttons that enable you to flip pages, zoom in and zoom out on the page, and change some common print settings. If your spreadsheet application displays a **Margins** button, click it to display margin and column markers; you can drag the markers to adjust column widths and page margins right onscreen. If your application displays a **Page Break Preview** button, click the button to see how the application plans on dividing your spreadsheet into pages; you can drag the page break bars to adjust the page breaks before printing.

Changing the Page Setup

If your spreadsheet is close to fitting on a single page, you usually can adjust the left and right margins to pull another column or two (or a couple of rows) onto the page. If the spreadsheet still doesn't fit, you may need to adjust the page setup, via the Page Setup dialog box. To display the Page Setup dialog box, open the **File** menu and click **Page Setup,** or click the **Setup** button on the Print Preview screen. In Excel, the Page Setup dialog box features the following four tabs:

- **Page.** This tab contains options for specifying the page orientation (portrait or landscape), the paper size, print quality, and the number at which Excel starts numbering the pages. This tab also offers an interesting feature that can shrink your spreadsheet to fit on one or more pages.

- **Margins.** This tab contains spin boxes for setting the top, bottom, left, and right margins and for specifying the distance between the top edge of the page and the header and the distance between the bottom edge of the page and the footer. You may prefer to set margins in Print Preview.

- **Header/Footer.** This tab provides options for printing a footer (on the bottom of each page) or a header (at the top of each page) that automatically numbers the spreadsheet pages for you and prints the file's name, the spreadsheet title, the date and time, and any other information you want to include.

- **Sheet.** The Sheet tab enables you to specify the order in which you want your pages printed and to designate one or more rows you want to print at the top of every page and one or more columns you want printed along the left side of every page. This tab includes several additional options, including an option for specifying a print area, so you can print only a select portion of the spreadsheet.

Printing Your Spreadsheets

When you're satisfied with the way your spreadsheet looks in Print Preview, you're ready to send it to your printer. The quickest way to print is to click the tab for the spreadsheet you want to print and then click the **Print** button. This sends the spreadsheet off to the printer, no questions asked. To print more than one spreadsheet or set additional printing preferences, open the **File** menu, click **Print,** and enter your preferences.

The Least You Need to Know

- A cell can contain any of the following entries: a row or column heading, a formula, a function with an argument, or a value.

- Formulas perform calculations on the values in the cells. Each formula consists of one or more cell addresses and a math operator.

- A function is a ready-made complex formula that performs calculations on a range of values.

◆ You can format the cells in a spreadsheet to control the text size and style, row height, column width, borders, and shading.

◆ Spreadsheet programs include several special page setup options to cram wide spreadsheets on narrow sheets of paper.

Chapter 14

Storing and Managing Information in a Database

In This Chapter

- ◆ Witness the power of a database management program
- ◆ Create a fill-in-the-blanks form to shovel information into your database
- ◆ Sort your database entries alphabetically or numerically, forward or backward
- ◆ Merge a database with a stick-on label to create and print mailing labels

Picture this. It's the year 2020. Frank Gifford has moved to FOX TV and is color man for Super Bowl LIV. It's the Cowboys against the Bills (yes, again), and you're in the booth with Frank. You purchased exclusive rights to the only sports trivia database on the planet, making you the most powerful (and highest paid) data broker in history. The Gif turns to you and says, "What was the last team to have lost four consecutive Super Bowls in a row?" You overlook the mild redundancy, type **Losses = 4,** and press the **Enter** key. A list of all the teams that lost four Super Bowls pops up on your screen, showing the dates of the losses. You say, "Holey moley, Gif! It was the Buffalo Bills in Super Bowls XXV through XXVIII!"

You have instant access to the most valuable information: pass completions, interceptions, third down conversions, even those salary figures that make your nose bleed. Ahhhh, the power of information is at your fingertips!

A database gives you such power by automating the process of organizing, storing, and retrieving piles of data. A database can search through thousands of records in the blink of an eye (no matter how useless or insignificant that data might be) and pick out just the data you need. This chapter reveals the power of the database and shows you the basics of creating one to manage your own information.

The Making of a Database: Behind the Scenes

Before you get mired in the gory details of what it takes to create a database, familiarize yourself with the overall process. Creating a database consists of two steps:

> **Step 1: Create a fill-in-the-blanks form.** Forms simulate on the computer screen, the paper forms you fill out with a pen or pencil (for example, an insurance claim, a tax return, or a Rolodex card). To create a form, you must enter *field names* to indicate where each piece of information should be typed; for example, LastName, FirstName, MI, SSN, Address, and so on.

> **Step 2: Fill in the blanks.** After you have a form, you can fill in the blanks with the information (or plant an ad in the paper for a data-entry operator). The blanks, in this case, are referred to as *fields*. By entering information into the fields, you create a *record*, as shown in Figure 14.1. A database is a collection of *records*.

def•i•ni•tion

A **record** is a collection of information about a person, place, or thing. It may contain specifications for a gear or the name, address, and accounting information for a client. A collection of records makes up a database.

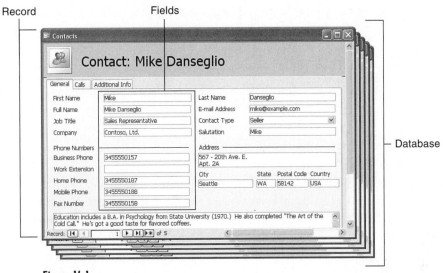

Figure 14.1

A database is sort of like a Rolodex.

Step 1: Designing the Perfect Form

The best way to start designing a form is to follow the paper system you're currently using—your Rolodex, phone book, calendar, list of employees, accounts receivable, inventory list, or whatever. Think up field names for each piece of information you'll need (or just lift the field names from the existing paper form). Weed out any unnecessary information—you don't want to turn your database into a junkyard. When you're designing the form and creating fields, keep the following guidelines in mind:

♦ **Use form numbers.** If you're using the database to store information such as invoices or purchase orders, include a field that gives each record a unique number. This enables you to arrange the records in the same order you entered them, just in case they get jumbled later.

♦ **Be logical.** Your form should present information in a natural flow, from left to right and top to bottom, in the order that you use it.

♦ **Leave space to the right.** Leave blank space for entering data to the right of the field name, not below it. Leave sufficient space for your entries. (Many database programs allow you to make a field expandable, so it will automatically stretch to accommodate long entries.)

♦ **Use brief field names.** Keep field names just long enough to explain the entry that follows. Long field names take space away from your entries.

◆ **Use examples.** If an entry can be typed a number of ways, include an example of how you want it entered—such as, Date (mm/dd/yyyy). It is likely that someone besides you will enter information into the database. By giving an example of how to format entries, you ensure consistency.

◆ **Break entries into parts.** If you place each piece of data into a separate field, it's easier to pull out individual pieces of data later. For example, to record a name create separate fields for the person's title (Mr./Ms./Mrs.), first name, last name, and middle initial.

You can design a form ahead of time, but before creating the form, you must create the desired fields. A field has three essential components: a field name, type (e.g., text, number, date/time, or currency), and field width. Newer, top-of-the-line database applications can help you create a custom database. When you start Microsoft Access, a dialog box appears, asking if you want to create a new database using the Database Wizard. The wizard leads you through the process of entering field names and even allows you to start with an existing form (such as an address book, recipe list, or home inventory record).

As shown in Figure 14.2, the database may display your fields as a form or as a table (sort of like a spreadsheet). In most database applications, you can switch between form and table view and use whichever view is easiest for you to type your entries.

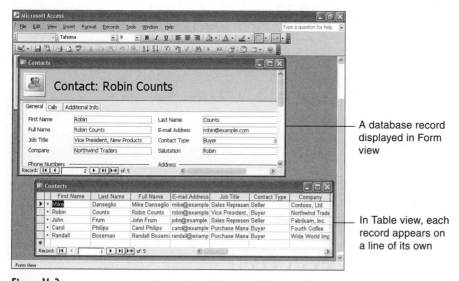

A database record displayed in Form view

In Table view, each record appears on a line of its own

Figure 14.2

You can enter information on a blank form or in a table.

Step 2: Filling in the Blanks

When you start filling out your forms, you feel as though you're spending an eternity in your doctor's office. Here's where you enter all the information that you want to include in your database: names, addresses, company contacts, part numbers, prices, inventory lists.

If you have to do it yourself, simply type an entry in each field. To move the insertion point from one field to the next, click in the field or press the **Tab** key. When you click the button to go to the next record or display a new record, the database saves the record you just entered and displays a blank form for your next record.

Computer Cheat

If you're using an application suite that includes a database manager and you already created a document that contains the information you want to use for your database, you may be able to export the data from the other application (word processor or spreadsheet, for example) rather than having to retype it. Check the application's help system for details. You can also drag and drop data entries from other documents into your database forms.

Ferreting Out Information in a Database

Now that you have this oversized filing cabinet sitting in your computer, how do you go about getting at those records? You have at least three options. You can browse through the records one at a time. You can list the information in every record according to field name. Or you can search for a specific record or range of records.

Just Browsing, Thanks

Browsing consists of flipping through the electronic pages of your database. It's a fairly slow process and is useful for finding a record when you don't know which record you're looking for. If you have even a vague notion of which record you need, you're better off using one of the other two methods.

Gimme the List

Instead of displaying each record on a single screen, the List (or Table) option displays each record on a single line (from left to right across the screen). Although some of the information for each record typically trails off the right side of the screen, you can see a small portion of each record.

In Search of a Single Record

The fastest and easiest way to search a database is to look for a specific record. You start by entering a command telling the database to search, and it responds by asking what you want to search for.

In most databases, you must specify the field in which you want to search and the information you want to find in that field. The entry you type is referred to as *search criteria*. For example, to look up the March sales total for one of your sales reps, Alan Nelson, you'd enter the following search criteria:

- ◆ Search the Month field for March.
- ◆ Search the LastName field for Nelson.
- ◆ Search the FirstName field for Alan.

Only one record matches your search criteria, so Alan Nelson's March sales total appears on the screen. You can review it to determine his total sales for the month.

Searching for a Range of Records

In addition to searching for an individual record, you can tell the database to search for a group of records. For example, to search for purchase order numbers 10013 to 10078, or companies with outstanding balances of $300 to $1,500, you enter a range in the field you want to search. Table 14.1 shows some sample search entries.

Table 14.1: Searches Within a Range

Search Criteria	Finds
K>W	Words beginning with K through V, but not A through J or W through Z
<=50	Numbers 50 or less
>=3/16/1991<=3/31/1991	Any record from March 16 to March 31 1991

Don't Know What You're Looking For?

After you've entered a hundred or a thousand records, no one can seriously expect you to remember the exact spelling of every entry in every field. You'll forget a few, and you need some way of finding these records. That's why most database programs let you use *wildcards* to search for records. (Wildcards stand in for characters you can't remember.)

Most programs support two wildcards: the asterisk (*) and the question mark (?). The question mark stands in for a single character; for example, to find all entries with Anderson or Andersen, you type **Anders?n.** The asterisk stands in for two or more characters; for example, to find any entry that ends in "son" (such as Anderson, Thompson, or Tyson), you type ***son.**

Get Organized! Sort Your Records

The database stores records in the order in which you entered them. If you entered a stack of records in no particular order, your database is a mess. Whenever you call up a list of records, they appear in no logical order. Fortunately, the database can *sort* your records in whatever order you specify and present you with a neat, orderly stack.

Like the Search feature, the Sort feature requires you to enter criteria that tell the program how to sort your records. You have to specify two things: the sort field and the sort direction. The sort field tells the database which field entries to use for sorting the records. For example, if you sort by postal code, the database rearranges the records using the numbers in the Postal Code field. You can also specify a second sort field that the database could use if the first field is the same for two or more records. (Phone book entries, for instance, are sorted by last name and then first name.) The sort direction tells the program whether to sort in ascending order (A B C ... or 1 2 3 ...) or descending order (Z Y X ... or 10 9 8 ...).

Figure 14.3 shows a sample form used to sort records in a database.

Figure 14.3

In Microsoft Access, you can enter sort instructions for one or more fields.

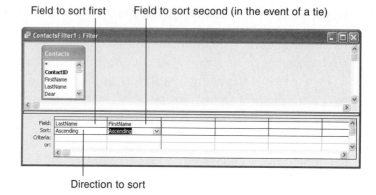

Field to sort first   Field to sort second (in the event of a tie)

Direction to sort

Creating Form Letters and Mailing Labels

You've seen how much power the field names give you in searching and sorting your records, but that's not the half of it. You can also use field names to yank information out of your records and stick it in other documents. This allows you to create form letters, reports, invoices, mailing labels, and much more.

To create a form letter, you would use your word processor to type a generic letter. In place of the recipient's name and address, you type field names, such as the following:

> <Title> <FirstName> <LastName>
> <Address>
> <City>, <State> <Zip>

Then you merge your letter with your database. The merge process looks up information in your database and inserts it in the form letter, creating a separate letter for each selected record in the database (see Figure 14.4).

Analyzing Data with Queries

In addition to pulling data out of a database, you can combine data from two or more database files to demonstrate trends and analyze the data. Suppose you have one database file that contains a list of products, their ID numbers, and their prices. You have another database file that contains a list of customers and the quantity of each type of product they order each month. You want to find out which product is bringing in the most money.

Using a *query*, you can combine the data from the two database files. The query adds the number of each item ordered, multiplies it by the price of each item, and then lists the totals from largest to smallest.

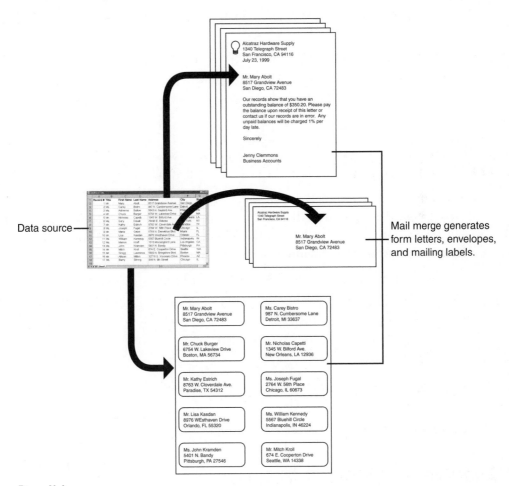

Data source

Mail merge generates form letters, envelopes, and mailing labels.

Figure 14.4

You can merge your database with a document created in your word processor to generate a stack of personalized letters.

The Least You Need to Know

◆ A database consists of records, each of which is made up of multiple field entries.

◆ To build a database, you create a form and then fill out the form to create records.

◆ When you save a record, you're storing information in your database.

◆ You can search your database by browsing page by page, by displaying a list of records, or by entering search criteria for a specific record or range of records.

◆ Field names give you the power to pull information from your database and insert it into a document. This lets you generate comprehensive reports, personalized letters, and mailing labels.

Chapter 15

Getting Graphical ... Even if You're Not Artistic

In This Chapter

- ◆ Build custom slide show presentations
- ◆ Design greeting cards, newsletters, flyers, and other publications
- ◆ Decorate your documents with ready-made clip art
- ◆ Scan drawings, photos, or illustrations into your computer
- ◆ Draw your own illustrations in a paint or draw program

In this age of information overload, most of us would rather look at a picture than wade through a sea of words. We don't want to read a newspaper column to find out how many trillions of dollars we owe as a nation. We want a graph that shows how much we owed in 1960 and how much we'll owe in 2020, or maybe a map that shows how much of our nation we could have covered with $200,000 homes given the amount of our debt, maybe even a picture of a tax dollar that shows how much of each dollar goes to pay interest on the national debt. We want *USA Today!*

But what about your presentations and the documents you create? Are you as kind to your audience as you expect the media to be to you? Do you use pictures to present information more clearly and succinctly? Do you *show* as well as *tell?* After reading this chapter, you'll know about several types of programs that can help you answer "yes" to all of these questions.

Whipping Up Slide Shows, Overhead Transparencies, and Handouts

If you want to know how to create a computerized slide show, ask a junior high school student. Almost every kid over the age of 13 has learned how to create a "PowerPoint." That's short for PowerPoint presentation—interactive, often animated slide shows that you can display onscreen or play on a projector screen.

Microsoft PowerPoint is the most popular slide show presentation program on the planet. It leads you step by step through the process of creating a professional-looking presentation, and it handles all the fancy design stuff for you. All you do is supply the content. The following steps provide a brief overview of how to create a slide show in PowerPoint:

1. **Pick a look, any look.** PowerPoint provides a collection of attractive templates and color schemes. When you pick a template or color scheme, PowerPoint applies the design to all the slides, giving your slide show a consistent and professional look and feel, as shown in Figure 15.1.

2. **Add lists, pictures, and charts.** When the design is in place, you can add objects to each slide. Most slides contain a title, a bulleted or numbered list, and a clip art image or photo. Slides can also contain graphs (often called *charts*), illustrations, flow charts, and just about anything else that you can display on a computer screen.

3. **Shuffle your slides.** If the slides are not in the order in which you want to present them, you can switch to Slide Sorter view, which displays a miniature version of each slide. In Slide Sorter view, simply drag and drop the slides to the desired locations.

4. **Add sound, animation, and special effects.** You can add sound effects to each slide, play background music, add animation to transition smoothly from one slide to the next, or create *builds*—an animation effect that adds items to a slide during your presentation. You simply select the desired effect in PowerPoint and enter a few settings that tell PowerPoint exactly how to execute the special effect.

Inside Tip

To make your slides more effective, consider following these good-practice guidelines:

◆ **The 6x6 rule:** Use no more than 6 words per line and no more than 6 lines per slide, to keep your slides less "busy."

◆ **The 20-point or larger rule:** Use a 20-point or larger font to ensure that the audience can read the words. The slide should guide the presentation rather than include detailed information provided in your speech.

5. **Produce a slide show, overhead transparencies, or audience handouts.** PowerPoint provides several ways to output your presentation. You can create a standard onscreen presentation, save your presentation as a file that you can play on other computers, convert your slide show into web pages for viewing on the Internet, print audience handouts, create your own overhead transparencies, or send the file to a photo shop to have it transformed into 35mm slides!

def•i•ni•tion

PowerPoint uses a **master slide** to control the appearance of all slides in the presentation. If you adjust the master slide, the change appears in all other slides.

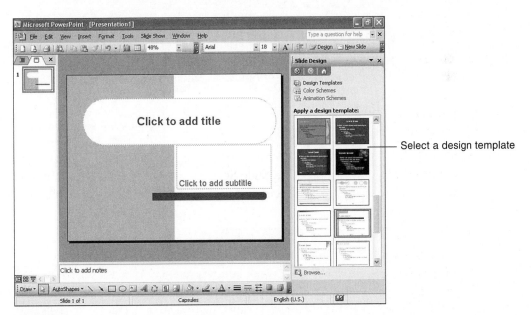

Select a design template

Figure 15.1

In PowerPoint, you can pick a design template or color scheme to apply to every slide in your presentation.

Laying Out Pages in a Desktop Publishing Program

You've probably received computer-generated greeting cards or invitations from friends showing off what they can do with their computers. Now that you have a computer (and hopefully a color printer and a desktop publishing program), you, too, can create your own greeting cards, invitations, brochures, flyers, business cards, calendars, newsletters, and any other fancy documents you can imagine.

If you're slapping together a standard publication, few skills are required. The desktop publishing program does most of the heavy lifting. In Microsoft Publisher, for example, a Publishing Wizard leads you step by step through the process of choosing the type of publication you want to create, entering your text, and positioning graphics and other objects on the page.

When you're done, you have a page or several pages, each of which is decorated with several objects—typically *text boxes* and clip art. A text box, as explained later in this chapter, is a box with text in it. You can move the box anywhere on the page and resize and reshape it to fit in the allotted space. You can do the same with the clip art image, as shown in Figure 15.2.

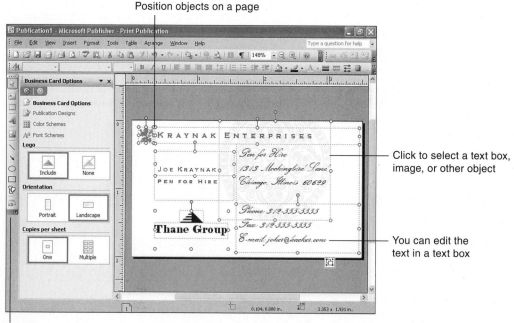

Position objects on a page

Click to select a text box, image, or other object

You can edit the text in a text box

These tools can add other objects to a page

Figure 15.2

In a desktop publishing program, you place and arrange objects on a page to create your publication.

Later in this chapter, you discover how to use the various drawing tools available in a desktop publishing program. You find many of these same tools in graphics programs, word processors, and other applications that offer graphics features.

Inside Tip

You can lay text and graphics on a page in a word processor, but a desktop publishing program supports more precise positioning of objects on a page. With a desktop publishing program, for example, you can print objects upside down and right side up on the same page so that when you fold the page, you end up with a greeting card. In a word processor, you might be able to pull off that same feat, but it would take the better part of the day. Word processors are better for creating long documents that don't require intricate formatting and layout.

Inserting Ready-Made Clip Art Images

The easiest way to begin adorning your documents with graphic objects is to insert *clip art images*—small images rendered by professional artists. With clip art, illustrating your publications is easy. Suppose you're creating a newsletter and you want to spruce it up with some pictures. Nothing fancy; maybe a picture of a fireworks display for a company newsletter or a drawing of a baseball player to mark upcoming games for your softball league. You create the newsletter and then enter a command telling the program to insert a piece of clip art. You select the piece you want, click **OK,** and voilá, instant illustration, no talent required!

Get It Where You Can: Sources of Clip Art

Some programs (desktop publishing, word processing, presentation, and spreadsheet programs) come with a collection of clip art on the installation disks or CDs. Microsoft Office, for example, includes a huge collection of clip art that you can use in all programs in the suite.

You also can purchase separate clip art libraries on disk, just as you would purchase a program. These libraries typically include hundreds or even thousands of clip art images that are broken down into several categories: borders and backgrounds, computers, communications, people and places, animals, productivity and performance, time and money, travel and entertainment, words and symbols—you name it.

Inside Tip _____

You can find gobs of graphics on the Internet, as you'll see in Part 4. You can use a web search tool, as explained in Chapter 19, to find clip art libraries and samples. When you see an image you like, just right-click it and choose **Save Picture As.** (One warning, though: you shouldn't use a picture someone else created in your own publication without the artist's permission.) You can purchase clip art at Clipart.com or subscribe to the site and download a number of clip art images every day for a fixed fee.

Pasting Clip Art on a Page

Now that you have a satchel full of clip art, how do you get it from the satchel into your documents? Well, that depends. Sometimes you have to open the library, cut the picture you want, and paste it onto a page. Other times, you import or insert the image by specifying the name of the file in which the image is saved (it's sort of like opening a file). In Microsoft Word and other Office applications, you position the insertion point where you want the image inserted and then open the **Insert** menu, point to **Picture,** and click **Clip Art.** This opens the Clip Art task pane, shown in Figure 15.3. Click in the **Search for** text box, type a brief description of the desired image, and press **Enter.** The Clip Art task pane displays all the images in the collection that match your search term. Scroll down the list to check out the images, and then click an image to insert it.

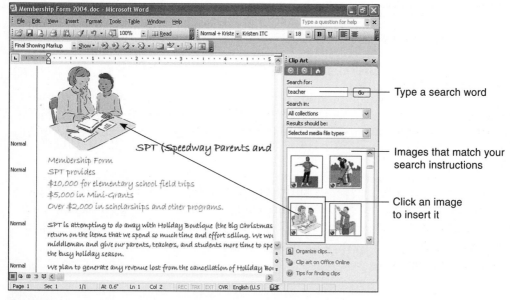

Figure 15.3

You can paste a piece of clip art onto a page.

Hey, the Picture's Blocking My Text

When you lay a picture on top of text, the text typically moves to make room for the picture. In most programs you can set *text wrap* options to control the way that text behaves around the picture. To set the text wrap options, click the picture and then enter the command for formatting the picture (for example, click **Format, Picture**). The following list explains common text wrap options:

♦ **Square.** Places the picture on an imaginary rectangle and wraps the text around the rectangle. For example, if you have a circular picture, you can set text wrapping to square to make the text wrap in a more regular pattern around the image.

♦ **Tight.** Makes the text follow the contour of the picture.

♦ **None.** Places the picture right on top of the text. Choose this only if you have a see-through picture that you want to use as a watermark. Otherwise, it hides your text.

♦ **Top and Bottom.** Places text above and below the picture but does not wrap it around the sides.

♦ **Distance from Text.** Specifies how close the text can get to the image.

Panic Attack

Your choice in how to wrap text around an image seriously affects how the image moves when you drag it. Choosing no text wrapping gives you the most freedom—you can drag the image anywhere, even on top of a chunk of text. If the image refuses to budge when you drag it, the text wrap setting may be restricting its movement.

Resizing and Reshaping Images

When you plop a picture in a document, it rarely places itself in the perfect position. It's usually too big or too small, too far up or too far down, too far to the left or too far to the right. Fortunately, you have full control over the size and placement of the picture.

Changing the size of an image is a fairly standard operation. When you click the picture, squares or circles (called *handles*) surround it, as shown in Figure 15.4. To move the image, position the mouse pointer over the image itself (not over its handles) and drag the image to the desired location. To change the size and dimensions of the image, use the following techniques.

- Drag a top or bottom handle (not in the corner) to make the picture taller or shorter.

- Drag a side handle (not in the corner) to make the picture thinner or wider.

- Drag a corner handle to change both the height and width proportionally.

- If the image has a green circle handle floating above it, drag the green handle to spin the image around its center point.

- Hold down the **Ctrl** key while dragging to increase or decrease the size of the image from the center out.

Figure 15.4

You can quickly resize and reshape an image.

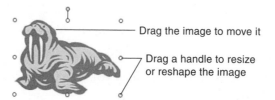

Drag the image to move it

Drag a handle to resize or reshape the image

For more control over the size and dimensions of an image, right-click the image, click **Format Picture** (or **Format Object,** where *Object* is the name of the selected object), and click the **Size** tab. This page of options enables you to enter specific measurements for your picture. (The Size tab typically has an option called Lock Aspect Ratio, which is on by default. This ensures that when you change the height or width of a picture, the corresponding dimension is resized proportionally.)

Many programs also feature a cropping tool that lets you "trim" the edges off an image. Click the **Crop** button, and then drag a handle toward the center of the image to trim an edge off the image. (If you crop too much, drag the handle away from the image to uncrop it.) In Microsoft Office applications, you can find the **Crop** button on the Picture toolbar. (To turn on a toolbar, right-click any toolbar or the menu bar and click the name of the desired toolbar.)

Inserting Other Pictures

Clip art galleries are not the only source of graphic images. You can obtain digitized photos using a digital camera (as explained in Chapter 27), draw your own images, obtain images someone else has created and sent to you, or copy images from the web.

Digitized images are stored in a variety of *file formats.* The file format is computer code that a program uses to render a particular image onscreen and in print. Not all programs can translate all file formats, but most programs support numerous common and uncommon graphic file formats, including WMF (Windows Meta File), TIFF (Tagged Image File Format), GIF (Graphics Interchange Format), JPG or JPEG (Joint Photographic Experts Group), and BMP (Bitmap), to name a few.

Inside Tip _____

You can tell a particular file's format by looking at its file name extension—the three characters tacked on to the end of a file name, after the period. Your computer may be set up to hide file name extensions, but if you right-click a file or a thumbnail view of the image and click **Properties** or **Preview/ Properties,** you can see the complete file name, including its extension.

Though you can obtain images from numerous sources, the process for inserting an image in most programs is fairly standard:

1. Change to the document on which you want the picture inserted.

2. Open the **Insert** menu, point to **Picture,** and click **From File.** An Insert Picture dialog box appears.

3. Select the image file you want to insert and click the **Insert** button.

Scanning Photos, Drawings, and Illustrations

Another way that we, the artistically challenged, overcome our artistic handicap is to scan photos and other images into the computer using a gadget cleverly called a *scanner.* A scanner is sort of like a copy machine, but instead of creating a paper copy of the original, it creates a digital copy that can be saved as a file. You can then print the image, fax it, or even insert it in a document.

Most scanners on the market are *flatbed* scanners. You lay the picture face down on the scanner's glass, and then run the scan program by pressing a button on the scanner or selecting the program from the **Start, All Programs** menu. Another popular type of scanner is the *sheet fed.* With a sheet fed scanner, you load the original picture into a slot on the scanner, and the scanner pulls the original past its scanning mechanism to create the copy.

Whichever way you choose to scan, the scanning program typically displays a dialog box, like the one shown in the Figure 15.5, which prompts you to specify the type of document you're scanning and any preferences.

Figure 15.5

Enter your scanning preferences.

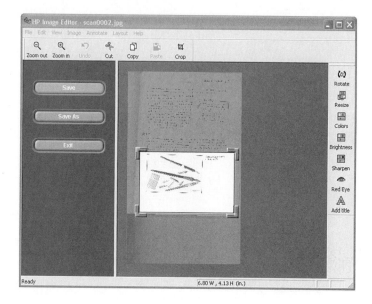

If you have an application that features TWAIN (Technology Without An Interesting Name) support, you can scan an image directly into a document. For example, in Microsoft Word, you position the insertion point where you want the image inserted and choose **Insert, Picture, From Scanner or Camera.** Word runs your scanning program and scans the image. When you exit your scanner's program, the scanned image appears in your Word document.

Drawing and Painting Your Own Illustrations

Clip art, photos, and scanned images are a great source of ready-made art; but when you need a custom illustration, draw it yourself. Most word processors and desktop publishing, spreadsheet, and presentation programs include their own *drawing tools* that enable you to draw lines, arrows, basic shapes, and other objects. In addition, Windows includes its own *paint program* that transforms your monitor into a virtual canvas on which you can paint using an onscreen brush, pen, and "can" of spray paint. The following sections teach you the basic techniques for using paint and draw tools.

def•i•ni•tion

Paint programs and drawing tools differ in how they treat objects. In a paint program, objects consist of thousands of tiny colored dots that comprise the image. **Drawing tools** treat each shape as a continuous line. Drawn objects are easier to resize and move, because you manipulate the shape rather than trying to move a bunch of dots.

Drawing Lines, Squares, Circles, and Other Shapes

Drawing tools consist of onscreen pens, rulers, and templates that enable you to draw lines and basic shapes to create your own custom illustrations. By assembling a collection of these lines and shapes, you can create sophisticated illustrations to adorn your documents. But first you need to know how to draw a line or shape onscreen. The following steps show you how to draw lines and shapes in most programs. If you're working in a Microsoft Office application, you can access the drawing tools by right-clicking the menu bar or any toolbar and clicking **Drawing.** To draw a line or shape, follow these steps:

1. Click the button or select the command for drawing the desired line, arrow, or shape on the Drawing toolbar. When you move the mouse pointer over the page, it changes into a crosshair pointer.

2. Move the crosshair pointer to the position where you want one corner or one end of the object to appear.

3. Hold down the mouse button and drag the pointer away from the starting point in the desired direction until the object is the size and shape you want, as shown in Figure 15.6.

4. Release the mouse button.

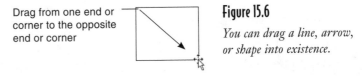

Drag from one end or corner to the opposite end or corner

Figure 15.6

You can drag a line, arrow, or shape into existence.

To save some time and reduce frustration when drawing objects, read through the following list of drawing tips:

◆ To draw several objects of the same shape, double-click the desired button and then use the mouse to create as many of those shapes as you like.

◆ To draw a uniform object (a perfect circle or square), hold down the **Shift** key while dragging.

◆ Hold down the **Ctrl** key while dragging to draw the object out from an imaginary center point. Without the Ctrl key, you drag the object out from its corner or starting point.

◆ To select an object, click it.

- To delete an object, select it and press **Del.**

- To move an object, select it and drag one of its lines.

- To resize or reshape an object, select it and drag one of its handles.

- To copy an object, hold down the **Ctrl** key while dragging it.

- To quickly change the appearance of an object, right-click it and select the desired option from the shortcut menu.

After you have an object on the page, you can use some of the other buttons in the Drawing toolbar to change qualities of the object, such as its fill color and the color and width of the line that defines it. First select the shape whose qualities you want to change, and then click the button for the aspect of the object you want to change (line thickness, line color, or fill color) and choose the desired option.

Painting the Screen with Tiny Colored Dots

Have you ever seen a painting by Georges Seurat, the famous pointillist? His magnificent paintings consist of thousands of tiny dots. Paint programs use the same technique to generate an image. Each image you create in a paint program consists of thousands of tiny, onscreen colored dots called *pixels.*

def•i•ni•tion

Your computer screen is essentially a canvas made up of hundreds of thousands of tiny lights called **pixels.** Whenever you type a character in a word processing program or draw a line with a paint or draw program, you activate a series of these pixels so that they form a recognizable shape onscreen.

Windows comes with a paint program, called Paint, which you can find on the **Start, All Programs, Accessories** menu. Run Paint to display a screen like the one shown in Figure 15.7.

When you have the Paint screen up, play around with some of the line, shape, and paint tools. The procedure is pretty basic: click a line, shape, or paint tool (such as the Airbrush tool), choose a line thickness, and click a color. Then drag the mouse pointer over the "canvas." To create a filled shape, click the desired color for the inside of the shape, right-click the color for the outside of the shape, and then drag your shape into existence. To fill a shape with color, click the paint can, click a color, and click anywhere inside the shape.

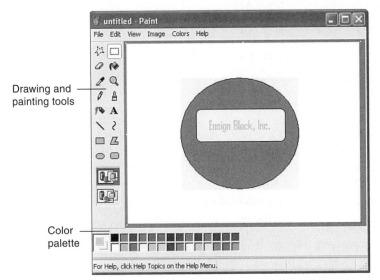

Drawing and
painting tools

Color
palette

Figure 15.7

Paint is a paint program that comes with Windows.

Adding Text in a Box

As you saw earlier in this chapter, you can place text and images on the same page and have text wrap around the image. However, in some cases, you might need to add a label to an image or position a block of text in a precise location on a page. In such cases, you should add the text inside a *text box*. To place text in your publication, you must first draw a text box and then type something in that box. As you fine-tune your publication, you can drag and stretch the box as needed to position it on the page and accommodate your text.

To create a text box, click the **Text Tool** or **Text Box** button. The mouse pointer turns into a cross-hair pointer. Position the pointer where you want the upper-left corner of the box to appear, and then drag down and to the right to create a box of the desired height and width. When you release the mouse button, your program inserts the text box. Type your text in the box, and use the Formatting toolbar to style the text.

 Inside Tip

Moving a text box is kind of tricky. You can't just drag the center of the box, as you do when you move a picture. First click the outline of the box so that handles appear around it. Then drag the border that defines the box.

Manipulating Overlapping Objects

Working with two or more objects on a page is like making your own collage. The trouble with objects is that when you place one object on top of another, the top object blocks the bottom one and prevents you from selecting it. You have to flip through the stack to find the object you want.

Most programs that enable you to stack objects on a page offer tools to help you rearrange the objects in a stack. You can send an object that's up front back one layer or all the way to the bottom of the stack, or you can bring an object from the back to the front. First click the object you want to move (if possible). Some objects are buried so deep that you can't get to them. In such a case, you have to move objects from the front to the back to get them out of the way until you find the one you want.

After selecting the object that you want to move, open the **Arrange** menu, point to **Order,** and select the desired movement: **Bring to Front, Send to Back, Bring Forward, Send Backward, Bring in Front of Text,** or **Send Behind Text.**

Inside Tip _____

If you have a half-dozen objects on a page and you want to nudge them all to the right, you don't have to move each object individually. **Shift+click** each object you want to move. Drag one of the objects, and all the rest follow like little sheep. To group the objects and make them act as a single object, right-click one of the objects and click **Group.** (To ungroup the objects, right-click a grouped object and click **Ungroup.**)

The Least You Need to Know

◆ A presentation program simplifies the process of building and showing slide shows.

◆ A desktop publishing program enables you to create your own greeting cards, business cards, flyers, brochures, newsletters, and other publications.

◆ When you need some professionally drawn, ready-made art, check out the clip art collections included with your word processor and other programs and on the Internet.

◆ To move an image, drag any part of the image.

◆ To resize an image while retaining its relative dimensions, drag a corner handle.

◆ In any of the Office applications, you can insert images from the Internet or from a scanner, digital camera, or graphics program by using the **Insert, Picture, From File** command.

◆ To draw a line, shape, or text box onscreen, click the button for the object you want to draw, position the mouse pointer where you want one end or corner of the object to appear, and drag away from that point.

Chapter **16**

Managing Your Finances with a Personal Finance Program

In This Chapter

♦ Computerize your banking and investments

♦ Draw up a monthly budget

♦ Transfer money between accounts without having to drive to the bank

♦ Pay your bills over an Internet connection

♦ Use financial calculators to make sound financial decisions

The whole concept of money was supposed to simplify things, to make it easier to exchange goods. Instead of trading a fox pelt for a lobster dinner, you could sell the pelt to someone and then take the money to your local seafood restaurant and pay for your lobster dinner.

Somewhere in history, things got all fouled up. We now buy and sell money, store our money in banks and use checks and debit cards to get at it, and even have chunks of our money removed from our paychecks before we've even touched it to cover taxes and pay monthly bills! To help manage your money in these trying times, consider using a personal finance program, as described in this chapter.

Setting Up Your Accounts

To start using a personal finance program, you first need to supply the program with information about your accounts. This typically includes the account name, type of account (savings, checking, cash, and so on), and the current balance or the balance according to your most recent statement.

To set up an account, you enter the command for creating an account and then follow the onscreen instructions, as shown in Figure 16.1, to supply the requested information.

Figure 16.1

Your personal finance program gathers the information it needs to set up and manage your accounts.

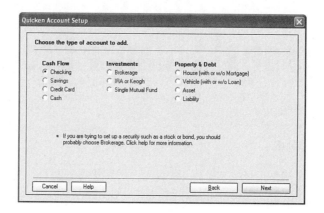

Whoa! _____

Before you attempt to set up your account online, check with your bank or credit union to determine whether it supports online banking. Tell the bank what program you plan to use, so they can supply you with specific instructions on how to proceed. When you're setting up new accounts, you may be able to automate the account setup by having your personal finance program obtain information directly from the bank. Not only does this save you some time, but it can also prevent costly errors.

Automating the Process of Writing Checks

The problem with writing checks by hand is that you have to enter a lot of duplicate information. You write the date, the name of the person or business, the amount of the check (both numerically and spelled out), and a memo reminding you what the check is for. Then, you flip to your check register and enter all the same information again. If you happen to make a mistake copying the information from your check to your register, you'll have loads of fun at the end of the month when you try to reconcile your register with your bank statement.

With a personal finance program, your computer enters the date automatically. You enter the name of the person or business to whom you're writing the check. The program spells out the amount for you, copies the required information into the register, and calculates your new balance, as shown in Figure 16.2. This eliminates any discrepancy between what's written on the check and what's recorded in the register. It also eliminates any errors caused by miscalculations.

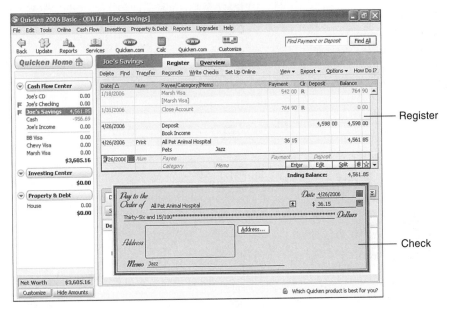

Figure 16.2

When you write a check, the personal finance program automatically transfers the information to the register.

Inside Tip

Printing checks sounds good until you realize some of the ramifications of such a move. You have to get special checks designed for a printer, and some printers require that you print a full page of checks (up to three) at a time. If your printer jams, you may need to void the damaged checks and shred them. If you go grocery shopping, you need to fetch checks from the printer. Many users continue writing checks by hand and use the personal finance program to record the checks, reconcile their balances, and manage their budgets.

Reconciling an Account with a Statement

Back in the old days, reconciling your checking account with the bank statement was an exercise in frustration. You calculated and recalculated till you started seeing double. With a personal finance program, you simply enter the ending balance (from your most recent statement) and then mark the checks that have cleared, mark the deposits, and record any service charges and interest, as shown in Figure 16.3. The program takes care of the rest, determining whether or not your register matches your bank statement.

Mark checks that have cleared   Mark cleared deposits

Figure 16.3

Your personal finance program takes the complexity out of reconciling your account.

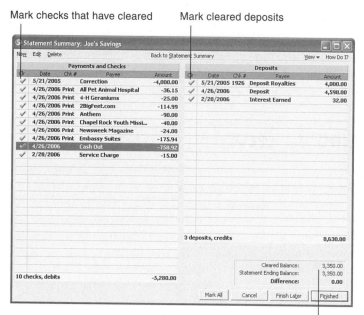

The program determines the balance

If the total on your register doesn't match the total on your bank statement, the program lets you know. If you have to correct an entry in the register, the program automatically recalculates the total, saving you the time of starting over from scratch.

Doing Your Banking Online

Most banks and credit unions offer online banking, and they don't even require you to use a personal finance program to access it. You simply connect with your Web browser, as explained in Chapter 19, and you can bring up a list of recent transactions, transfer funds between accounts, and even pay bills online.

If you use a personal finance program to manage your finances, however, it makes sense to do your online banking through the program. The program can automatically retrieve information from your bank, mortgage company, or credit card company and record it, so you don't have to manually enter the information. This keeps your account information current and relatively error-free.

Paying Your Bills Online

If your computer has a modem or other connection to the Internet, you may be able to pay your bills without the hassle of writing a check and the expense of mailing it. Your personal finance program can connect to your bank or an online bill-paying service and remit payments electronically. You can often use online bill paying to pay your utility bills and make credit card and loan payments. If you owe money to a person or business that's not connected to the system, the online bill-paying service can print and mail out an old-fashioned paper check for you!

Setting Up Recurring Entries

If you get paid the same amount every two weeks or you have a bill that's the same amount each month (such as a mortgage payment, rent, or budgeted utility payment), you can set up a recurring entry that automatically records the transaction at the scheduled time or reminds you to enter it. If you're set up to pay bills online, you can even automate the payment.

When you enter the command to create a new recurring entry, the program displays a dialog box, like the one shown in Figure 16.4, requesting details about the transaction. Enter the requested information.

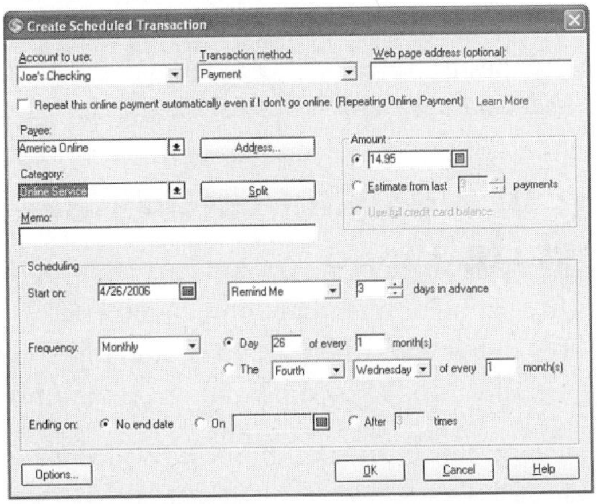

Figure 16.4

With a recurring entry, the personal finance program automatically records the transaction on schedule.

Tracking Your Budget

To take control of your financial destiny, you have to figure out where all your money is going. For instance, you can't decide if you're spending too much on car repairs unless you know exactly how much you're spending. Would you save money by buying a new car instead? Is there any way you can set aside some money for investments? With accurate budget information, you can make financially sound decisions.

With most personal finance programs, you can have the program keep track of each expense for you. Many programs come with a set of home or business expense categories you can use when recording your transactions. If an expense is not listed, you can create a new category. Whenever you record a transaction (check, cash, credit card, debit), you specify the category. At the end of the month, you tell the program to generate a budget report, as shown in Figure 16.5. The report displays the total for each category and helps you spot the pork in your budget.

Figure 16.5

A personal finance program can generate a budget report that helps you track your income and expenses.

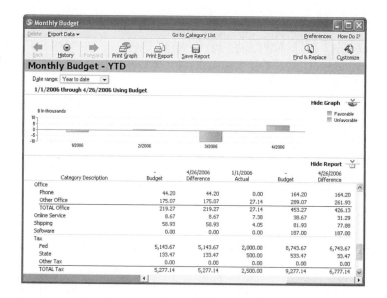

Tapping the Power of Financial Calculators

Personal finance programs typically include several financial calculators that can help you determine the monthly payment on a loan, how much you need to invest to retire comfortably at 65, and how much you can save by refinancing your mortgage for a shorter term or a lower interest rate. You simply plug in the numbers you know, and the calculator supplies you with the missing figures.

Inside Tip _____

If you purchase the basic version of a personal finance program, it may not be equipped with calculators. When you're shopping for a program, make sure you get the version that includes the calculators. They're indispensable … I guess that's why the software developers charge extra for them.

Preparing Your Annual Tax Return

About the only thing a personal finance program can't do (financially speaking) is your taxes. However, assuming you did a good job of recording all your transactions, accounting for every penny of income and expenses, and assigned a category to each transaction, the program can package up your financial data and ship it off to a tax preparation program, such as TurboTax.

TurboTax and similar tax preparation programs lead you through the process of preparing your taxes by asking you a series of questions, as shown in Figure 16.6. You simply answer the questions and supply the requested data, and the program fills out the tax forms for you. The program can even submit your tax returns online, so you get your refund sooner.

Figure 16.6

TurboTax leads you through an interview to gather the information necessary to complete your tax return.

Inside Tip

In a tax preparation program, all the forms are linked, so you enter a piece of data only one time. For example, you enter your name, address, and social security number one time. The tax program transfers that information to every form that requires it. If you fill out the form to itemize your deductions, the tax program automatically transfers the total amount of your deductions to your 1040 form.

The Least You Need to Know

◆ A personal finance program can help you track your income and expenses and manage your bank accounts.

◆ When you write a check in a personal finance program, the program automatically records it in the register.

◆ Check with your bank to determine if it offers online banking and to find out how to access its features with your personal finance program.

◆ By assigning a category to each transaction, you enable your personal finance program to account for every penny of income and expenses and generate a monthly budget report.

◆ You can set up recurring entries to have your personal finance program automatically enter transactions on schedule.

◆ A personal finance program can help you gather all your financial data for the year, simplifying the task of preparing your taxes.

Printing Documents and Other Creations

In This Chapter

◆ Installing a printer in Windows

◆ Previewing your document before you print

◆ Tweaking the page margins

◆ Printing your masterpiece

◆ Troubleshooting common printer problems

When printing goes as planned, it's a snap. You click the **Print** button and then kick back and play Solitaire while the printer spits out your document. However, not all print jobs proceed without a hitch. You finish your game of Solitaire only to find a stack of papers covered with foreign symbols. Or you get an error message saying the printer's not ready. After hours of fiddling and fumbling, you find and correct the problem only to face a new problem: getting your printer back online. In this chapter, you learn all you need to know to print glitch free and recover from the occasional print failure.

Setting Up Your Printer in Windows

You can't just plug your printer into the printer port on your system unit and expect it to work. No, that would be far too easy. You also need to install a printer driver— instructions that tell your programs how to use your printer. (If you have a printer that supports plug-and-play, Windows leads you through the installation at startup.)

In Windows, you install one printer driver that tells Windows how to communicate with the printer. All of your applications then communicate with the printer through Windows. When you set up a printer, Windows asks for the following information:

♦ **Printer make and model.** Windows comes with printer drivers for most common printers. In addition, your printer might include a CD containing an updated printer driver.

♦ **Printer port.** This is the connector at the back of the system unit into which you plug the printer. Standard printers connect the LPT1 (*parallel* printer) port, but many newer printers use the *USB* (Universal Serial Bus) port. (A few oddball printers connect to the *serial* port.) If you're not sure which port to select, but you know that the printer is plugged into the port labeled with a tiny printer icon, try LPT1. If the printer is plugged into the serial port, try COM1, COM2, or COM3.

def•i•ni•tion

All printers are commonly categorized as either **parallel, serial,** or **USB.** Parallel printers connect to one of the system unit's parallel printer ports: LPT1 or LPT2. A serial printer connects to the system unit's serial port: COM1, COM2, or COM3. USB printers plug into one of the computer's USB ports. Most people use parallel or USB printers because they're faster; parallel and USB cables can transfer several instructions at once, whereas a serial cable transfers them one at a time. Wireless printers are also available for wireless-enabled systems.

When you installed Windows, the installation program asked you to select your printer from a list. If you did that, Windows is already set up to use your printer. If you're not sure, open the **Start** menu and click **Printers and Faxes.** If there's an icon for your printer, right-click it and make sure there's a check mark next to **Set As Default Printer.** If no icon is available for your printer, you must install a printer driver.

If your printer came with its own installation disk or CD, install the printer driver from that disk or CD. Insert the disk or CD, click the **Start** button and click **Run.** When the Run dialog box appears, click the **Browse** button, change to the disk drive and folder that contains the Setup or Install file, double-click the **Setup** or **Install** file, and then click the **OK** button. Follow the onscreen instructions to complete the installation.

If you do not have a disk or CD for your printer, try installing one of the printer drivers included with Windows. Windows comes with printer drivers for hundreds of printers currently on the market (and many older printers, too). To install one of the Windows printer drivers, take the following steps:

1. If the Printers window is not displayed, open the **Start** menu and click **Printers and Faxes.**

2. Double-click the **Add a Printer** icon. The Add Printer Wizard appears.

3. Click the **Next** button. The next dialog box asks if you want to set up a network or local (desktop) printer.

4. Make sure **Local printer** is selected and click the **Next** button.

5. Select the port into which you plugged your printer. This usually is LPT1 or USB. Click the **Next** button. A list of printer manufacturers and printer makes and models appears.

6. Click the manufacturer of your printer in the Manufacturers list, click the specific printer model in the Printers list, and then click the **Next** button, as shown in Figure 17.1. You now are asked to type a name for the printer.

7. This step is optional. Type a name for the printer. If you want to use this printer as the default printer, click **Yes;** then click the **Next** button. Windows asks if you want to print a test page.

8. Make sure your printer is on and has paper and then click **Yes** and click the **Finish** button. If you don't have a disk for the printer, a dialog box might appear telling you to insert the Windows CD. If prompted to insert the Windows CD, insert the CD into your computer's CD-ROM drive and click **OK.** Windows copies the specified printer driver and prints a test page to make sure the printer is working properly.

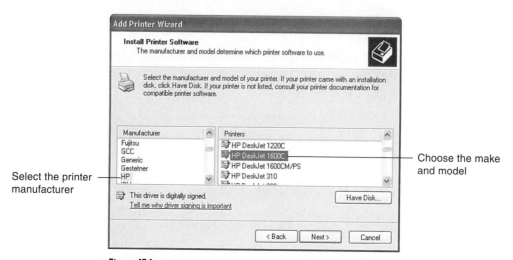

Select the printer manufacturer

Choose the make and model

Figure 17.1

Windows includes printer drivers for most printers.

Preprint Checklist

 Most programs display a print button in the toolbar that allows you to quickly send your document to the printer. It's tempting to click the button and see what happens. Resist the temptation. You can avoid 9 out of 10 printing problems by checking your document in Print Preview first. Open the **File** menu and click **Print Preview** (or its equivalent command), or click the **Print Preview** button in the toolbar. Figure 17.2 shows a sample document in Word's Print Preview window. Flip through the pages to see how they will appear in print and look for the following:

- ◆ **Chopped text.** Many printers have a nonprinting region near the margins. If you set your margins so that the text falls in these areas, the text will be chopped off (not printed).

- ◆ **Strange page breaks.** If you want a paragraph or picture to appear on one page and it appears on the next or previous page, you might need to insert a page break manually. Position the insertion point where you want the page break inserted and then press **Ctrl+Enter.**

- ◆ **Overall appearance.** Make sure your fonts look good next to one another, that text is aligned properly, and that no pictures are lying on top of text.

Make sure the text and graphics don't overlap

Check the margins to see if text falls in the nonprinting region

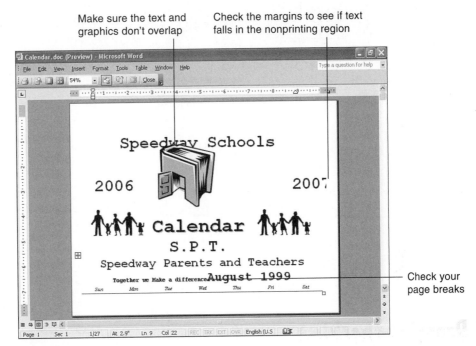

Check your page breaks

Figure 17.2

Print Preview can reveal many problems you should correct before printing.

Setting Your Margins and Page Layout

You can correct many undesirable page layout issues by checking and adjusting the page margins and layout settings in your program. To display the page setup options, open the **File** menu and select **Page Setup.** The Page Setup dialog box appears, presenting numerous options for changing the page layout and print settings. In the following sections, you learn how to use a typical page setup dialog box to set margins and control how your program prints text on the pages. (If you checked your document in Print Preview and it looks fine, feel free to skip ahead to the section "Sending Documents to the Printer," to start printing your document.)

Setting the Page Margins

A typical Page Setup dialog box displays the Margins tab up front, as shown in Figure 17.3. If it's hiding, click the **Margins** tab to bring it to the front. This tab lets you change the top, bottom, left, and right margins. Click the up or down arrow to the right of each margin setting to change the setting in increments of .1 inch, or click in a margin setting text box and type the desired margin setting (usually measured in inches).

Figure 17.3

Set the page margins for the entire document.

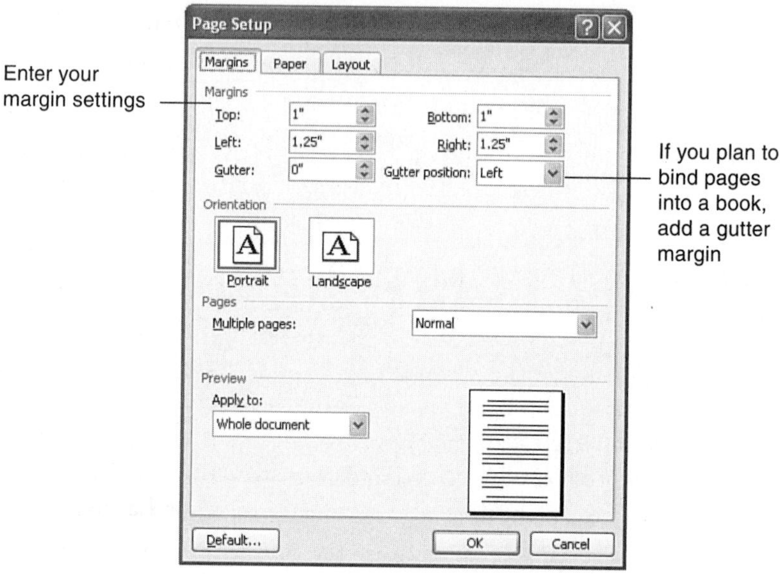

Enter your margin settings ⎯

If you plan to bind pages into a book, add a gutter margin

The Margins tab offers several additional options for special printing needs:

◆ **Gutter** lets you add margin space to the inside margin of the pages, in case you plan to insert the pages into a book or binder.

◆ **From edge** specifies the distance from the top of the page to the top of the *header* and from the bottom of the page to the bottom of the *footer*. (The From edge options are on the Layout tab in recent versions of the Microsoft Office applications.)

def•i•ni•tion

A **header** is text that appears at the top of every page in a document. A **footer** is the same thing, but it appears at the bottom of every page. To add a header or footer, open the **View** menu and click **Header and Footer**. A word processor typically hides headers and footers in Normal view. To see how your header or footer looks on a page, change to Print Layout (or Page Layout) view, as explained in Chapter 12.

◆ **Mirror margins** proves useful if you plan to print on both sides of a sheet of paper. When this option is on, your printer makes the inside margins of facing pages equal.

◆ **2 pages per sheet** or **Multiple pages** shrinks the pages of your document so that your printer can print two pages on a single sheet of paper.

◆ **Apply to** lets you apply the margin settings to the entire document, from this point forward in the document, or to only selected text. This proves useful for long documents that might require different page layouts for some sections.

Picking a Paper Size and Print Direction

Usually, you print a document right side up on an 8½ × 11-inch piece of paper. In some cases, however, you might need to print on legal-size paper or print a wide document, such as an announcement or sign, sideways on the page. If that's the case, check out the **Paper** or **Paper Size** tab. On this tab, you can pick from a list of standard paper sizes or specify a custom size. You can also select a print orientation: **Portrait** (to print normally, as in this book) or **Landscape** (to print with the longer edge of the paper at the bottom). **Landscape** is especially useful if you choose the **2 pages per sheet option.** (In recent versions of the Office applications, you can find the **Portrait** and **Landscape** options on the **Margins** tab.)

Where's Your Paper Coming From?

If you always print on standard 8½ × 11-inch paper, you don't really need to worry about where the paper is coming from. Your printer is set up to use the default paper tray, which is typically loaded with 8½ × 11-inch, and all your programs know that. However, if you need to print envelopes, banners, or any other paper that's not 8½ × 11-inch, check the **Paper** or **Paper Source** tab before you start printing just to be sure that your program is set up to use the right tray.

Laying Out Your Pages

The last tab in the Page Setup dialog box is the **Layout** tab. You can safely ignore most of the options on the **Layout** tab. Just be sure you don't miss the following three options:

- ◆ **Vertical alignment.** The **Vertical alignment** list is very useful for making one-page documents (such as cover pages and short letters) look good on the page. Open the list and select **Center** to center the document on the page.

- ◆ **Line Numbers.** The **Line Numbers** button is useful for legal and literary pieces. These types of documents often contain line numbers so that people can refer to the line numbers when discussing the documents instead of quoting entire lines and sounding really boring.

- ◆ **Borders.** The **Borders** button opens the **Borders and Shading** dialog box, which allows you to add a border around your entire page or at the top, bottom, left, or right margin.

Sending Documents to the Printer

 After your printer is installed and online, printing is a snap. Although the procedure for printing might vary, the following steps work in most Windows programs. If you just want to print one copy of your document, using the default settings click the **Print** button on the toolbar. If you need to customize a bit, follow these steps:

1. Open the document you want to print.

2. Open the **File** menu and click **Print.** The Print dialog box appears, prompting you to enter instructions. Figure 17.4 shows a typical Print dialog box.

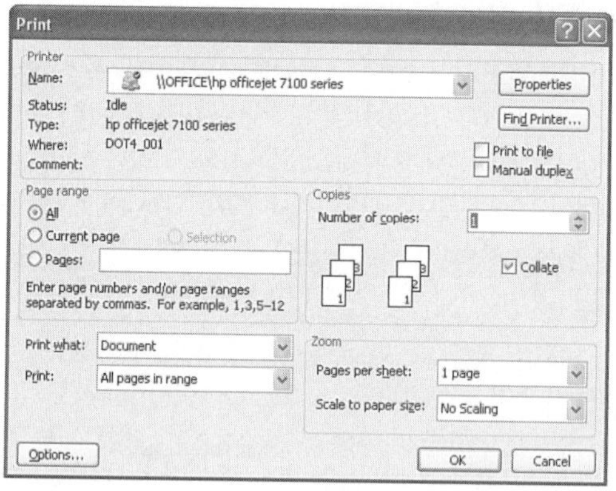

Figure 17.4

The Print dialog box lets you enter specific instructions.

3. In the **Print range** section, select one of the following options:

   ♦ **All** prints the entire document.

   ♦ **Selection** is available only if you highlighted text before choosing the Print command. Selection prints only the highlighted portion of the document.

   ♦ **Pages** prints only the specified pages. If you select this option, type entries in the **From** and **To** boxes to specify which pages you want to print. Some programs display a single text box into which you type the range of pages you want to print; for example, 3-10 or 3,5,7.

4. Click the arrow to the right of the **Print Quality** option (or click the **Options** or **Properties** button), and select the desired quality. (If you have a color printer, you might have the option of printing in grayscale or black and white.)

Inside Tip _____

To enter default settings for your printer (including the quality settings), click **Start**, **Printers and Faxes**, and then right-click the icon for your printer, and click **Properties**. Enter your preferences and click **OK**. The default settings control the operation of the printer for all programs. You can change settings in individual programs without affecting the default settings used for other programs.

5. To print more than one copy of the document, type the desired number of copies in the **Copies** text box.

6. Click **OK**. The program starts printing the document. This could take a while, depending on the print quality and on the document's length and complexity; documents that have lots of pictures can take a long time.

Whoa! _____

Did your printer spit out an extra blank page at the end of your document? If it did, you might have told it to by pressing the **Enter** key three or four times at the end of your document. Doing this adds extra blank lines to your document, which can cause the program to insert a page break. If you see an extra page in Print Preview, delete everything after the last line of text in your document. Some programs also offer an option of spitting out a blank page to separate multiple documents. Check your printing options.

Managing Background Printing

If you ever need to stop, cancel, or resume printing, you must access the *queue* (a waiting line in which documents stand to be printed). Whenever you print a document in Windows, a picture of a printer appears next to the time in the taskbar. Double-click the printer icon to view the print queue, as shown in Figure 17.5. You then can perform the following steps to stop or resume printing:

♦ To pause all printing, open the **Printer** menu and select **Pause Printing.**

♦ To pause the printing of one or more documents, **Ctrl+click** each document in the queue, open the **Document** menu, and select **Pause Printing.**

♦ To resume printing, open the **Printer** or **Document** menu and click **Pause Printing.**

♦ To cancel all print jobs, open the **Printer** menu and select **Purge Print Jobs.**

♦ To cancel individual print jobs, **Ctrl+click** each print job you want to cancel, open the **Document** menu, and select **Cancel Printing.**

♦ To move a document in the print queue, drag it up or down.

If you choose to cancel printing, don't expect the printer to immediately cease and desist. Fancy printers have loads of memory and can store enough information to print several pages. If you're serious about canceling all printing, press the Cancel button on your printer.

The Printer menu has options for controlling all printing

Figure 17.5

You can supervise and control printing using Print Manager.

The Document menu controls printing for selected documents

Panic Attack

If you chose to print only one copy of a document but your printer spits out several copies, this usually indicates that you printed the document more than once. When the printer doesn't start printing right away, many people lose patience and keep clicking the Print button. Each time you click the Print button, another copy of the document is sent to the queue, and your printer dutifully prints it.

Hey, It's Not Printing!

If your printer refuses to print your document, you must do a little troubleshooting. The following questions can help you track down the cause:

- Is your printer plugged in and turned on?

- Does the display on the printer indicate a problem, such as a paper jam? Refer to your printer's manual for information on clearing paper jams and solving other common printer-related problems.

- Does your printer have paper? Is the paper tray inserted properly?

- Is the printer's On Line light on (not blinking)? If the On Line light is off or blinking, press the **On Line** button to turn on the light and make the printer print.

- Display the Print dialog box again and be sure **Print to file** is not selected. This option sends the document to a file on your disk instead of to the printer.

- Is your printer marked as the default printer? In My Computer, double-click the **Printers** icon. Right-click the icon for your printer and be sure that **Set As Default** is checked. If there is no check mark, select **Set As Default.**

- Is the printer paused? Double-click the printer icon on the right end of the task-bar, open the **Printer** menu, and be sure that **Pause Printing** is not checked. If there is a check mark, click **Pause Printing.**

- Is the correct printer port selected? In My Computer, double-click the **Printers** icon and then right-click the icon for your printer and choose **Properties.** Click the **Details** tab and be sure that the correct printer port is selected—LPT1 in most cases.

The Least You Need to Know

- Before you print a document, click the **Print Preview** button to see how it will appear when printed.

- To check the page layout settings, open the **File** menu and click **Page Setup.**

- To quickly print a document, no questions asked, click the **Print** button. For more control over printing, choose **File, Print.**

◆ To pause or cancel printing, double-click the printer icon on the right end of the taskbar to display the Print Manager, and then choose the desired option from the **File** menu.

◆ If your document doesn't start printing, double-click the printer icon on the right end of the taskbar to determine what's wrong.

Part 4

Tapping the Power of the Internet

Faster than the U.S. Postal Service. More powerful than the Home Shopping Network. Able to leap wide continents in a single click. Look, up on your desktop. It's a phone! It's a network! No, it's the Internet!

With your computer, a modem, and a standard phone line, you have access to the single most powerful communications and information network in the world: the Internet. The chapters in this part show you how to get wired to the Internet and use its features to exchange electronic mail, chat with friends and strangers, shop for deals, manage your investments, plan your next vacation, research interesting topics, and even publish your own creations via the web!

Chapter 18

Getting Wired to the Internet

In This Chapter

- ◆ Grasp the overall idea of how your computer accesses the Internet and its various features

- ◆ Pick the right type of connection for your needs and budget

- ◆ Set up the hardware your computer needs to establish a connection

- ◆ Find an entrance ramp to the Internet's information superhighway

- ◆ Check out your connection speed and see how it stacks up with other types of connections

How would you like to access the latest news, weather, and sports without stepping away from your computer? Track investments without having to call a broker or wait for tomorrow's newspaper? Connect to an online encyclopedia, complete with sounds and pictures? Order items from a computerized catalog? Send a postage-free letter and have it arrive at its destination in a matter of seconds? Mingle with friends and strangers in online chat rooms? Transfer files from your computer to a colleague's computer anywhere in the world?

With your computer, a modem, and a subscription to an online service or Internet service provider, you can do all this and more. This chapter introduces you to the wonderful world of the Internet and shows you how to connect your computer to the outside world.

Understanding How This Internet Thing Works

The Internet is a worldwide network of computers that can communicate with one another and share resources. The computers are all interconnected by a massive collection of fiber optic cables, phone lines, and wireless signals that enable the Internet to transfer data at lightening-fast speeds. The network of cables, phone lines, and wireless connections that carry the data are known as the Internet's *backbone*.

For your computer to plug into this network and tap its resources, it needs a modem and an ISP (Internet service provider). The modem is the hardware that your computer uses to send and receive data on the Internet—it's sort of like a telephone for your computer. The ISP functions as a communications hub between your computer and the Internet. Using the modem, your computer connects to the ISP, and the ISP connects to the Internet, as shown in Figure 18.1.

Figure 18.1

Your computer uses a modem to connect to your ISP, which connects your computer to the Internet.

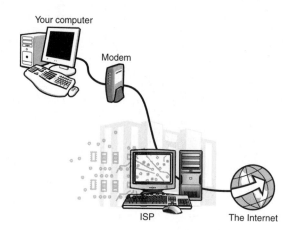

Your computer

Modem

ISP

The Internet

Picking a Connection Type

Although myriad options are available for connecting to the Internet, they boil down to two choices: *dial-up* or *broadband*. Dial-up is a relatively slow connection, but it's available wherever you have access to a phone line, which is pretty much everywhere. Dial-up stinks, but sometimes it's your only choice. Broadband is a fast connection, which you can get through some cable companies, digital satellite services, phone companies, and wireless ISPs, but keep in mind that "fast" is a relative term. Wireless is typically the fastest followed by cable, DSL (Digital Subscriber Line), and then satellite, but several factors can affect the actual speed at which your computer connects. One user's DSL connection may be faster than another user's cable connection.

If you live in a major metropolitan area, you have plenty of Internet connection types from which to choose: dial-up using a standard modem over your existing phone line, DSL modem, cable modem, satellite, and perhaps even a wireless connection. Your choice hinges on the following three factors:

- **Availability.** You might not have cable or DSL service in your area, so that can significantly limit your choices. Dial-up service over an existing phone line and satellite service are almost universally available.

- **Speed.** You should choose the fastest connection you can afford. You may think you won't use the Internet that much, but when Windows or your other programs need to download huge software updates, you'll be wishing you had a faster connection.

- **Price.** Monthly service charges range from less than $10 per month for dial-up service (plus the cost of local phone service) to more than $60 a month for cable or satellite service. (Satellite also costs about $600 up front for the installation.)

def•i•ni•tion

Connection speeds are measured in kilobits per second (**Kbps**), which is equivalent to 1,000 bits per second, and megabits per second (**Mbps**), which is roughly equivalent to a million bits per second. Dial-up connections top out at about 44Kbps. Cable modem speeds range from 512Kbps to 20Mbps, but you're likely to see speeds of about 3–6Mbps. DSL is generally a little slower than cable with speeds ranging from 1.5–9Mbps. Wireless is super fast, at least in theory—about 30Mbps. Satellite service tops out at about 6Mbps, although the connection is typically much slower, especially when you're sending data (uploading) from your computer to the Internet. A newer technology called **BPL** (Broadband over Power Lines) enables computers to connect to the Internet at speeds ranging from 500Kbps to 3Mbps over existing electrical lines.

The following sections provide a brief overview of your choices, but you need to shop around to find out what's available in your area and to compare prices.

Chugging Along with Standard Modems

Because standard modems are the least expensive of the lot and because they can send and receive signals over existing phone lines, they remain the most popular type of modem. However, not all standard modems are created equal. As you shop for a modem, consider the following features:

◆ **Speed.** Don't settle for anything slower than 56Kbps.

◆ **Internal versus external.** Most computers come with an internal modem that's built into the computer. All you see of the modem are jacks for connecting the modem to a phone line and (optionally) plugging in a phone so you can use the line for phone calls when you're not connected to the Internet. An external modem sits outside the computer and connects to the computer's serial (COM, or communications) port or a USB (Universal Serial Bus) port using a cable. External modems are typically more expensive.

def•i•ni•tion

Your computer has a big circuit board inside it that everything else plugs into. This board is called the **motherboard.** The motherboard typically has five or more **expansion slots** that are about a half-inch wide and 4 to 6 inches long, depending on the slot type. On most computers, the expansion slots are located in the back. You can plug smaller circuit boards, called **expansion cards,** into these slots to upgrade your computer and add capabilities. An internal modem is an expansion card.

◆ **Serial port or USB connection.** If you decide to purchase an external modem, and your computer is equipped with one or more USB ports, consider a USB modem. USB allows you to connect up to 127 devices to a single port, giving your computer virtually unlimited expandability. This leaves your sole serial port open for other devices.

◆ **ITU or V.90 support.** ITU or V.90 is the international standard for 56K modems. You might find modems that advertise the x2 standard. In the past, these modems did not conform to the V.90 standard, but newer x2 modems support V.90.

◆ **Fax support.** Like fully equipped fax machines, a fax/modem allows you to exchange faxes with a conventional fax machine or another computer that has a fax/modem.

◆ **Voice support.** If you plan to have your computer answer the phone and take messages, be sure the modem offers voice support. Without voice support, your modem can answer the phone, but it can only emit annoying screeching noises, which is useful for making telemarketers back off.

◆ **Videoconferencing support.** Some modems are also designed to handle video calls, sort of like on *The Jetsons*. Of course, you'll need a video camera to take advantage of this feature.

Standard modems offer three benefits: the modem itself is inexpensive and easy to install, the modem plugs into a standard phone jack, and online services offer modem connections at bargain rates. However, for speedy Internet connections, consider the options described in the following sections.

Avoiding Speed Bumps with ISDN

Unlike standard modems that must perform analog-to-digital (voice-to-data) conversions, ISDN (Integrated Services Digital Network) deals only with digital signals, supporting higher data transfer rates: 128Kbps, which is more than twice as fast as 56K modems. ISDN modems use two separate 64Kbps channels, called *B channels*, that, when used simultaneously, achieve the 128Kbps transfer rates. This two-channel approach also lets you talk on the phone while surfing the web; one channel carries your voice while the other carries computer signals at 64Kbps (half speed). When you hang up, the modem can use both channels for computer communications. A third, slower, channel (channel D) is used by the phone company to identify callers and to do basic line checking, so you don't really need to think about it.

Shop for the ISDN service before you shop for an IDSN modem or adapter and ask your phone company for recommendations. The performance of your ISDN connection relies on how well your ISDN adapter works with your phone company's connection.

Speeding Up Your Connection with DSL

DSL can achieve data transfer rates of 1.5–9Mbps over standard phone lines by using frequencies not used by voice signals. The only catch is that your computer has to be within about 3 miles of the phone company's switching station.

Several types of DSL are available, including ADSL and SDSL. In North America, ADSL (Asynchronous DSL) is most common. "Asynchronous" indicates that the system uses different data transfer rates for upstream (uploading) and downstream (downloading) communications—typically 1 to 2Mbps for downstream traffic and 32Kbps to 1Mbps for upstream traffic. In Europe, SDSL (Symmetric DSL) is most common. SDSL lines use the same data transfer rates for both upstream and downstream traffic (typically about 3Mbps).

Whoa!

Before you jump on the DSL bandwagon, do some research and ask your phone company to provide details on the cost, reliability, and performance boost you can expect from the service.

Because there is no single DSL standard, don't purchase a modem without first checking with your phone company. Most DSL providers market their service as a package deal and include a DSL modem that works with the service.

Turbo Charging Your Connection with a Cable Modem

Like cable television connections, a cable Internet connection supports high-speed data transfers to your PC, allowing you to cruise the Internet at the same speed you can flip TV channels. In addition to speed, cable modems are relatively inexpensive (starting at about $100) and are easy to install. You can expect to pay about $20 to $60 per month for cable Internet access, which makes it competitive with DSL service. If your cable company offers broadband Internet service, I strongly recommend that you at least try it for a month.

The main drawback with cable service is that you share the bandwidth with other users in your area, so the speed of your connection can fluctuate depending on how many users are currently using the service and how much data they're transferring over the connection. Still, in most areas, broadband cable is the fastest and most reliable option available.

Zipping Along with a Satellite Connection

In a major metropolitan area where plenty of broadband options are available, satellite is rarely a rational option. Installation costs are upward of $600, you may pay $60 to $100 a month for the service depending on how much speed and reliability you can afford, and you have to hang one of those ugly satellite dishes on your house.

However, if you're living out in the boonies, where cable, DSL, and wireless service are unavailable, satellite might be the only broadband connection option. It's pretty quick, but it doesn't quite stack up to cable service.

Plugging in Wirelessly with WiFi

The latest craze in Internet connectivity is WiFi (wireless fidelity). Many hotels, airports, coffee shops, bookstores, colleges, and other places where people like to tote around their notebook computers and pretend they're working offer WiFi service. WiFi enables computers equipped with wireless modems to connect to the Internet whenever they're in range of the WiFi network.

Supporting connection speeds of up to 30Mbps, WiFi is definitely the way to go, assuming you have ready access to a WiFi *hotspot*. Although WiFi is popular in corporations, university settings, and businesses that cater to the mobile computing crowd, it hasn't become readily available for residential use.

def•i•ni•tion

Many businesses that offer wireless Internet connectivity advertise themselves as hotspots. A **hotspot** is a wireless adapter that's hardwired to the Internet. As many as 100 computers within range of the hotspot can use it to access the Internet at any one time. Most new notebook computers are equipped with a wireless Internet adapter that enables them to connect to a WiFi hotspot.

Installing a Modem

To establish any type of Internet connection, your computer needs a modem. Most computers come equipped with a standard internal modem (the 56Kbps variety). To connect to the Internet, you connect a standard phone cord to the modem and plug it into a phone jack, just as you would plug in a phone. Your computer can then use the modem to dial the ISP and establish a connection to the Internet.

If your computer is not equipped to use the type of Internet connection you plan on using, you need to install the required modem and perhaps some additional equipment. In most cases, you connect a modem to your computer using one of the following options:

- ◆ **Install an internal modem.** An internal modem is an expansion card that plugs into one of the expansion slots inside your computer. Installation requires turning off your computer, popping the hood, and properly inserting the card.

- ◆ **Install an external modem.** Some modems plug into the Ethernet (networking port). Others connect to the USB port or the serial port on your computer. Connecting an external modem is pretty easy. You plug the modem into the correct port and then plug the modem into the power supply.

- ◆ **Insert a PC card.** Notebook computers have PC card slots that enable you to easily upgrade the computer and add optional devices. You can purchase a standard modem for dial-up access or a wireless adapter for WiFi connectivity.

Whenever you install a new device, you must install the software that tells Windows how to use that device. See Chapter 34 for details on upgrading your computer.

Shopping for an Online Service

The best way to shop for an online service is to connect to the Internet and search the Web for services in your area. That certainly sounds like a chicken-and-egg scenario, doesn't it? How can you shop online for an Internet service provider if you don't yet have a connection to the Internet? Well, you can use a friend's or relative's computer or head down to the public library and use one of its computers. Windows can also help you track down an ISP and install the software necessary to connect to the service. All you need is a modem, your computer, and a valid credit card. Once you have those items, take the following steps to locate an ISP and set up an account:

1. Click **Start, All Programs, Accessories, Communications, New Connection Wizard**. The New Connection Wizard appears.

2. Follow the wizard's onscreen instructions to complete the installation and setup. The wizard dials in to Microsoft's ISP referral service, prompts you to select an ISP, as shown in Figure 18.2, and then downloads the software you need to install to use the service. The ISP's software leads you through the process of setting up an account using your credit card.

Figure 18.2

Windows's Internet Connection Wizard can help you find an ISP, set up an account, and establish a dial-up connection.

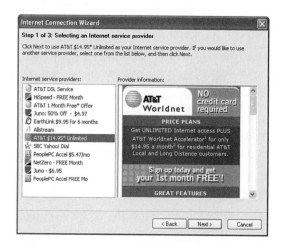

If you don't like the idea of shopping for an ISP using the Windows Internet Connection Wizard, employ one of the following old-fashioned techniques to track down an ISP:

- **Call your phone company.** Most phone companies feature an ISP service, and if they don't, they'll have plenty of suggestions on where to go.

- **Call your cable or satellite company.** If you have cable or satellite TV service, your cable or satellite company may also be able to provide you with Internet service.

- **Look in your yellow phone book under "Internet."** Most phone books list the Internet service providers in the area.

Computer Cheat

One of the best ways to acquaint yourself with the Internet is to sign up for a service that provides you with a free month of Internet service. If you decide you don't like the service, simply call and cancel before your first month is up. Be careful, though. Some services make it very difficult to cancel; when you call to cancel, you have to be assertive.

- **Ask your neighbors.** Neighbors love to swap horror stories and success stories about their Internet service. They've probably tried several local services and can steer you clear of the less-reliable ones.

If you choose to use a local company as your ISP, the ISP may provide you with some Internet connection settings you need to enter to establish a connection. The Internet Connection Wizard can lead you step by step through the process of entering these settings and specifying the phone number your modem needs to dial in order to connect. Click **Start, All Programs, Accessories, Communications, New Connection Wizard,** and then follow the wizard's lead.

Connecting to Your ISP

If you set up a broadband connection, your computer remains connected to the Internet as long as the computer and modem remain turned on.

With a dial-up connection, your modem must dial in to the ISP and log on to connect before you can access the Internet. When you install software for most ISPs, the installation places an icon on the desktop that you can click or double-click whenever you want to connect. If you don't see an icon for connecting to the service, click **Start,** right-click **My Network Places,** and click **Properties.** Then double-click the icon for connecting to the service and click the **Dial** button.

After you've established a connection, a Dial-Up icon typically appears in the system tray (in the lower-right corner of the Windows desktop). It looks like two overlapping computers. Rest the mouse pointer on the icon to check out your connection speed or click the icon for additional details. You can right-click the icon and click **Disconnect** to hang up.

Inside Tip _____

Dial-up connections are typically configured to disconnect after a specified period of inactivity. You can disable this feature and change other settings for your dial-up connection. Click **Start,** right-click **My Network Places,** and click **Properties.** Right-click the icon for your dial-up connection and click **Properties.** When the Properties dialog box appears, click the **Options** tab and enter the desired settings.

Testing Your Connection Speed

No matter how your computer connects to the Internet, connection speeds can vary depending on the speed of your modem, the condition of the phone and fiber-optic cables, the amount of traffic on the network, and various other factors outside your control. If your Internet connection seems more sluggish than usual, you can check your connection speed. Click **Start,** right-click **My Network Places,** and click **Properties.** Right-click the icon for your Internet connection and click **Status.** The Status dialog box appears, as shown in Figure 18.3, showing the speed of your connection and how long your computer has been online.

Inside Tip _____

Several websites enable you to test a broadband Internet connection to determine how fast it transfers files to and from the Internet. This provides a more accurate estimate of your connection speed. Go to www.dslreports.com to test your broadband connection.

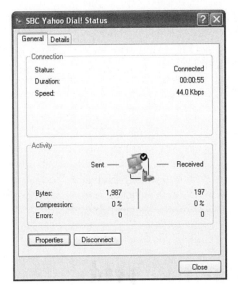

Figure 18.3

Check the status of your connection to determine the speed at which your computer is currently connected to the Internet.

The Least You Need to Know

◆ To connect to the Internet, your computer needs a modem to establish a connection and an ISP to open a line of communications between your computer and the Internet.

◆ A dial-up connection is slow, but it enables a computer to connect to the Internet over a standard phone line.

◆ Cable Internet service is typically the fastest and most reliable, but it can be a bit costly.

◆ The process for installing a modem varies on the type: an Internal modem requires that you install an expansion card inside the computer; an external modem plugs into one of the computer's ports; a PC card modem slides into the PC card slot on a notebook computer.

◆ To set up an Internet connection, run the Internet Connection Wizard and follow its instructions.

◆ To check the speed of your Internet connection, click **Start,** right-click **My Network Places,** click **Properties,** right-click the icon for your Internet connection, and click **Status.**

Chapter 19

Poking Around on the World Wide Web

In This Chapter

- ◆ Launching your web browser on its virgin voyage
- ◆ Opening specific web pages by entering addresses
- ◆ Skipping from one web page to another with links
- ◆ Finding stuff on the web
- ◆ Bookmarking web pages for quick return trips

The single most exciting part of the Internet is the World Wide Web (or web for short), a loose collection of interconnected documents stored on computers all over the world. What makes these documents unique is that each page contains a link to one or more other documents stored on the same computer or on a different computer down the block, across the country, or overseas. You can hop around from document to document, from continent to continent, by clicking these links.

When I say *documents*, I'm not talking about dusty old scrolls or text-heavy pages torn from books. Web documents contain pictures, sounds, video clips, animations, and even interactive programs. When you click a multimedia link, your modem pulls the file into your computer, where the web browser or another program plays the file. As you'll see in this chapter, the web has plenty to offer, no matter what your interests—music, movies, finance, science, literature, travel, astrology, body piercing, shopping—you name it.

Browsing for a Web Browser

To navigate the web, you need a special program called a *web browser*, which works through your service provider to pull documents up on your screen. You can choose from any of several web browsers, including the most popular browser, Internet Explorer. In addition to opening web pages, browsers contain advanced tools for navigating the web, finding pages that interest you, and marking the pages you might want to revisit.

Windows comes with Internet Explorer, which should already be installed on your computer. To keep things simple, I use Internet Explorer in the examples throughout this chapter. However, if you're using a different browser, don't fret. Most browsers offer the same basic features and similar navigation tools. Be flexible, and you'll be surfing the web in no time.

Steering Your Browser in the Right Direction

To run your web browser, click or double-click its icon on the desktop or choose it from the **Start, All Programs** menu. If you're using Internet Explorer, click the icon named **Internet Explorer** on the Windows desktop or click the big "e" icon in the Quick Launch toolbar.

Panic Attack

If you're not connected to the Internet when you start your browser, it might display a message indicating that it cannot find or load the page. If you have a standard modem connection, reestablish your connection as discussed in Chapter 18.

When your browser starts, it immediately opens a page that's set up as its starting page. For example, Internet Explorer opens Microsoft's or MSN's (Microsoft Network's) home page. You can start to wander the web simply by clicking links (typically, blue underlined text; buttons; or graphic site maps). You can tell when the mouse pointer is over a link because the pointer changes from an arrow into a pointing hand. Click the **Back** button (on the button bar just above the page display area) to flip to a previous page, or click the **Forward** button (the button with the right-pointing arrow) to skip ahead to a page that you've visited but backed up from (see Figure 19.1).

Click the Back button to
display the previous page   Click a link to flip to a page

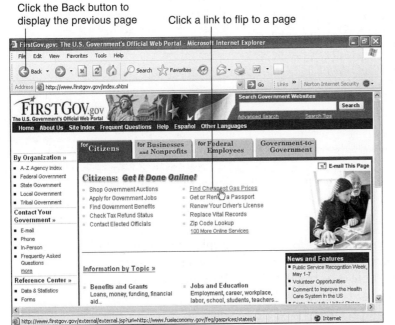

Figure 19.1

A web browser displays and helps you navigate web pages.

If you click a link and your browser displays a message that it can't find the page or that access has been denied, don't freak out. Just click the **Back** button and then try the link again. If that doesn't open the page, try again later. In some cases, the web page creator (*webmaster*) might have mistyped the page address that the link points to or might have moved or deleted the page. On the ever-changing web, this happens quite often. Be patient, be flexible, and don't be alarmed.

A Word About Web Page Addresses

Every page on the web has an address that defines its location, such as www.si.edu for the Smithsonian Institution or www.walmart.com for Wal-Mart. The next time you watch TV or flip through a magazine, listen and keep your eyes peeled for web page addresses. Not only do these addresses look funny in print, but they sound funny, too; for instance, www.walmart.com is pronounced "doubleyou-doubleyou-doubleyou-dot-walmart-dot-kom."

Web page addresses are formally called *URLs* (*Uniform Resource Locators*). They allow you to open specific pages. You enter the address in your web browser, usually in a text box called **Go to** or **Address,** near the top of the window, and your web browser pulls up the page.

def•i•ni•tion

Every web page **URL** starts with http://. Newsgroup sites start with news://. FTP sites (where you can get files) start with ftp://. You get the idea. HTTP (short for Hypertext Transfer Protocol) is the coding system used to format web pages. The rest of the address reads from right to left (from general to specific). For example, in the URL http://www.mitsubishi.co.jp, jp stands for Japan, co stands for corporation (a company in Japan), mitsubishi stands for Mitsubishi (a specific company), and www stands for World Wide Web (or Mitsubishi's web server, as opposed to its FTP server or mail server). Addresses that end in .edu are for pages at educational institutions. Addresses that end in .com are for commercial institutions. You can omit the http:// when entering web page addresses, but omitting ftp:// or news:// causes the browser to attempt to connect to a website.

All you really have to know about a URL is that if you want to use one, type the URL exactly as you see it. Type the periods as shown, use forward slashes, and follow the capitalization of the URL. If you make any typos, the browser either loads the wrong page or displays a message indicating that the page doesn't exist or that the browser cannot locate the specified page.

Finding Stuff with Google and Other Search Tools

The web has loads of information and billions of pages, and this vast amount of information can make it difficult to track down anything specific. The web often seems like a big library that gave up on the Dewey decimal system and piled all its books and magazines in the center of the floor. How do you sift through this mass of information to find what you need?

The answer: use an Internet search tool. You simply connect to a site that has a search tool, type a couple of words that specify what you're looking for, and click the **Search** button (or its equivalent). The following are the addresses of some popular search sites on the web:

www.google.com

www.yahoo.com

www.ask.com

www.lycos.com

www.go.com

www.altavista.com

www.excite.com

Most web browsers have a **Search** button that connects you to various Internet search tools. For example, if you click **Search** in Internet Explorer, Internet Explorer displays a form that you can use to enter your search query. Simply type a couple of key words that describe what you're looking for and click the **Search** button, as shown in Figure 19.2.

The Search bar   The Search button

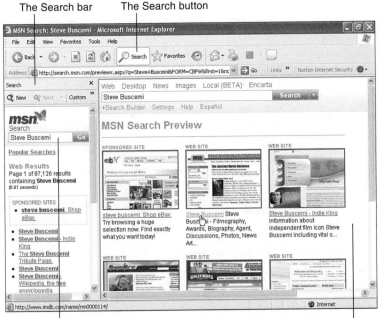

Type your search query here

The search returns links to pages that match your query

Figure 19.2

Use the Search bar to find the desired web content.

Locating People Online

You can also use special search tools to find long-lost relatives and friends on the Internet. These search tools are electronic telephone directories that can help you find mailing addresses, phone numbers, and even e-mail addresses. To search for people, check out the following sites:

www.whitepages.com

www.anywho.com

people.yahoo.com

www.bigfoot.com

www.infospace.com

Opening Multiple Browser Windows

You're hot on the trail of a fabulous website when you encounter a site that catches your eye. Do you stop and explore the site, forsaking the path to your original destination, or do you forge ahead and take the risk of never being able to return to the site?

Whoa!

Every program window you open consumes valuable system resources. When resources run low, your computer gets slow. If your computer seems to be slowing down, close some windows.

Neither. Your browser offers some better options:

◆ Bookmark the page and quickly return to it later by selecting it from a menu (see "Marking Your Favorite Web Pages for Quick Return Trips" later in this chapter).

◆ Complete your journey to your original destination and then, later, use the Back button or the history list to return to the site that caught your eye (see the next section).

◆ Open a new browser window, use it to complete your journey to your original destination, and then return to the other window when you have time. To open a new browser window in Internet Explorer, open the **File** menu, point to **New**, and click **Window** (or press **Ctrl+N**); or right-click the desired link and click **Open in New Window.**

◆ Click a tab. The current generation of web browsers employs tabbed navigation, enabling you to open several web pages in a single window and flip to a page by clicking its tab.

Going Back in Time with History Lists

Although the Back and Forward buttons will eventually take you back to where you were, they don't get you there in a hurry or keep track of pages you visited yesterday or last week. For faster return trips and a more comprehensive log of your web journeys, check out the history list:

In Internet Explorer, click the **History** button to display the History bar on the left side of the window. Click the day or week during which you visited the website, and then click the website's name to see a list of pages you viewed at that site. To open a page, click its name, as shown in Figure 19.3.

Whoa!

If you share your computer with someone, you might not want that person to know where you've been on the web. To cover your tracks, clear the History list. In Internet Explorer, choose **Tools, Internet Options,** and then click the **Clear History** button.

Click the day or week icon   History button

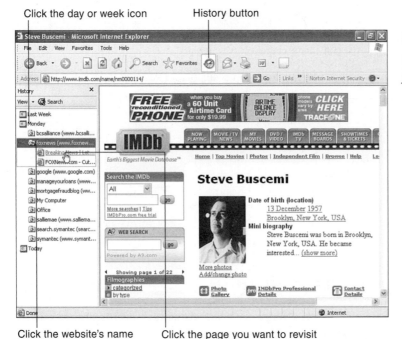

Figure 19.3

Use the history list to retrace your steps.

Click the website's name   Click the page you want to revisit

Marking Your Favorite Web Pages for Quick Return Trips

As you wander the web, you pull up pages that you know you want to return to in the future. When you happen upon such a page, flag it by bookmarking the page as one of your *favorites*. This adds the page's name to the **Favorites** menu. The next time you want to pull up the page, you simply select it from your customized menu.

Computer Cheat

Right-click a blank area of the page and click **Create Shortcut**. This places a shortcut icon for the page on your desktop.

To mark a page, simply right-click a blank area of the page and select **Add to Favorites.** Other browsers have similar features but may refer to favorites as *bookmarks.*

In Internet Explorer, when you choose to add a page to the Favorites menu, the Add Favorite dialog box appears, asking if you only want to add the page to your **Favorites** menu or have Internet Explorer make the page available offline (when you're not connected). If you choose the option for making the page available offline, you can click the **Customize** button and enter settings to have Internet Explorer automatically download updates at a scheduled time (typically when Internet traffic is light) or you can download updates at any time by opening the **Tools** menu and selecting **Synchronize.** When you choose to open the page, Internet Explorer quickly loads it from the cache (a temporary storage area on your computer's hard drive) rather than from the web.

After you have added a page to the **Favorites** menu, you can quickly open the page by opening the menu and clicking the name of the page.

Inside Tip

After bookmarking several web pages as Favorites, the list can become rather lengthy. To make it more manageable, consider creating separate folders for related web pages. To create a folder, click **Favorites, Organize Favorites, Create Folder,** type a name for the folder, and click **Close.** You can move existing Favorites into the new folder by dragging and dropping them onto the desired Favorites menu submenu.

Changing the Starting Web Page

Whenever you fire up your browser, it opens with the same page every time. If you have your own favorite page you'd like your browser to load on startup, just let your browser know. To change your starting page in Internet Explorer, take the following steps:

1. Open the page you want to view on startup.

2. Click **Tools, Internet Options.**

3. On the **General** tab, under **Home page,** click **Use Current.**

4. Click **OK.**

Can Cookies Hurt Me?

When you visit some websites, they automatically send an electronic passport, called a *cookie*, to your computer. As you browse the site, use its tools, or order products, the site "stamps" your passport to keep track of your interests, passwords, and any products you ordered. Whenever you revisit the site, the site can grab the cookie and immediately identify you. Think of it as living in a small town where everyone knows your business.

Because cookies are used to track your web habits, they give many people the heebie-jeebies and inspire allusions to the "futuristic" novel *1984*. Admittedly, cookies work behind the scenes to track your movements, but most cookies are designed to enhance your web browsing experience and allow companies to target advertisements to your tastes (rather than pitching products you probably wouldn't be interested in).

In short, cookies are either good or bad, depending on how they're used and how you view them. If you love to shop on the Internet, cookies are an essential tool, because they act as your shopping basket, keeping track of the items you ordered. On the other hand, if you're the kind of person who gets nervous around security cameras, cookies might bother you.

So can you refuse a cookie when a site tries to send you one? Of course—you have the option of blocking all cookies or having your browser ask for your permission before accepting a cookie. All browsers have tools for regulating how the browser handles cookies. In Internet Explorer, take the following steps to set your preferences:

1. Click **Tools, Internet Options.**

2. Click the **Privacy** tab.

3. Click the **Advanced** button.

4. Drag the slider to set the desired privacy level.

5. Click **OK.**

Inside Tip _____

For additional details about cookies, check out www.cookiecentral.com.

If you've done plenty of web surfing with the cookies feature enabled, you probably have several cookies on your computer. To get rid of cookies in Internet Explorer, open the **Tools** menu, click **Internet Options,** click the **General** tab, and click the **Delete Cookies** button.

The Least You Need to Know

◆ To start Internet Explorer, double-click its icon on the Windows desktop or select it from the **Start, All Programs** menu.

◆ Links typically appear as buttons, icons, or specially highlighted text (typically blue and underlined).

◆ Click a link to open the page that the link points to.

◆ If you know a web page's address, type it in your browser's **Address** or **Go to** text box and press **Enter.**

◆ To search for a topic or site on the web, use a search engine, such as www. google.com, and enter a few words to describe what you're looking for.

◆ To bookmark a page in Internet Explorer, right-click a blank area of the page and select **Add to Favorites.**

Chapter 20

Sending and Receiving E-Mail: Postage-Free, Same-Day Delivery

In This Chapter

- Addressing and sending e-mail messages
- Checking your electronic mailbox
- Jazzing up your messages with photos and fancy fonts
- Attaching files to outgoing messages
- Following proper e-mail etiquette

How would you like to send a message to a friend and have it arrive in a matter of seconds instead of days? Send dozens of messages every day without paying a single cent in postage? Never again stare out your window waiting for the mail carrier? Well, your dreams are about to come true. When you have a connection to the Internet and an e-mail program, all of these benefits are yours. In this chapter, you learn how to start taking advantage of them.

Running Your E-Mail Program for the First Time

The hardest part about e-mail is getting your e-mail program to connect to your Internet service provider's *mail server*, an electronic post office that routes your incoming and outgoing messages to their proper destinations. If you are using one of the major commercial online services, such as America Online or AT&T Yahoo!, you can relax; the installation program took care of all the details for you. You simply click the e-mail or mailbox button and start using it. However, if you connect through an ISP, you must use a separate e-mail program (such as Outlook Express) and enter settings that tell it how to connect to the *mail server*. Before you start your e-mail program, be sure you have the following information from your ISP:

◆ **E-mail address.** Your e-mail address is usually all lowercase and starts with your first initial and last name (for example, jsmith@iway.com). However, if your name is John Smith (or Jill Smith), you might have to use something more unique, such as JohnHubertSmith@iway.com. (All e-mail addresses must contain the @ sign to separate the recipient's name from the mail server's address.)

◆ **Outgoing mail (SMTP).** The SMTP (Simple Mail Transfer Protocol) server is the mailbox into which you drop your outgoing messages. It's actually your Internet service provider's computer. The address usually starts with mail or smtp, such as mail.iway.com or smtp.iway.com.

◆ **Incoming mail (POP3).** The POP (Post Office Protocol) server is like your neighborhood post office. It receives incoming messages and places them in your personal mailbox. The address usually starts with pop, such as pop.iway.com.

◆ **Account.** This one is tricky. It could be your user name, the name you use to log on to your service provider (for example, jsmith), or something entirely different assigned to your account by your ISP.

◆ **Password.** Typically, you use the same password for logging on and for checking e-mail. I can't help you here; you pick the password or have one assigned to you.

After you have the preceding information, you must enter it into your e-mail program. To enter e-mail settings in Outlook Express, for example, take the following steps:

1. Click the **Outlook Express** icon on the Windows desktop or on the Quick Launch toolbar, or run the program from the **Start, All Programs** menu. When you first run Outlook Express, the Internet Connection Wizard starts and steps you through the process of entering the required information, as shown in Figure 20.1.

2. Follow the onscreen instructions. If the Internet Connection Wizard does not start, or you need to enter information for a different e-mail account, open the **Tools** menu in Outlook Express and click **Accounts.** Click the **Add** button, click **Mail,** and follow the onscreen instructions to enter your settings.

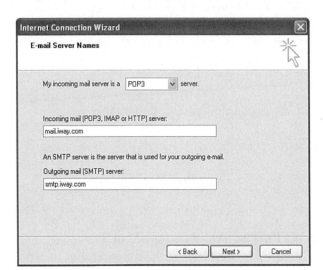

Figure 20.1

Before you can use Outlook Express, you must enter connection settings.

Addressing an Outgoing Message

The procedure for sending messages over the Internet varies, depending on which e-mail program or online service you're using. In most cases, you first click the button for composing a new message. For example, in Outlook Express, you click the **Create Mail** button. A window appears, prompting you to compose your message. Click in the **To** box and type the person's e-mail address (see Figure 20.2). Click in the **Subject** box and type a brief description of the message. Click in the large box near the bottom of the window and type your message. When you're ready to "mail" your message, click the **Send** button.

Some e-mail programs send the message immediately. Other programs place the messages you send in a temporary outbox; then, when you're ready to send the messages, you click the button to initiate the send operation. For example, in Outlook Express, you click the **Send/Recv** button. Outlook Express then sends all messages from the outbox and checks for incoming messages.

Click here to send the message

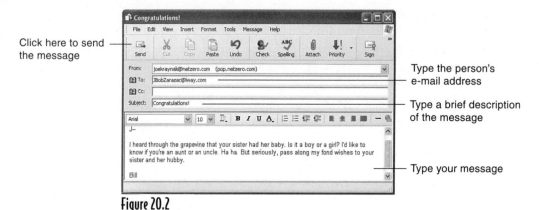

Type the person's e-mail address

Type a brief description of the message

Type your message

Figure 20.2

Sending mail with a typical Internet e-mail program (Outlook Express).

Inside Tip

Most e-mail programs, including Outlook Express, include e-mail address books. Instead of typing the person's e-mail address, you simply select it from a list. To quickly display the address book in Outlook Express, press **Ctrl+Shift+B**. To add someone to your address book, click the button for creating a new contact, and then enter the person's name, e-mail address, and other contact information.

Checking Your E-Mail Box

When someone sends you an e-mail message, it doesn't just pop up on your screen. The message sits on your service provider's mail server until you connect and retrieve your messages. There's no trick to connecting to the mail server—assuming that you entered the correct connection settings. Most programs check for messages automatically on startup or display a button you can click to fetch your mail. The program retrieves your mail and then displays a list of message descriptions. To display a message, click or double-click its description, as shown in Figure 20.3.

Inside Tip

Most e-mail programs use several folders to help you keep your messages organized. For example, Outlook Express stores the messages you receive in the Inbox folder, messages that are waiting to be sent in the Outbox folder, messages you sent in the Sent Items folder, messages you deleted in the Deleted Items folder, and messages you composed but chose not to send in the Drafts folder. To switch from one folder to another, click the desired folder. To display a message you received, for instance, click the Inbox folder and then click the description of the message.

Double-click the message to display it in its own window

Click the message to preview its contents

The contents of the message appear in the preview pane

Figure 20.3

You can quickly display the contents of messages you receive.

Sending Replies

To reply to a message in most e-mail programs, you select the message and then click the **Reply** or **Respond To** button. This opens a window that automatically inserts the e-mail address of the person who sent the message, along with the sender's description of the message (usually preceded by Re:). Many e-mail programs also include the contents of the received message so everyone who receives your reply can easily follow the conversation. To differentiate between the sender's original message and your reply, some e-mail programs add a right angle bracket (>) at the beginning of each line of the original message. To respond, type your message in the message area, and then click the **Send** button.

If you received a message that you would like to pass along to other recipients, you can *forward* the message. First click the message you want to forward, and then click the **Forward** button. This opens a window that automatically inserts the sender's description of the message (usually preceded by Fwd:).

Inside Tip

When replying to a long message, delete most of the original material from the message you received, leaving only one or two lines to establish the context. This makes the message travel faster and takes up less disk space on the recipient's computer.

In the **To** text box, enter the e-mail addresses of the people to whom you want to forward the message. Your e-mail program automatically inserts the original message in the message area. If you would like to add an introduction to or comment about the original message, type this text in the message area. When you're ready to forward the message, click the **Send** button.

Adding Photos and Other Cool Stuff

How would you like to add a photo to your message or jazz it up with some fancy fonts? Most e-mail programs let you use special type styles and sizes, add backgrounds, insert pictures, and embellish your messages with other formatting options.

Whoa!

When you send a message that has pictures, lines, and fancy fonts, the e-mail program sends it as a web page. The recipient's e-mail program must support web page formatting (most do); otherwise, the message will appear to be packed with cryptic codes.

Inside Tip

Most e-mail programs automatically convert any web page addresses or e-mail addresses you type in the message area into links. Just type the address and press the **spacebar** or **Enter** key.

Outlook Express offers a toolbar that contains buttons for the most common enhancements. You can use the toolbar to make text bold or italic, add bulleted and numbered lists, and insert pictures, horizontal lines, links, and other objects. (If the toolbar does not appear, check the **Format** menu for an **HTML** or **Rich Text** option. HTML stands for Hypertext Markup Language, the coding system used to format web pages.)

The buttons for inserting pictures and formatting text work the same way as in your word processing and desktop publishing programs. The only new thing here is the button for inserting links. (A *link* is highlighted text that points to another web page.) To insert a link, first you drag over the text you want to appear as the link. You then click the button for inserting the link, type the address of the web page you want it to point to, and click **OK.** You can also drag links from a web page into the message area and plop them right down in the message area. (For more about links, see Chapter 19.)

Attaching Documents to Your Messages

You can fit most e-mail messages on a Post-it note. A person typically fires off a message or reply in less than a minute. However, there are times when you might want to send something more substantial—perhaps an outline for a book, a photo of yourself, a copy of an article you found on the web, or a document with its formatting intact.

Whatever the case, you can send files along with your messages by creating *attachments*. An attachment is a file in its original condition and format that you clip to the message. For instance, if you have a resumé you created in Word, you can e-mail it as an attachment to a prospective employer. That person could then open the resumé in Word and view or print it. Without attachments, you would need to copy the text of the resumé and paste it into your e-mail message, losing any formatting you applied to the text and any graphics you inserted.

The process for attaching a file is fairly simple, but the steps vary, depending on which e-mail program you use. In most e-mail programs, you follow the same steps as you do for composing and addressing the message. To attach a file to the message, you click a button (for example, **Attach** or **Insert File**). This displays a dialog box that lets you select the file you want to send. The dialog box looks just like the dialog box you use to open or save files. Change to the folder that contains the file you want to send, and then double-click the file's name. When you're ready to send the message, along with the attachment, simply click the **Send** button.

Many word processing and spreadsheet programs have built-in support for e-mail, allowing you to send a document right from the program. In Word, for instance, you open the document you want to send, and then open the **File** menu, point to **Send To**, and click **Mail Recipient**. This displays the e-mail program's toolbar with text boxes for typing the recipient's e-mail address and a description of the message.

If you receive a message that contains an attached file, your e-mail program usually displays some indication that a file is attached. For example, Outlook Express displays a paper clip icon. If you double-click the message (to display it in its own window), an icon appears at the bottom of the window or in an attachments text box. You can double-click the icon to open the file, or right-click and choose **Save** to save the file to a separate folder on your hard drive.

In many cases, when someone forwards a message to you, the person's e-mail program sends the forwarded message as an attachment. If the message has been forwarded several times, you might need to meander through a long line of attachments to view the original message.

Panic Attack

When you receive an attachment, you should use an antivirus program to scan the file before opening it (if it's a document) or running it (if it's a program). Programs are especially notorious for carrying viruses, but documents can contain macro viruses, which can cause as much havoc. (Most antivirus programs are set up to run in the background and automatically scan attachments when you choose to open them or save them to disk.)

What About Hotmail and Other Free E-Mail Services?

You probably have heard of "free e-mail" services, such as Gmail (Google Mail), Yahoo!, and Juno, and wondered why anyone would need free e-mail. Isn't all e-mail free? Does your ISP charge extra for it? Of course, your e-mail account is included with the service that your ISP provides; your ISP does not charge extra for it. But there are several good reasons to explore these free e-mail services:

♦ Free e-mail is typically web based, allowing you to send messages and check your mail on the web. If you travel, you can manage your e-mail from anywhere in the world using any computer that's connected to the Internet. You don't need a computer that has your e-mail account settings on it.

♦ Free e-mail lets everyone in your home or business have his or her own e-mail account. When Junior starts corresponding with his chat room buddies, he'll want his privacy, and he can have it with his own e-mail address.

♦ Free e-mail gives you another e-mail address for registering "anonymously" for free stuff. Whenever you register for contests, shareware, and other freebies on the Internet, you must enter your e-mail address. Use your free e-mail account to register so that companies will send any junk mail to that address, and keep your real e-mail address private.

♦ Free e-mail provides you with a stable e-mail address. In the event that you change ISPs, you don't need to notify all your friends, relatives, and colleagues that you changed your e-mail address.

To get a free e-mail account, connect to any of the following sites, click the link for free e-mail, register, and follow the instructions at the site to start using your free e-mail account:

Gmail	mail.google.com
MSN Hotmail	www.hotmail.com
ICQ Mail	www.icqmail.com
Yahoo!	mail.yahoo.com
Excite	mail.excite.com

To find more free e-mail services, use your favorite web search page to search for the phrase "free e-mail."

E-Mail Shorthand and Emoticons

If you want to look like an e-mail veteran, pepper your messages with any of the following *emoticons* (pronounced *ee-mow-tick-ons*); these are icons that look like facial expressions or act as abbreviations for specific emotions. (You might need to turn your head sideways in order for them to look like tiny faces.) You can use these symbols to show your pleasure or displeasure with a particular comment, to take the edge off a comment you think might be misinterpreted, and to express your moods:

:) or :-)	I'm happy, it's good to see you, or I'm smiling as I'm saying this. You can often use this to show you're joking.
:D or :-D	I'm really happy or laughing.
;) or ;-)	Winking.
:(or :-(	Unhappy. You hurt me, you big brute.
;(or ;-(	Crying.
:| or :-|	I don't really care.
:/ or :-/	Skeptical.
:# or :-#	My lips are sealed. I can keep a secret.
:> or :->	Devilish grin.
;^)	Smirking.
%-)	I've been at this too long.
:p or :-p	Sticking my tongue out.

<g>	Grinning. Usually takes the edge off whatever you just said.
<vbg>	Very big grin.
<l>	Laughing.
<lol>	Laughing out loud.
<i>	Ironic.
<s>	Sighing.
<jk>	Just kidding (these are also my initials).
<>	No comment.

In addition to the language of emoticons, Internet chat and e-mail messages are commonly seasoned with a fair share of abbreviations. The following is a sample of some of the abbreviations you'll encounter and be expected to know:

AFAIK	As far as I know
BRB	Be right back
BTW	By the way
CUL8R	See you later
F2F	Face to face (usually in reference to meeting somebody in person)
FAQ	Frequently asked questions. (Many sites post a list of questions that many users ask, along with the answers. They call this list a FAQ—pronounced like *fact* without the "t.")
FOTCL	Falling off the chair laughing
FTF	Another version of face to face
FYA	For your amusement
FYI	For your information
HHOK	Ha ha; only kidding
IMHO	In my humble opinion
IMO	In my opinion
IOW	In other words

KISS	Keep it simple, stupid
LOL	Laughing out loud
MOTOS	Member of the opposite sex
OIC	Oh, I see
PONA	Person of no account
ROTFL	Rolling on the floor laughing
SO	Significant other
TIC	Tongue in cheek
TTFN	Ta ta for now

E-Mail No-No's

To avoid getting yourself into trouble by unintentionally sending an insulting e-mail message, you might want to consider the proper protocol for composing e-mail messages. The most important rule is to NEVER EVER TYPE IN ALL UPPERCASE CHARACTERS. This is the equivalent of shouting, and people become edgy when they see this text on their screen. Likewise, take it easy on the exclamation points!!!

Secondly, avoid sending bitter, sarcastic messages (*flames*) via e-mail. When you disagree with somebody, a personal visit or a phone call is usually more tactful than a long e-mail message that painfully describes how stupid and inconsiderate the other person is. Besides, you never know who might see your message; the recipient could decide to forward your message to a few choice recipients as retribution.

def•i•ni•tion

When you strongly disagree with someone on the Internet, via e-mail or (more commonly) in newsgroups, it's tempting to **flame** the person with a stinging, sarcastic message. It's even more tempting to respond to a flaming message with your own barb. The resulting flame war is usually a waste of time and makes both people look bad. Also, don't bombard your enemy's e-mail account with a billion messages in an attempt to make the person's e-mail server crash. Even if it works, it's not very nice.

If you are in marketing or sales, avoid sending unsolicited ads and other missives. Few people appreciate such advertising. In fact, few people appreciate receiving anything that's unsolicited, cute, "funny," or otherwise inapplicable to their business or personal life. In short, don't forward every little cute or funny e-mail message, "true" story, chain letter, joke, phony virus warning, or free offer you receive. And no matter what business you're in, avoid inserting emoticons in your messages—some professionals consider this unprofessional.

Finally, avoid forwarding warnings about the latest viruses and other threats to human happiness. Most of these warnings are hoaxes, and when you forward a hoax, you're just playing into the hands of the hoaxers. If you think that the warning is serious, check the source to verify the information before you forward the warning to everyone in your address book.

The Least You Need to Know

- ◆ To set up a new e-mail account in Outlook Express, open the **Tools** menu, click **Accounts,** click the **Add** button, choose **Mail,** and follow the onscreen instructions.

- ◆ To create a new e-mail message, click the **Create Mail** or **New Message** button or its equivalent in your e-mail program.

- ◆ Incoming e-mail messages are often stored in the Inbox. Simply click the **Inbox** folder and then click the desired message to display its contents.

- ◆ To reply to a message, select the message and then click the **Reply** button.

- ◆ To attach a document to an outgoing message, click the button for attaching a file and then select the desired document file.

Chapter 21

Chatting Online with Friends, Relatives, and Complete Strangers

In This Chapter

◆ Contacting friends and relatives with instant messages

◆ Adding other dimensions with audio and video

◆ Experiencing the lively banter in chat rooms

◆ Chatting in private rooms

◆ Setting up a group site to keep in touch

Instant messaging and online chat provide fun and inexpensive ways to meet people and converse with friends, relatives, colleagues, and complete strangers. With an instant messaging program and an Internet connection, you can exchange text messages with any of your "buddies" who happen to be connected at the time. If you both have a microphone and speakers connected to your computers, you can carry on a voice conversation without the expense of placing a long distance phone call. With the addition of a digital camera, you can even videoconference like *The Jetsons!*

If you prefer to party online with groups of friends or complete strangers, then chat rooms may be more to your liking. When you're in a chat room, you simply type and send a message, and it immediately pops up on the screen of every person in the room. When anyone else in the chat room sends a message, it pops up on your screen. This makes for a frenetic conversation that can be quite stimulating.

This chapter shows you how to use various instant messaging and chat tools on the Internet. You learn how to use AIM (America Online's Instant Messaging program) to chat privately with friends, relatives, and colleagues, and use the audio and video features of your computer to place voice and video "phone calls" across the Internet. This chapter also introduces you to online chat rooms, where you can engage in a verbal free-for-all, and shows you how to set up a group site to keep in touch with friends, classmates, and your other circles of friends, colleagues, and acquaintances.

Instant Messaging with AIM

AIM, America Online's Instant Messaging program, is the most popular program of its kind. Millions of people, most likely including some of your friends and relatives, use it daily to keep in touch with one another. In the following sections, you learn how to download a free copy of AIM to your computer, install it, and start using it to communicate with your other computer-savvy pals.

Inside Tip _____

Most instant messaging programs enable you to exchange messages only with people who are using the same program. If all your friends are using AIM, you should use AIM, too. If your friends are using another program, download and use that program instead. Here's a list of popular instant messaging programs along with the websites where you can find them:

AIM at www.aim.com

MSN Messenger at messenger.msn.com

Yahoo! Messenger at messenger.yahoo.com

ICQ at www.icq.com

Trillian at www.ceruleanstudios.com

Some instant messaging programs, including ICQ and Trillian, enable users of different instant messaging programs to communicate with one another.

Grabbing and Installing a Free Copy of AIM

Most instant messaging programs, including AIM, are free for the taking. To download and install a copy of AIM and create a screen name that identifies you on the instant messaging network, take the following steps:

1. Connect to the Internet and run your web browser.

2. Click in the Address bar, type **www.aim.com,** and press **Enter.** AIM's home page appears.

3. Click **Download Now.**

4. Follow the onscreen instructions to install AIM and obtain a screen name and password.

Signing On with AIM

AIM starts automatically after you install it and whenever Windows starts. If you exit the program and decide to restart it later, click **Start, All Programs, AIM,** and then click the icon for running AIM. When AIM starts, it prompts you to enter your screen name and password, as shown in Figure 21.1.

Click in the **Screen Name** box, type your screen name, and then click in the **Password box** and type your password. To have AIM remember your password so that you don't have to enter it next time, click the **Save Password** box to place a check in the box. You can also click the **Auto Sign In** option to have AIM automatically sign you in whenever you start the program. Click the **Sign In** button to go online. At this point, anyone who knows your screen name can contact you by sending you a message.

Inside Tip _____

To remain signed on but hidden, click **I am Available** and click **Invisible.** You'll be able to see your friends, but they won't be able to see that you're signed in. To step away from your computer and notify your friends that you're unavailable, click **I am Available** and click **Away.**

Figure 21.1

AIM prompts you to sign in.

Text-Messaging with AIM

If you know someone's AIM screen name, you can click the **IM** button to text-message that person, assuming he or she is online. When you click the IM button, a window appears prompting you to enter the person's screen name. Type the person's screen name and then click **View Status**. If the person is available, you can type a message in the IM box, as shown in Figure 21.2, and then click **Send** or press **Enter** to initiate a conversation.

In addition to typing text, you can format the text to use a different type style, shrink or enlarge the text, add enhancements such as bold and italics, apply highlighting, insert a link to a web page, or even insert small icons that represent your emotional reactions. Use the toolbar just above the area where you type your message to give it a personal touch.

Type the person's screen name here   Click View Status

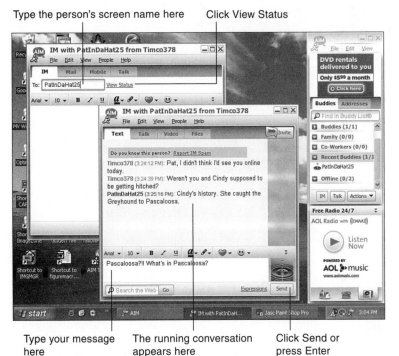

Figure 21.2

Start text-messaging!

Type your message here   The running conversation appears here   Click Send or press Enter

Building Your Own Buddy List

Although you can click the IM button and then type a person's screen name to contact them, it's a whole lot easier if you can select the person's screen name from a list. That's why AIM provides a feature called the *Buddy List.* To add a buddy to your list, follow these steps:

1. Click **Actions.**

2. Click **Add Buddy.** The New Buddy window appears, as shown in Figure 21.3.

3. Type your buddy's AIM screen name or ICQ number or in the IM box. (You can send text messages to a mobile phone by typing +1 followed by the 10-digit phone number; but your buddy must enter the required settings to receive the message.)

> **Inside Tip**
>
> If you have loads of buddies, create your own buddy groups to make your buddy list less crowded and overwhelming. To create a new group, click **Actions,** click **Add Group,** type a descriptive name for the group, and click **Save.**

4. To assign the person to a specific buddy group, click the arrow to the right of the Buddy Group box and click the desired group.

5. (Optional) Type the person's first and last name in the boxes at the top of the New Buddy window.

6. Click **Save**.

Figure 21.3

Add a buddy to your buddy list.

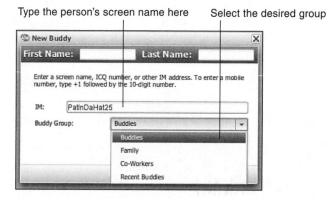

Type the person's screen name here   Select the desired group

Whenever you sign on to AIM, AIM checks to see which of the people on your buddy list are currently online and willing to accept messages. When a buddy's online, you simply click that person's screen name in your buddy list and start chatting.

Voice-Messaging with AIM

Plug a set of speakers and a microphone into your computer, and AIM can transform your computer into an overpriced phone that you can use to talk to your buddies online. You might even be able to trim that long-distance bill! Depending on the speed of your connection and computer and on the quality of your microphone and speakers (and the speed of your buddy's connection and computer and the quality of your buddy's microphone), it might even sound pretty good. Over slow connections, however, the conversation can get a little choppy.

To engage in a voice chat with a buddy who has the proper equipment, simply click your buddy's name and click **Talk**. If you're already text messaging, click the **Talk** tab in the message box, as shown in Figure 21.4, and click **Start**.

Click the Talk tab   Click Start

Figure 21.4

Assuming you and your buddy have the right equipment, you can carry on a voice conversation.

Videoconferencing with AIM

If that voice thing didn't impress you, AIM has another trick up its sleeve. By equipping your computer with an affordable webcam, you can videoconference with colleagues and loved ones. Again you need a fairly speedy Internet connection and excellent equipment for a smooth conference, but when everything works right, you not only hear the person you're talking with, but you see the person, too, and that person gets a peek at you.

To videoconference with AIM, click the **Video** tab and then click **Start.** A message pops up on your buddy's screen inviting him or her to a video chat. Assuming your buddy accepts the invitation, his or her image appears on your screen, as shown in Figure 21.5, and your image appears on your buddy's screen.

Computer Cheat

Have you ever sent a large file to someone via e-mail and had it rejected because it was too large? With AIM, you can send someone a file, large or small, while conversing with that person. Simply click the **Files** tab, click the **Send File** button, and select the file or folder you want to send. Assuming your friend chooses to accept the file or folder, AIM transfers it over your current connection.

You need to be a little careful with this feature, however. Don't accept files or folders from suspicious sources, and always scan an incoming file or folder for viruses before opening it. For details about how to protect yourself on the Internet, see Chapter 24.

Figure 21.5

With video chat, you and your buddy can see and hear one another chat.

Click the Video tab

Your image appears here

Your buddy's image appears here

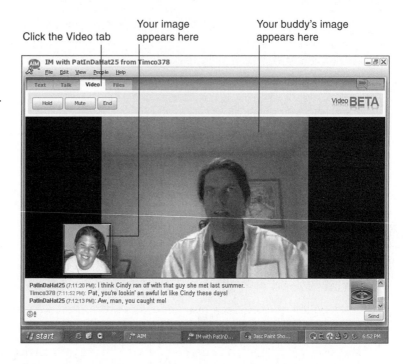

Exploring the Wild and Wacky World of Online Chat Rooms

When America Online first introduced chat rooms, at any time of the day or night you could find hundreds of chat rooms packed with thousands upon thousands of complete strangers engaged in witty and often witless repartee. America Online members can still skip from chat room to chat room to party online with other members, but now you can find chat rooms scattered all across the Internet, from large communities such as Yahoo! and SpinChat to individual sites where members with similar interests can discuss specialized topics.

Panic Attack

Online services typically limit the capacity of a chat room so that the conversation doesn't become too overwhelming. In most cases, if a popular room, such as The Flirts Nook, is full, the service automatically spins you off into a similar room, such as Flirts Nook Two, where you can immediately begin conversing.

The web chat tools vary from service to service. AIM users can use AIM to access a collection of rooms at www.aim.com/chats.adp. (When I was writing this book, however, the latest version of AIM was in development, and it couldn't connect to chat rooms.)

Yahoo! also offers chat rooms that you can access using Yahoo! Messenger, covered in the following sections. Some sites have their own built-in chat rooms that use other tools to enable members to chat online.

Chatting It Up at Yahoo!

Yahoo! has injected the power and simplicity of its search tools into its Internet chat rooms. The best way to access these chat rooms is to use Yahoo! Messenger, an instant messaging program that's very similar to AIM. Take the following steps to download and install Yahoo! Messenger for free and register for a user name and password:

1. Connect to the Internet and run your web browser.

2. In the Address box, type **messenger.yahoo.com** and press **Enter.** Internet Explorer opens and displays the Yahoo! Messenger page.

3. Click **Get It Now.**

4. Follow the onscreen instructions to download and install Yahoo! Messenger and register for a user name and password.

Signing In to Yahoo!

After you have installed it, Yahoo! Messenger runs automatically whenever you log on to Windows. If you exit the program and need to run it later, you can find it on the **Start, All Programs** menu. When you run Yahoo! Messenger, it displays a Sign In window. Simply enter your Yahoo! ID and password, and click **Sign In.** You can then exchange instant messages with your friends and acquaintances, make voice calls, and videoconference, just as you can with AIM.

Entering Chat Rooms

With Yahoo! Messenger and Yahoo! Chat, you're never at a loss for someone to talk to. Yahoo! Chat features hundreds of active chat rooms you can prowl at any time of the day or night. To enter a chat room, take the following steps:

1. In Yahoo! Messenger, open the **Messenger** menu, point to **Yahoo! Chat,** and click **Join a Room.** The Join Room window appears, displaying a list of chat room categories.

2. Browse through the list for the desired category. Click the plus sign next to a category to view a list of subcategories.

3. Click the desired category. A list of available rooms appears on the right.

4. Double-click the desired room or click the room's name and click **Go to Room.** The chat room's window appears, as shown in Figure 21.6.

Messages from all chat room participants appear here

Screen names of people currently in the room

Figure 21.6

Yahoo! brings chat rooms to the web.

Type your message and click Send

After you are in a chat room, you can start chatting. The ongoing discussion is displayed in the large frame in the upper left. To send a message to the other chatters, click in the text box just below the ongoing discussion, type your message, and press **Enter** or click **Send.** When you tire of this simple banter, try the following:

◆ Click the smiley face icon (below the message area) and click the desired smiley face to send it to the room.

◆ Right-click the name of someone in the room. This displays a menu with options that let you find out more about the person, send the person a private message or a file, add the person to a list of friends, or ignore the person (prevent the person's messages from appearing on your screen).

◆ Just above the message area are several menus. Use the various options on these menus to display your Friends List (see which of your friends are online), turn voice chat on or off, turn webcam on or off, change the chat room settings, or create a list of your favorite chat rooms.

◆ To move to a different room, open the Chat menu and click **Change Chat Room.** This opens the Join Room window where you can choose the desired chat room category and a specific room. (When I was writing this book, the ability to create your own rooms was unavailable.)

◆ To edit your own profile, return to the Yahoo! Messenger window, open the **Messenger** menu, and click **My Profiles.** This displays a link with your username that you can click to go to Yahoo! Messenger on the web and change your profile.

◆ To learn other maneuvers, ask the people in the chat room. Most of them are happy to answer your questions, and it's definitely more fun than reading about it.

Inside Tip _____

Although Yahoo! is on the cutting edge of web chat, you can check out some other web chat services:

www.spinchat.com

www.talkcity.com

www.flirt.com

www.chatting.com

www.chat-web.com

Keeping in Touch with Friends and Family

Developers have come up with an innovative communications feature for the web that allows people to create their own online community centers, family circles, or special-interest groups to keep in touch. For example, if you have a large extended family, you can create a family circle and have all your family members (at least those who have Internet access) join the circle. Members can then post messages, digitized photos, announcements, and calendar dates in a special area where everyone in the family can check them out. Many of these "community" centers also allow you to set up a members-only chat room and exchange electronic greeting cards and virtual gifts.

One of the best online community centers I know of is Yahoo! Groups, which you can find at groups.yahoo.com. If you already registered for Yahoo! Chat, you are registered for Yahoo! Groups, too. If you didn't register, you must register to obtain a member name and password. Use your member name and password to log in. You can then create your own group or join existing groups, invite others to join, create your own online photo albums, enter important dates, post messages, and much more. To create your own group, click the **Start a group now** link, as shown in Figure 21.7, and then follow the onscreen instructions.

Figure 21.7

At Yahoo! Groups, you can create your own online community to stay in touch with friends and family.

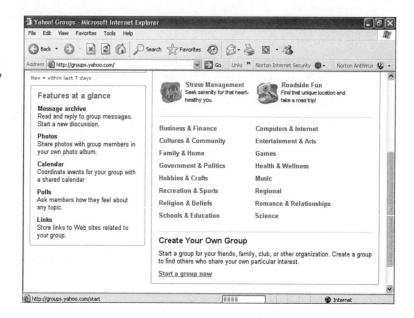

 Inside Tip

Although Yahoo! Groups is one of the best places to set up your club or family circle, other places on the web host groups. Check out the following:

www.faceparty.com

groups.msn.com

www.classmates.com

Instead of hosting groups on services such as Yahoo! Groups and MSN Groups, many web users are beginning to use blogs for the same purpose. For details on blogs, skip to Chapter 23.

The Least You Need to Know

◆ AIM and other instant messaging programs enable you to chat with others on the Internet using text messages, voice, and video.

◆ After connecting to the Internet and signing on with AIM, you can send a text message to a buddy by double-clicking your buddy's name, typing the message, and clicking **Send.**

◆ Online chat rooms enable groups of people to gather and converse online via text messaging, voice, and webcams.

◆ In a chat room, you can typically check out a member's profile, assuming the member supplied a profile.

◆ Yahoo! Groups and similar services provide families and other groups of people who have shared interests with a central meeting place to swap messages, photos, and calendars.

Rubbing Elbows with Newsgroups, Message Boards, and Mailing Lists

In This Chapter

◆ Tell the difference between a newsgroup and a coffee klatch with Katie Couric, Charles Gibson, and Anderson Cooper

◆ Read and post messages in a newsgroup

◆ Read and post messages on website message boards

◆ Sign up to get your name on a free e-mailing list or newsletter

◆ Have the latest news broadcast to your computer with RSS news feeds

As you've already gleaned from Chapters 20 and 21, the Internet is an incredible communications tool. It enables you to e-mail and chat with your circle of friends, converse with voice and video, and mingle with complete strangers.

But that's not all.

The Internet also enables people to share common interests in slightly less personal ways through newsgroups, message boards, mailing lists, newsletters, and RSS news feeds. With newsgroups and message boards, people post messages where anyone (or members only) can read them. On message boards, you can commonly find answers, solutions, guidance, support, and camaraderie without having to know someone's e-mail address or screen name. With mailing lists and newsletters, organizations can keep members posted of the latest news and information, notify members of upcoming events, and call members into action. And with RSS news feeds, you can create your own custom newspaper that updates itself!

In this chapter, you learn how to stay in the loop with these powerful communication tools.

Reading and Posting Newsgroup Messages

You would think that a newsgroup would consist of a bunch of guys with typewriters sitting around smoking cigars and typing news stories. Well, newsgroups aren't quite like that. A newsgroup is more like a bulletin board where people can share ideas, post questions and answers, and support one another.

The Internet has thousands of newsgroups, covering topics from computer programming to cooking, from horses to cars, from politics to tattoos. With your Internet connection and a newsreader, you have access to newsgroups 24 hours a day, 7 days a week. In the following sections, you learn how to connect to newsgroups, subscribe to newsgroups that interest you (for free), and read and post newsgroup messages.

Setting Up Your Newsreader

The best way to access newsgroups is to use a specialized program called a *newsreader*, whose sole purpose is to connect to newsgroups and display messages. This chapter focuses on Outlook Express, the e-mail/newsreader program that's included with Windows. If you are using a different newsreader, the options should be similar enough to Outlook Express for you to make the transition.

To access newsgroups you must set up your newsreader to connect to your service provider's *news server*. This consists of entering the news server's address (for instance, news.internet.net)—ask your service provider for the address.

The first time you run your newsreader it should lead you through the process of setting up a news server account. You can check your settings or create a new account in Outlook Express by performing the following steps:

1. Open the **Tools** menu and select **Accounts**. The Internet Accounts dialog box appears.

2. Click the **News** tab. If you have not set up a newsgroup account, the News list should be blank.

3. Click the **Add** button and click **News.** The Internet Connection Wizard appears, prompting you to type your name.

4. Type your name as you want it to appear in messages that you post to newsgroups, and then click **Next.**

5. Type your e-mail address and click **Next.** Sometimes instead of or in addition to posting a reply in a newsgroup, a person will reply to your post through e-mail.

6. Type your news server's address, as shown in Figure 22.1.

7. If the news server requires you to log on to use it, click the check box next to **My News Server Requires Me to Log On**, and then click the **Next** button.

8. If in Step 7 you indicated that you are required to log on, enter your username and password in the appropriate text boxes and click **Next.** Otherwise, skip to Step 9.

9. Click **Finish.** Outlook Express creates a new newsgroup account for you and displays its name in the News list.

10. Click the **Close** button.

Computer Cheat

If you don't know your news server's address, stick **news** at the beginning of your service provider's domain name. For example, if your service provider's domain name is internet.com, the news server address likely would be news.internet.com.

Enter the news server's address

Figure 22.1

To connect to a news server you must enter its address.

Subscribing to Newsgroups (It's Free!)

Before you can start reading messages about do-it-yourself body piercing or other topics of interest, you must download a list of the newsgroups available on your news server and subscribe to the newsgroups that interest you. Your newsreader might automatically download the list the first time you connect. Be patient; even over a fairly quick modem connection, it might take several minutes to download this very long list. You then can subscribe to newsgroups to create a list of newsgroups that interest you.

> **Inside Tip**
>
> You usually can determine a newsgroup's focus by looking at its address. Most addresses are made up of two or three parts. The first part indicates the newsgroup's overall subject area; for example, **rec** is for recreation and **alt** stands for alternative. The second part of the address specifically indicates what the newsgroup offers. For example, **rec.arts** is about the arts. If the address has a third part (most do), it focuses even further. For example, **rec.arts.bodyart** discusses the art of tattoos and other body decorations.

Although the steps you take to subscribe to newsgroups vary depending on the newsreader you're using, the procedure is fairly straightforward in any newsreader. Let's take a look at just how easy it is by following the procedure in Outlook Express:

1. Click the **Outlook Express** icon on the Windows desktop or on the Quick Launch toolbar.

2. At the bottom of the folder list (left pane), click the name of your news server.

3. Click the **Newsgroups** button in the toolbar. The Newsgroups dialog box appears, as shown in Figure 22.2, displaying a list of available newsgroups. (You can update the list at any time by clicking the **Reset List** button.)

4. In the **Display Newsgroups Which Contain** text box, type a topic (for example, type **cats**). This filters the list to show only those newsgroups that have "cats" in their name.

5. Double-click the name of the newsgroup to which you want to subscribe. A newspaper icon appears next to the name. (You can unsubscribe by double-clicking the newsgroup's name again.)

6. Repeat Steps 3 and 4 to subscribe to additional newsgroups and then click the **OK** button.

Click Newsgroups

Type a topic that interests you
to narrow the list

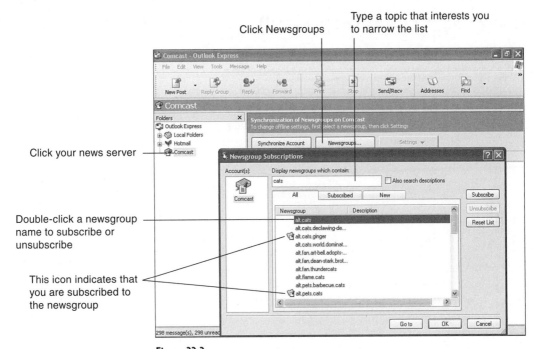

Click your news server

Double-click a newsgroup
name to subscribe or
unsubscribe

This icon indicates that
you are subscribed to
the newsgroup

Figure 22.2

Outlook Express displays a list of newsgroups.

7. In the folder list (left pane), click the plus sign next to your news server to display a list of subscribed newsgroups.

8. Click the newsgroup's name to display a list of posted messages in the upper-right pane.

Reading and Responding to Posted Messages

Although the names of newsgroups can provide hours of entertainment by themselves, you didn't connect to a news server just to chuckle at the weirdoes. (Well, maybe you did.) You connected to read what people have to say and to post your own messages. If you used Outlook Express to read e-mail messages in the previous chapter, you find that the steps for reading newsgroup postings are similar:

1. Click the plus sign next to your news server's name to display a list of subscribed newsgroups.

2. Click or double-click the name of the desired newsgroup. Descriptions of posted messages appear.

3. Click a description to display the message contents in the message pane as shown in Figure 22.3, or double-click the message to display it in its own window.

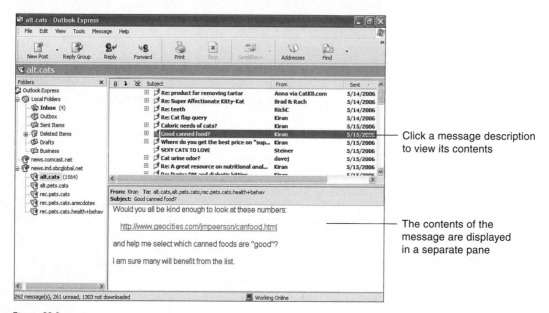

Click a message description to view its contents

The contents of the message are displayed in a separate pane

Figure 22.3

Outlook Express displays a list of messages in the selected newsgroup.

Following a Meandering Discussion

As people post messages and replies, they end up creating *discussions*. Most newsreaders are capable of displaying related messages as *threads*, so you can follow the discussion from its beginning to its end. If you see a message that has a plus sign next to it you can click the plus sign to view a list of replies to the original message. You then can click the descriptions of the replies to view their contents.

Replying Publicly and Privately

When you read a message that inspires you to write a reply, you have two choices: you can reply to the group by posting your reply in the newsgroup or reply to the individual through e-mail. Some people request that you reply through e-mail for privacy or just because they're too lazy to check for replies in the newsgroup itself.

In Outlook Express you can reply to the group by clicking the **Reply Group** button. This displays a window that addresses the message to the current newsgroup and to any other newsgroups in which the original message was posted. It also quotes the contents of the original message. (If the original message was long, you should delete some of the quoted material to be polite.) Type your reply and click the **Post Message** button.

To reply privately, click the **Reply** button. This displays a message window addressed to the person who posted the original message. Type your reply and click the **Send** button, as you normally would do to send an e-mail message. The reply is sent directly to the author and is not posted in the newsgroup.

Inside Tip

Before you post a message in a newsgroup, get a feel for its culture and history, as if you were visiting a foreign country. See if the newsgroup has a FAQ (frequently asked questions list) to determine whether the question you want to ask or the issue which you want to address has already been addressed. And don't pick a fight, unless, of course, that's what the newsgroup is all about.

Starting Your Own Discussions

Newsgroups are great for expressing your own ideas and insights, having your questions answered by experts, and finding items that might not be readily available in the mass market (for example, books that are no longer in publication, parts for your 1957 Chevy, and so on). When you need help or you just feel the overwhelming urge to express yourself, you can start your own discussion by posting a message.

Posting a message is fairly easy. First you connect to the newsgroup in which you want the message posted. Click the **New Post** button (or select the command for posting the new message). Your newsreader automatically addresses the message to the current newsgroup, as shown in Figure 22.4. (You also can add newsgroup addresses to post the message in other newsgroups.) Type a brief but descriptive title for your message, type the contents of your message, and click the **Post** button.

Computer Cheat

Most newsreaders enable you to attach files to your messages. Although most messages consist of simple text, people post graphics in some newsgroups such as hk.binaries.portrait.photography. (For details on how to work with file attachments, see Chapter 20.)

Your message is posted in the newsgroup, where anyone can read it. It might take awhile for people to reply, so check back every day or two for responses. (Sometimes nobody responds, so don't expect too much.)

The newsreader addresses the message to the current newsgroup

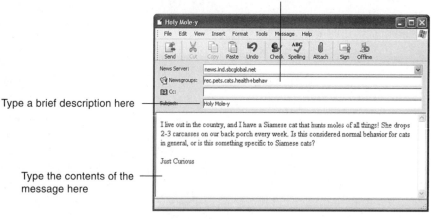

Type a brief description here

Type the contents of the message here

Figure 22.4

You can start a discussion by posting your own message.

Pulling Up Message Boards on the Web

Many websites have their own *message boards* (commonly called *discussion groups* or *forums*), which are nearly identical to newsgroups but may not show up in your newsreader. To access a message board, you simply click its link and follow the trail of links until you come upon a list of posted messages, as shown in Figure 22.5.

Inside Tip

To keep out the riffraff, many sites require you to register to gain access to their message boards.

To read a message, click the message description or whatever link the site provides for reading the message. You can then choose to reply to the message by posting a response (in most cases) or reply to the originator of the message via e-mail (in some cases). You can also choose to start a new discussion by posting your own message. The steps vary depending on the message board, but they're usually fairly intuitive.

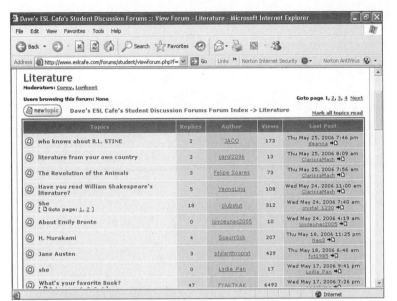

Figure 22.5

A message board is basically a web-based newsgroup.

Registering for E-Mail Mailing Lists

Many websites have a huge following and thousands of members and other interested parties. Rather than communicating with members individually, the site often enables members and sometimes even nonmembers to subscribe to its mailing list or newsletter. You typically click a link to subscribe to the site and then enter your name and e-mail address and perhaps some additional information. In many cases, clicking the Subscribe link runs your e-mail program and simply addresses a message from you to the site, as shown in Figure 22.6. To subscribe, you just send the message. Your e-mail address is added to the list, and whenever the next scheduled mass mailing occurs, you receive your copy via e-mail.

Most legitimate companies insert a message, typically near the bottom of the mail message or newsletter, providing instructions about how to unsubscribe and remove yourself from the mailing list.

Panic Attack

If you don't completely trust the website you're visiting, don't subscribe for its newsletter or mailing list. Some sites pass your e-mail address to other sites, in which case, you begin to be inundated with unsolicited messages. Create a separate (free) e-mail account, as discussed in Chapter 20, and use it to register, to protect your primary email account from spam.

Figure 22.6

At many websites, you can subscribe to the mailing list or newsletter.

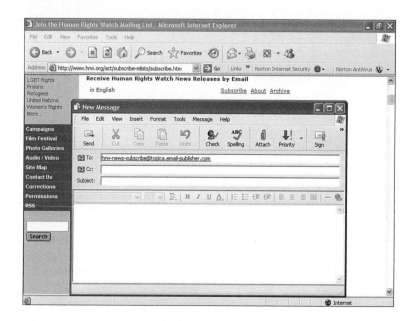

Getting Up-to-the-Minute RSS News Feeds

As you're cruising around the web, you might encounter some sites that offer RSS news feeds. RSS stands for Really Simple Syndication. News feeds are typically flagged with an orange icon that has the letters RSS or XML or an icon that looks like radio broadcast waves. With an RSS newsreader, you can subscribe to RSS content and have sites deliver late-breaking news directly to your newsreader rather than having to visit the site and poke around for what you want. It's sort of like creating your own custom newspaper that's automatically updated 24/7. Several newsreaders are available on the web for free, including the following:

◆ Awasu at www.awasu.com

◆ RssReader at www.rssreader.com

◆ Pluck RSS Reader at www.pluck.com

Awasu comes complete with its own *channel packs*, which enable you to quickly subscribe to RSS feeds from popular sites. After downloading and installing Awasu, the program leads you through the process of choosing the desired content, as shown in Figure 22.7.

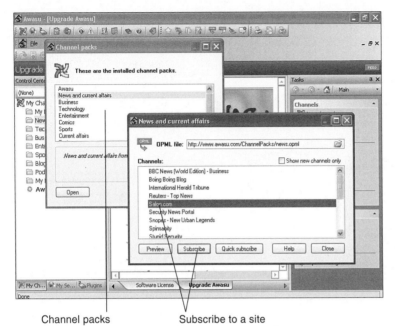

Figure 22.7

With an RSS newsreader you can subscribe to RSS content on the web.

Channel packs   Subscribe to a site

If you stumble on a site that features news feeds, you can right-click the link for the feed and select **Subscribe** in Awasu to initiate a wizard that leads you step-by-step through the process of subscribing to the feed. During this process, you can specify the frequency of updates and enter other preferences.

The Least You Need to Know

- To connect to your ISP's news server, you must specify the news server's address in your newsreader. In Outlook Express choose **Tools, Accounts.**

- When you first connect to a news server, your newsreader downloads a list of available newsgroups.

- To display the contents of a newsgroup message, click the description of the message. Double-click the description to display the message in its own window.

- Message boards on the web are nearly identical to newsgroups, although they may not show up in your newsreader.

- You can subscribe to mailing lists and newsletters on the web to have news and notices e-mailed to you.

- With an RSS newsreader, you can subscribe to content on several websites and have it delivered to a single location.

23

Publishing Your Own Web Page or Blog

In This Chapter

- ◆ Understanding how the web works
- ◆ Sneaking a peek at the codes behind web pages
- ◆ Slapping together your own cool web page
- ◆ Finding free enhancements for your web page
- ◆ Publishing your thoughts and insights through a blog

You wandered the web. Perhaps you sent out a few electronic greeting cards, played some audio and video clips, and even ordered products online. You can use search tools to track down information about the most obscure topics, and you can monitor the progress of all your stocks and mutual funds.

But now you want more. You want to establish a presence on the web, publish your own stories or poems, place pictures of yourself or your family online, show off your creativity, and communicate your ideas to the world.

def•i•ni•tion

A **blog** (short for web log) is a publicly accessible personal journal that enables an individual to voice his or her opinions and insights, keep an online record of experiences, and gather input from others. People also use blogs to share photos with friends and family and function as online clubs.

Where do you start? How do you create a web page or *blog* from scratch? How do you insert photos and links? How do you add a background? And after you've created the page, what steps must you take to place the page on the web for all to see?

This chapter shows you a quick and easy way to whip up your first web page or blog right online, without having to learn a special program or deal with any cryptic web page formatting codes. And because you create the page online, you don't have to worry about publishing your web page when you're done.

What Makes a Web Page So Special?

Behind every web page is a text document that includes codes for formatting the text, inserting pictures and other media files, and displaying links that point to other pages. This system of codes (commonly referred to as *tags*) is called *HTML* (Hypertext Markup Language).

Most codes are paired. The first code in the pair turns on the formatting, and the second code turns it off. For example, to type a heading such as "Apple Dumplin's Home Page," you would use the heading codes like this:

```
<h1>Apple Dumplin's Home Page</h1>
```

Inside Tip

Even if a browser is set up to display all level-one headings in a particular way, HTML codes can override the browser's setting and give the heading a different look. For example, they might make the heading appear in a different color or font.

The <h1> code tells the web browser to display any text that follows the code as a level-one heading. The </h1> code tells the web browser to turn off the level-one heading format and return to displaying text as normal. Unpaired codes act as commands; for instance, the <p> code inserts a line break or starts a new paragraph.

Web browsers use HTML codes to determine how to display text, graphics, links, and other objects on a page. Because the browser is in charge of interpreting the codes, different browsers might display the same page slightly differently. For example, one browser might display links as blue, underlined text, whereas another browser might display links as green and bold.

Forget About HTML

A basic introduction to HTML is helpful in understanding how the web works, troubleshooting web page formatting problems, and customizing web pages with fancy enhancements, but you don't need a doctorate in HTML to create your first web page. Many companies have developed specialized programs that make the process of creating a web page as easy as designing and printing a greeting card.

You can use programs such as Web Studio, FrontPage, and HotDog to create and format web pages on your computer and then upload (copy) the pages from your computer to a web server (typically your ISP's web server). Or you can create and format your web pages right on the web simply by specifying your preferences and using forms to enter your text. The next section shows you just how easy it is to create and publish your own web page online at Yahoo! GeoCities.

Making a Personal Web Page Right on the Web

When it comes to publishing your own web page, you have simple needs—a single web page that lets you share your interests with others and express yourself to the world. For someone with such simple needs, the web offers free *hosting* services, such as Yahoo! GeoCities. These services provide tools for building your web page online, along with access to a web server where you can publish your page.

So let's get on with it and publish a simple web page at Yahoo! GeoCities:

1. Run your web browser and go to geocities.yahoo.com.

2. Unless you registered with Yahoo! earlier (for example, for Yahoo! Chat), follow the series of links required to sign up as a new user. (Because websites are notorious for changing steps and commands, specific instructions would only confuse you. You have to wing it.)

3. Fill out the required form, read the legal agreement(s), and jump through whatever hoops you need to jump through to get your free membership. This gives you an ID (member name) and password so that you can sign in.

def•i•ni•tion

A web host is a server on which you can store your web page and all files related to it, such as photos and other graphics. Think of it as a neighborhood in which you can build your home. Your ISP might provide free hosting services, but in most cases you must create the web page yourself and then upload it to the web server.

4. Use your ID and password to sign in to Yahoo! GeoCities. Your browser loads the Yahoo! GeoCities welcome page, asking you for some general information, including the type of page you intend to create and where you heard about Yahoo! GeoCities.

5. Enter the requested information and click **Submit.** Yahoo! displays your user name and the address (URL) of your website.

6. Click **Build your web site now!** Yahoo! displays several options, including an option to build a web site or blog.

7. Click **Create a Web Site.** Yahoo! gives you the option of building your web site by filling out forms on the web or by the Yahoo! PageWizards, as shown in Figure 23.1.

Figure 23.1

Yahoo! GeoCities gives you a choice of tools.

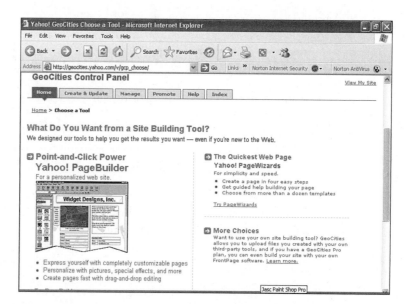

8. Click the **Try PageWizards** link. Yahoo! displays a list of predesigned web page templates you can use to get started.

9. Click one of the Page Wizard designs. Yahoo! GeoCities displays a brief introduction to the wizard, as shown in Figure 23.2. (If you change your mind and decide to use a different template, click the **Cancel** button and choose another.)

10. Click **Launch Yahoo! PageWizard** to start the wizard with the selected design, or click one of the alternative color schemes or designs near the bottom of the page. The first PageWizard dialog box appears, welcoming you to the wizard.

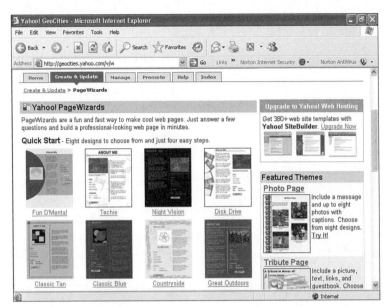

Figure 23.2

Yahoo! GeoCities provides a brief introduction to the selected wizard.

11. Click the **Begin** button. The wizard prompts you to select a color scheme.

12. Click the desired color scheme, and then click **Next.**

13. Follow the wizard's instructions to complete your web page and save it to the Yahoo! GeoCities web server. (The steps vary, depending on which wizard you're running.)

You can change your page at any time. Just go to Yahoo! GeoCities at geocities.yahoo.com, sign in, and run the PageWizard. When the PageWizard appears this time, it displays an option for editing an existing page. Click **Edit Existing Page,** and then open the drop-down menu and click the name of the page you want to edit. Click **Next** and follow the onscreen instructions to enter your changes.

For more options and control over your web page design and layout, use Yahoo! PageBuilder. This is a full-featured web page creation and editing tool. To run PageBuilder, simply open the Yahoo! GeoCities home page and click **Yahoo! PageBuilder.** This displays an introduction to PageBuilder. Click the **Launch Page-Builder** link to run the program.

Inside Tip

To delete a web page on Yahoo!, whether you created it with a wizard or with Page-Builder, you must use PageBuilder. Run PageBuilder, and then open the **File** menu and click **File Manager.** Click the check box next to the file you want to delete and then click the **Delete** button.

Finding Cool Stuff to Put on Your Page

You can decorate your web page with everything from floral-print backgrounds to cartoon clip art. You can even add clocks, counters that mark the number of times people have visited your page, video clips, audio clips, and even small programs that allow visitors to perform calculations or play games.

Where do you find all this stuff? On the web, of course. Check out the following websites for some cool free stuff you can use to enhance and enliven your website:

- ◆ **#1 Free Clip Art at www.1clipart.com.** This site features 10,000 free clip art images organized in more than 300 categories, including Animals, Cartoons, Games, Sports, and Transportation. Follow the trail of categories and subcategories until you find the desired image, and then right-click the image and choose **Save Picture As** to save it to your computer, as shown in Figure 23.3.

Figure 23.3

#1 Free Clip Art features thousands of free clip art images.

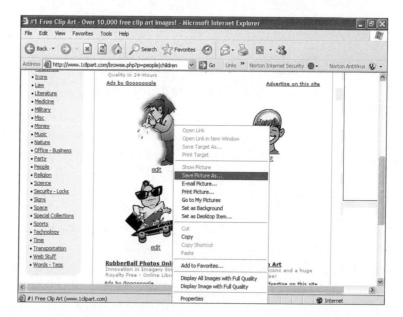

- ◆ **CLIPART.COM at www.clipart.com.** This site is one of the best places to go for web graphics, photos, and animations. Here you can purchase thousands of clip art images and other graphics for nearly every category you can imagine.

- ◆ **c|net at download.cnet.com.** This site provides plenty of free web page creation and development tools. Click the **Development Tools** link for access to tools for creating and enhancing web pages.

◆ **Free-Backgrounds.com at www.free-backgrounds.com.** This site specializes in custom background designs. New backgrounds are added every day. However, this is also a great place to pick up free clip art and animated graphics.

Computer Cheat _____

If you see something you like on a web page, write to the web page author via e-mail (if the person has his or her e-mail address on the page) and ask for permission to use the object. You can drag most clip art images, icons, and other objects right off a page displayed in your browser and drop them onto your page displayed in your web page editor, but ask for permission first.

Building a Blog and Speaking Out on the Internet

In the not-so-distant past, publishing your insights and words of wisdom was nearly impossible. Unless you won a few poetry contests or tirelessly submitted high-quality articles to magazines or manuscripts to book publishers, your hopes of being published were slim to none. With the advent of electronic publishing, via the web, anyone with a little technical expertise can publish his or her own writings; but creating and managing a website and keeping it up-to-date are both challenging and time-consuming.

Relatively recently (sometime in the late 1990s), self-publishing on the web became easier with the introduction of web logs (or blogs for short). These relatively simple web pages are primarily text based, and you can create and update them by filling out a form. You type a message, comment, or other text and then *post it* to the blog. The most recent posting appears at the top of your blog followed by prior postings. As your list of posted messages grows, old messages are pushed off the main blog and are archived.

The first blogs focused on news and commentary. Bloggers would read an article online and then post a link to the article along with their comments, insights, questions, and sometimes corrections or additional facts concerning the article. Over the years, the scope of blogs has broadened considerably. Now people commonly use blogs to publish their own poetry and fiction; broadcast news stories that are overlooked by the mainstream media; communicate with family members, friends, and colleagues; promote grassroots movements; keep an online journal; and much more.

Slapping Together a Blog at MySpace

The easiest way to create your own blog is to build it on a site that specializes in blogs, such as MySpace. Using your web browser, you register at MySpace and then use its online forms to create your blog and keep it up to date. The following steps show you just how easy it is to create your own blog at MySpace:

1. Open your web browser, click in the **Address** box, type **www.myspace.com,** and press **Enter.** The MySpace home page appears.

Panic Attack

Sign up for a separate e-mail account at Yahoo!, Google, MSN Hotmail, or some other site that offers free e-mail and use that address to register for an account, so you don't end up getting a bunch of unsolicited mail sent to your primary e-mail address.

2. Click the **Sign Up!** button and follow the onscreen instructions to register for a free blog. After you sign up, MySpace leads you step by step through the process of creating your blog, first prompting you to upload a digital photo of yourself.

3. If you have a digital photo of yourself, click the **Browse** button and use the resulting dialog box to select it, as shown in Figure 23.4. (If you don't have a digital photo of yourself, click **Skip for now,** and proceed to Step 5.)

Figure 23.4

Click the Browse button and choose the photo you want to use.

4. Click the **Upload** button. MySpace displays a form you can use to send a message to your friends inviting them to visit your new MySpace site.

5. Complete the form and click the **Invite** button or click **Skip for now.** MySpace displays a page that enables you to manage your blog, as shown in Figure 23.5. Scroll down the page to find the address of your blog—you might want to jot this address down somewhere for future reference.

Options for modifying your MySpace page

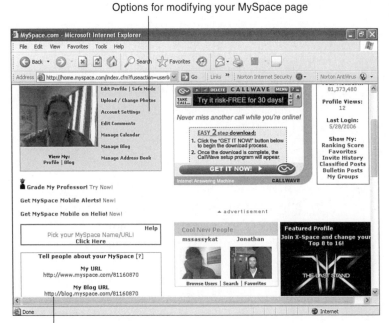

Your blog's address on the web

Figure 23.5

MySpace displays a page containing options for managing your blog.

6. Click the links and follow the onscreen cues to compose your profile, upload or change photos, change your account settings, manage your calendar and blog, and create a custom address book for your contacts. (You can click the **Home** link at any time to return to the page shown in Figure 23.5.)

7. To post a blog entry, click **Blog.** This displays your blog. The first time you visit, a message appears, indicating that you haven't yet posted a blog.

8. Click **Post New Blog.** The Post a New Blog Entry Page appears, as shown in Figure 23.6.

Panic Attack

If you post a blog and live to regret it later, you can delete it. Simply pull up your blog, scroll down to the end of the entry you want to delete, and click **Remove** or click **Edit** to change your entry.

9. Type a title for your blog entry, type your entry and format it however you wish, enter any additional preferences, and then click **Preview & Post.** MySpace displays your entry as it will appear on your blog.

10. Read the entry again and check for any typos, and then click **Post Blog.** MySpace posts your blog entry where everyone who visits your blog can read it.

Figure 23.6

Posting a blog entry is as easy as sending an e-mail message.

Type a title for your blog entry

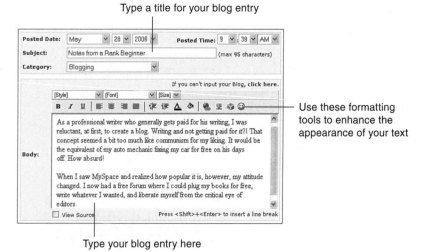

Use these formatting tools to enhance the appearance of your text

Type your blog entry here

Inside Tip

The MySpace message area features no spelling checker, so consider typing your blog post in your word processor and then copying (highlight the message and press Ctrl+C) your message, clicking in the message area, and pressing Ctrl+V to paste it. Remember to click **Preview & Post** to save your message and place it on your blog.

To check out some other online blogging sites, try the following addresses:

www.livejournal.com

www.blogger.com

www.typepad.com

wordpress.com

Professional-Strength Blogging Tools

A simple text-based blog, such as the blog you created in the previous section, is sufficient to get you started in the wonderful world of blogging; if you would like to jazz up your blog to make it act more like a full-fledged website, however, consider using a more robust blog building and management application.

Most blog building applications function like web page editors, inserting the necessary HTML codes for you behind the scenes. You simply create and format your blog as if you were using a word processor or desktop publishing application. In addition, the blog building application typically posts your updated blog to the host site, so you don't need to use a separate application. Following is a list of popular standalone blog building applications along with website addresses where you can learn more about them and possibly download a shareware version of the software:

- **Greymatter at www.noahgrey.com/greysoft** is a user-friendly blogging application that features powerful search tools, file uploading, image handling, customizable templates, multiple-author support, commenting, and additional features. Best of all, it's free.

- **Moveable Type at www.movabletype.org** is another easy-to-use blogging application that enables you to create, edit, and publish your blog simply by filling out a form on your computer. The opening screen displays a list of your blogs and links for creating new blogs, editing your blogs, deleting a blog, adding or deleting contributing authors, editing your profile, and much more.

- **Radio at radio.userland.com** is a powerful blogging application that enables you to create and edit blogs on your computer and upload updates over a dial-up connection in a matter of minutes. The application costs about $40 and includes a one-year subscription to Userland, a blog-hosting service. Radio also features a tool that can collect posts from several of your favorite blogs and present them on a single page, enabling you to keep up on any current posts. Radio offers a free 30-day trial.

The Least You Need to Know

- HTML (Hypertext Markup Language) is a system of codes used to format web pages.

- You don't need to master HTML in order to create your own attractive web pages.

♦ The easiest way to create a page at Yahoo! GeoCities is to use one of the Yahoo! PageWizards. To edit your Yahoo! GeoCities web page, sign in at geocities. yahoo.com and click the link for running the PageWizard.

♦ For gobs of web page clip art, go to www.clipart.com.

♦ An easy way to establish a presence on the Internet is to create and maintain your own blog at MySpace.

Chapter **24**

Protecting Your Computer and Your Children on the Internet

In This Chapter

- ◆ Spelling out the rules for your child
- ◆ Spying on … er … supervising your kids
- ◆ Blocking undesirable web content with a censoring program
- ◆ Avoiding deviants in chat rooms and via e-mail
- ◆ Scanning incoming files for viruses
- ◆ Blocking unauthorized access to your computer

The Internet is a virtual city packed with shopping malls, libraries, community centers, museums, newsstands, meeting rooms, and other valuable offerings. But like any city, the Internet has its dark side—a section of town ruled by pornography, violence, bigotry, vandalism, and theft. If you have children, you want to provide them access to all the positive material the Internet offers, but you're responsible for preventing them from accessing offensive material. In addition, you need to protect your computer from viruses and from unauthorized access, to prevent your files from being damaged or stolen. This chapter shows you how to protect your children and your computer from the various threats on the Internet.

Protecting Children on the Internet

As a society, we want our children to have the freedom to explore the Internet, but we have the responsibility of protecting them from media and individuals who threaten their innocence. We want our children to visit museums online, communicate with students in other parts of the world, take classes, visit political institutions, and research topics of interest. We don't want our kids or students pulling up porno pages, reading racist propaganda, hacking the Pentagon's computer system, or sitting in the Hot Tub chat room conversing with a bunch of old guys and gals who should know better. And we sure don't want our 11-year-olds corresponding via e-mail with deviants twice or three times their age.

The following sections serve as a parent/teacher guide to the Internet. These sections show you how to make your kids more street smart, so they won't fall prey to con artists, how to supervise their Internet use, and how to block access to offensive material by using various censoring tools. Along the way, you will become a little more savvy yourself and begin to understand the perils of the Internet.

Explaining the Rules of the Road

Most kids aren't rotten. They're confused, frustrated, careless, and selfish, but not intentionally bad. A child usually makes a wrong choice or breaks a rule either because he doesn't understand the rule, he's overly curious, or he faces no consequence for misbehaving. So before you let your child or student fire up the web browser, lay down the rules and explain the consequences. Here are a few rules to pass along to your kids:

- **Keep passwords secret.** Anyone who knows your user name and password can use your account, racking up charges, placing credit card orders, and performing illegal activities in your name.

- **Don't enter any personal information online without permission from a parent or guardian.** Using your real name, address, or phone number in your profile gives stalkers the information they want. Registering for contests and "free" stuff can make your private information public. Never tell someone your real name, address, or phone number in a chat room, where anyone can see it.

♦ **Don't use a credit card.** Leaving your teenager alone on the web with your credit card can be a disaster. The web is the biggest shop-at-home network in the world.

♦ **Don't run or install any programs without permission.** Downloading and running programs from unreliable sources can introduce computer viruses. You and your kids should also be careful with any program files you receive via e-mail.

♦ **Don't view sites that you wouldn't view with parents or guardians next to you.** Later in this chapter, I show you how to block undesirable content, but censoring programs do not block everything that's offensive. Be sure your kids know that you expect them to use good judgment.

♦ **Don't chat or correspond with creeps.** Some creepy adults use the Internet to prey on kids. Have your kids notify you immediately of any suspicious individuals or messages. Tell your kids not to send photos of themselves to strangers or post their photos on their web pages. Let your kids know that people on the Internet can pretend to be anybody; the 14-year-old girl your daughter thinks she is chatting with could be a 35-year-old guy.

♦ **Don't meet anyone in person known only from online contact.** If your child wants to meet a friend from the Internet, have your child schedule a meeting in a public place and take you along.

> **Inside Tip**
>
> Use computer time as a reward for proper behavior. If your child fails to follow the rules, reduce or eliminate the time your child spends on the computer. Your kid might claim that the punishment is harming his education. Don't buy it.

In addition to laying down the rules, specify limits on Internet use, just as you would limit TV viewing. Specify the time of day your child can access the Internet and the amount of time he or she can spend at the keyboard. Although the computer and the Internet can be great tools for education and entertainment, they can also interfere with a child's education and social and physical development.

A Little Personal Supervision Goes a Long Way

When my kids started watching TV, I was pretty naïve. I told them to watch only those shows that they would feel comfortable watching with me or their mom. A couple days later, I walked into the den and caught my 13- and 10-year-old watching MTV's *Celebrity Death Match*. Of course, they saw nothing wrong with it.

> **Whoa!**
>
> To be sure your kids can't surf the Internet without your permission, keep the password you use to connect to your ISP secret. Also remove the check mark from the **Save password** check box in the Connect to dialog box. If you have a cable connection (which is connected all the time), this trick isn't an option.

As a parent, it's your obligation not to be stupid. Don't stick a computer in your kid's bedroom and then celebrate because you now have more quality time to spend with your spouse. The reason your son isn't pestering you or picking on his kid sister is probably because he has found something much more sinister to do on the Internet.

Place the computer in a room that you can enter without looking like a spy. A room that's open to traffic, such as a living room or family room, is a good choice. If you have young children, spend some time exploring the Internet with them and supervising their activities. Your kids might balk and think you're a control freak, but that's your job.

Censoring the Internet

Over the years, people have debated whether the government should censor the Internet. As society wrestles with this issue, offensive material remains readily available. In the following sections, you learn what you can do on your end to prevent this material from reaching you and your children.

> **Computer Cheat**
>
> View the history list to see where your kids have been. In Internet Explorer, click the **History** button to display the History bar. Click the folder for the week or day you want to check. The History bar displays a list of sites visited during the selected week or day. Click the site folder to view a list of pages that were opened at the site, and then click the page name to view the page. If your kids are wise to the history list, they might know how to clear it, so if it's blank, suspect foul play.

Using Your Service Provider's Parental Controls

Many service providers offer parental controls that enable you to block some of the most offensive material and prevent access to the riskiest areas of the Internet. On America Online, for example, you can set restrictions on an account when you create or edit a screen name. With Comcast broadband Internet service, you can turn on website blocking and other features by accessing software that's built into the modem. When you're looking for ways to protect children on the Internet, your service provider should be your first source for options. All the tools you need may be included in the monthly subscription fee you already pay.

Every service provider has its own method for entering restrictions on Internet use, so I can't provide instructions that would work in every case. Check your service provider's online help system for detailed instructions.

Inside Tip

If you have a cable or DSL modem, you can often access security features of the modem through your Web browser. Start your browser, click in the address bar, type **192.168.0.1,** and press **Enter.** When prompted for a user name and password, try typing the user name and password your service provider supplied. Or try typing **admin** as the user name and **password** as the password. If that doesn't work, check your modem's or service provider's documentation.

Censoring the Web with Internet Explorer

If your service provider offers little or no help in protecting your children on the Internet, you have two options: you can use your Web browser's built-in features or install a censoring program that's designed specifically to block potentially offensive content.

The next section reviews some of the specialized censoring programs currently available. In the meantime, if you use Internet Explorer as your web browser, you can use its built-in Content Advisor to filter undesirable content. To enable the Content Advisor, perform the following steps:

1. Run Internet Explorer.

2. Open the **Tools** menu and click **Internet Options.** The Internet Options dialog box appears.

3. Click the **Content** tab, as shown in Figure 24.1.

4. Under Content Advisor, click the **Enable** button. The Supervisor Password Required dialog box appears.

5. Type the desired password, press **Tab,** type the password again to confirm it, and then click **OK.** Use a password that's easy for you to remember but impossible for your kids to guess. A dialog box appears informing you that the Content Advisor has been turned on.

Figure 24.1

Internet Explorer's Content Advisor can block potentially offensive web pages.

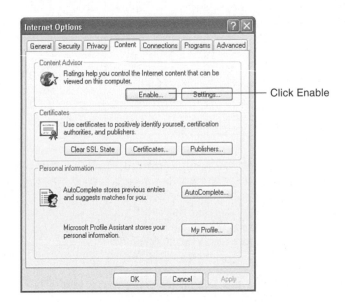

6. Click **OK.** You return to the Internet Options dialog box.

7. Under Content Advisor, click **Settings.** The Supervisor Password Required dialog box appears.

8. Type your password and click **OK.** The Content Advisor dialog box appears, as shown in Figure 24.2, enabling you to set the desired level of restrictions for four categories of potentially offensive content: Language, Nudity, Sex, and Violence. (By default, these are set to their strictest levels, which blocks almost every page you try to open. You may want to relax the settings a bit.)

9. To relax the level of censorship for a category, click the category and then drag the slider to the desired level.

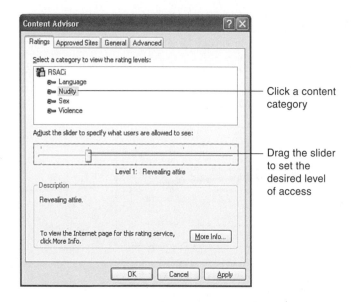

Figure 24.2

The Content Advisor enables you to set the desired level of access for four types of content.

Click a content category

Drag the slider to set the desired level of access

10. To omit a site from being censored, click the **Approved Sites** tab, type the site's address in the Allow This Site box, starting with **http://,** and click **Always.** (You can also add a site you want to block by typing its address and clicking **Never.** You may find it easier to visit the web page you want to allow and then copy its address from the Address bar and paste it into the Allow This Site box.)

11. Enter any additional preferences, as desired, and then click the OK button as many times as necessary to save your settings and exit out of all open dialog boxes.

Panic Attack

Unless you change the Content Advisor's settings, it'll block every unrated page on the web—just about every page you try to pull up.

Don't set the kiddies in front of the screen just yet. Test your setup first. Try going to www.playboy.com. If you see hot babes in various stages of undress, the Content Advisor is disabled. Close Internet Explorer, run it again, and then try going to the nudie page. You should see the Content Advisor dialog box, shown in Figure 24.3, displaying a list of reasons why you have been denied access to this site (as if you didn't know). Click **OK.**

Figure 24.3

The Content Advisor won't let you view the peep show.

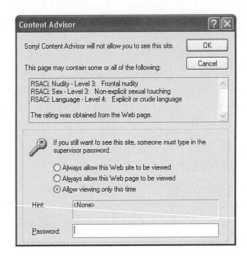

Panic Attack

Don't trust Content Advisor to block everything. For instance, when I tried to pull up the Playboy site, Content Advisor blocked it. When I went to Maxim Online, which is basically Playboy without actual nudity, Content Advisor let me right in. CyberPatrol and other standalone censoring programs, discussed in the next section, do a better job.

Using Censoring Software

If your web browser does not have a built-in censor, or if you want more control over the content and features your children can access, purchase a specialized censoring program. Following is a list of some of the better censoring programs, along with addresses for the web pages where you can find out more about them and download shareware versions:

- ◆ **CyberPatrol at www.cyberpatrol.com.** The most popular censoring program on the market, CyberPatrol uses a list of forbidden words to block access to objectionable material or uses a list of child-friendly words to block access to all web pages except those that contain one of the specified words. Passwords let you set access levels for different Windows User Accounts, and CyberPatrol can keep track of the amount of time each user spends on the Internet and can block or filter chat and Instant Messaging. It also enables parents to set time periods of when and how long their children can use certain Internet features and it enables parents to track attempts to access particular sites or features.

- **CYBERsitter at www.solidoak.com.**
  Another fine censoring program,
  CYBERsitter is a little less strict than
  CyberPatrol but is easier to use and
  configure. CYBERsitter has a unique
  filtering system that judges words in
  context, so it doesn't block access to
  inoffensive sites, such as the Anne
  Sexton home page.

> **Whoa!**
>
> No censoring program is
> perfect. Some objection-
> able content can slip through the
> cracks, and the program can
> block access to unobjectionable
> sites. Use the censoring program
> only when you personally are
> unable to supervise your kids.

- **Echo at www.pearlsw.com.** Not the
  best content blocker in the group,
  Echo's claim to fame is that it creates a comprehensive log of a user's Internet
  activity. The best way to use Echo is to install it and tell your kids that Echo is
  recording everything they do on the Internet. You might not even have to buy
  the program—the threat might be deterrent enough. Pearl Software, the developers of Echo, market it primarily for corporate use, so you might want to think
  twice before pulling up any questionable content at work. Echo might be watching you.

- **Net Nanny at www.netnanny.com.** Net Nanny is unique in that it can punish
  the user for typing URLs of offensive sites or for typing any word on the "no-
  no" list. If a user types a prohibited word or URL, Net Nanny can shut down
  the application and record the offense, forcing your child to come up with an
  excuse. To make the most of Net Nanny, however, you have to spend a bit of
  time configuring it; it's not the most intuitive program of the bunch.

Adjusting Your Web Browser's Security Settings

Your web browser has its own security guard on duty that checks incoming files for
potential threats. If you try to enter information (such as a credit card number) on a
form that's not secure, the web browser displays a warning message asking if you want
to continue. If a site attempts to install a program on your computer, your browser
displays a confirmation dialog box asking for permission to download and install the
program. At times, these warnings can become more annoying than useful, but they
do provide you with some confidence that your browser is on the lookout for security
threats.

Internet Explorer sets different security levels for different *zones*, enabling you to
relax the security settings for sites that you trust and tighten security settings for

untested sites or those that you don't trust. Internet Explorer offers the following four security zones:

- ◆ **Internet** enables you to specify security settings for untested sites. When you wander off to sites that you do not frequent, you might want to tighten security. All sites that are not in one of the other zones in this list fall into the Internet zone.

- ◆ **Local intranet** enables you to relax security for sites on your company's intranet or network so that you can freely access those sites without being bombarded with warnings. By default, the security level for local intranet sites is set at low.

- ◆ **Trusted sites** enables you to deactivate the security warnings for sites you trust. This prevents you from being inundated with warning messages at the sites you visit most frequently and trust completely.

- ◆ **Restricted sites** enables you to create a list of sites that you do not trust and tighten security for those sites. For example, you might want to prevent a particular site from automatically installing and running programs on your computer.

You can add sites to the Local, Trusted, and Restricted sites lists. To add a site to a list, open the **Tools** menu, select **Internet Options,** and click the **Security** tab. Click the desired zone at the top of the dialog box, as shown in Figure 24.4, and then click the **Sites** button. Click in the **Add this Web site to the zone** box, type the address of the site, starting with **http://,** and click **Add.** When you're done adding sites, click **OK** as needed to save your changes and close the dialog boxes.

Figure 24.4

You can add sites to the Local, Trusted Sites, or Restricted Sites lists.

To specify a security level for a zone, open the **Tools** menu, click **Internet Options,** and click the **Security** tab. Click the desired zone at the top of the dialog box and click the zone whose security level you want to change. Click the **Custom Level** button and then enter your preferences. You can enter individual settings to specify the type of content you want Internet Explorer to be able to download or you can open the **Reset To** list and choose the desired security level: **High, Medium, Medium-Low, or Low.**

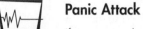

Panic Attack

If you use a browser other than Internet Explorer, the browser has its own security features that may be quite different. Check the browser's help system for information on how to enter your security preferences. All browsers have security features, although they all handle them a little differently.

Preventing Viruses from Entering Your System

Picking up a virus on the Internet is like coming home from vacation with some exotic illness. You were having so much fun; how could this happen? And how can you prevent it from happening again? First, follow a few simple rules:

♦ Download programs only from reputable and known sites. If you know the company that created the program, go to its web page or FTP server and download the file from there. Most reputable sites regularly scan their systems to detect and eliminate viruses.

♦ Don't accept copies of a program from another person (for example, by e-mail). Although the program might not have contained a virus when your buddy downloaded it, your buddy's computer could have a virus that infected the program. Ask your friend where he or she got the file and then download the file from its original location yourself.

♦ If your web browser displays a message indicating that a program it is being asked to download is unsigned or from a questionable source, click the button to cancel the download.

♦ If you receive a file attachment from someone you don't know or from a questionable source, delete the attachment. Do *not* open it.

♦ Keep an antivirus program running at all times. Antivirus programs scan any incoming program files for viruses and scan your computer on a regular basis to identify viruses before they can damage any files. Two of the best antivirus programs on the market are Symantec's Norton Internet Security and McAfee VirusScan. You can download a trial version of McAfee VirusScan at www. mcafee.com. Go to www.symantec.com for details about Norton Internet Security. I've used Norton Internet Security for about four years and have found that it does an excellent job of blocking viruses, adware, spyware, and attempts from hackers to access my computer.

Whoa!

If you receive e-mail you'll eventually receive virus warnings indicating that a nasty new virus is infecting thousands of computers all over the world and wiping out hard drives. Most of these warnings are hoaxes, and you should not forward the message as it instructs you to do. Check the source of the hoax first. Virus hoaxes are posted at www. symantec.com/avcenter/hoax.html and vil.mcafee.com/hoax.asp.

Keeping Hackers at Bay with a Firewall

Whenever you are connected to the Internet, you run the risk of having a mischievous hacker break into your system, steal information, and even damage some files. Hackers rarely break into home PCs that are connected to the Internet by dial-up connection, because you typically disconnect when you're done working. If you have a DSL or cable modem connection, which keeps your computer connected to the Internet at all times, consider installing a *firewall* to prevent unauthorized access to your system.

A firewall typically functions in one of two ways: it filters incoming and outgoing data to block anything that seems suspicious or it uses a *proxy server* between you and your Internet service provider to hide your computer, making it much more difficult for a hacker to find your computer.

Windows XP comes with its own firewall. The Windows XP Internet Connection Firewall (ICF) keeps track of every request for data your computer makes, and then checks incoming traffic to ensure that your computer initiated the transaction. If an outside source attempts to initiate communications, ICF drops the connection. Unlike many firewalls that display warnings of potential security breaches, ICF works in the background, automatically blocking unauthorized access. To turn on ICF, follow these steps:

1. Click the **Start** button and click **My Network Places.** The My Network Places window opens.

2. On the left side of the window, below Network Tasks, click **View network connections.** The My Network Places window displays icons for all of your computer's modem and network connections.

3. Right-click the icon for the network card or modem your computer uses to connect to the Internet, and then click **Properties.** The Properties dialog box for the selected connection opens.

4. Click the **Advanced** tab.

5. Under Windows Firewall, click **Settings.** The Windows Firewall Settings dialog box appears, as shown in Figure 24.5.

6. Click **On.**

7. Click **OK.**

Panic Attack

If you don't have Windows XP, you can download shareware versions of firewall software at any of the popular Internet add-on sites such as cws.internet.com, www.tucows.com, or download.cnet.com. If you already installed Internet security software, such as Norton Internet Security, chances are good that it includes a firewall and that the firewall is already active.

Click on →

Figure 24.5

Enable the Windows XP Internet Connection Firewall.

Panic Attack _____

A firewall can cause Internet connection problems for some features, including instant messaging, especially when you're trying to share files or videoconference. If you experience a connection problem after enabling the firewall, you may need to set up exceptions to exempt specific programs from firewall protection. In Windows XP, display the Windows Firewall Settings dialog box again, click the **Exceptions** tab, and use the options you find there to exempt the program that you're having problems with.

Dealing with Cookies

When you visit some sites on the Internet, the site automatically pins an identification badge, called a *cookie*, on your computer. This relatively small file can follow you on your journey, keeping track of the pages you visit, the information you enter, the products you order, and any other information it wants to gather concerning your activity on the Internet.

Most cookies are designed to make your web browsing experience more productive and enjoyable. Without cookies, you wouldn't be able to shop on the Internet and have the remote web server keep track of your order or remember your password. However, if you are concerned that cookies threaten your privacy, you can choose to disable them in your web browser or have a warning appear whenever a site tries to send you one. Just be aware that if you disable cookies, you can expect a warning to pop up on just about every site you visit.

Inside Tip _____

For additional details about cookies, search your browser's help system for "cookie" or go to www.cookiecentral.com.

To change your cookie settings in Internet Explorer, open the **Tools** menu, click **Internet Options,** and click the **Privacy** tab. Under Settings, drag the slider to set the desired security level for cookies—the higher the security level, the more cookies Internet Explorer blocks. You can click the **Sites** button to add sites from which you always want cookies blocked or always want them allowed.

The Least You Need to Know

◆ Before you unleash your kids on the Internet, lay down the rules you want them to follow.

◆ The most essential rule kids must follow is to never give out any personal or sensitive information, including passwords, phone numbers, addresses, credit card numbers, or even the name of the school they attend.

◆ No censor program can replace the supervision of a loving, caring parent or teacher.

◆ If you cannot supervise your kids every minute they're on the Internet (what parent can?), install CyberPatrol or CYBERsitter and learn how to use it.

◆ To protect your computer against viruses, purchase and install a good antivirus program and keep it updated with the latest virus definitions.

◆ To prevent unauthorized access to your computer, enable the Windows firewall or install third-party firewall software on your computer.

Part 5

Going Digital with Music, Photos, and Video

Although you may think that your food processor is the most versatile tool in your home, your computer has it beat. With the right software and accessories, your computer can moonlight as a powerful jukebox, photo lab, and video studio.

The chapters in this part introduce you to the most popular home-based computer gadgets. Here you learn how to download and play music clips from the Internet, burn your own custom music CDs, transfer music to a portable MP3 player, snap and print photos, and edit your home movies. This part takes you from tech weenie to tech wizard in just a few short chapters.

Chapter 25

Playing CDs, DVDs, MP3s, and Other Audio/Video Media

In This Chapter

- ◆ Playing your favorite audio CD tracks on your computer
- ◆ Finding and installing a free MP3 audio player
- ◆ Copying MP3 audio clips to a portable MP3 player
- ◆ Burning your own audio CDs
- ◆ Watching DVD movies on your computer

If you thought the move from LPs to CDs was impressive, you're going to love the latest in audio and video technology. With your computer and a CD drive, a sound card, and a decent set of speakers, you can create your own computerized jukebox that can play hundreds of your favorite songs. Add an Internet connection, and you can download music clips to add to your collection. With a portable music player, you can take your favorite tunes wherever you go. And if you have a CD-R or CD-RW drive, you can even "burn" your own custom CDs and play them on any CD player! And that's not all. With a DVD drive—most new computers have them—you can watch your favorite movies on your computer!

This chapter steps you through the process of building your own "recording studio," points out the best places on the web to get free MP3 players and music clips, and shows you how to transform your computer into a personal DVD player, so you can watch movies while you pretend to work.

Understanding CD and MP3 Audio Basics

To understand CD and MP3 audio basics, you must first know that standard audio CD players and computers differ in how they store and play audio clips. On an audio CD, data is stored in a format called Red Book, which has been the standard format for more than 20 years. Computers, on the other hand, store audio data in various formats, the most popular of which is MP3. This format compresses an audio clip to about one twelfth of its Red Book size with an imperceptible loss of quality. MP3 and similar technologies enable users to download audio clips more quickly over the Internet and store them in less space on their computers' hard drives.

The only trouble is that a standard audio CD player cannot play such files. Fortunately, the following types of programs can handle the required format conversions for you:

- **MP3 player.** An MP3 player lets your computer play MP3 audio clips. You can copy MP3 clips from websites or convert audio clips from your CDs into MP3 files with a CD ripper, described next. An MP3 player converts MP3 files into a standard digital audio format (typically a WAV format) that your computer can play through its sound card and speakers.

- **CD ripper.** A CD ripper converts audio clips from a CD into the MP3 format or another format that a computer equipped with the required software can play. A CD ripper is commonly called a *jukebox*, because it stores all the clips you record and lets you play them simply by selecting them from a list or creating your own custom playlists.

- **CD burner.** A CD burner converts MP3 audio clips stored on your computer into the standard Red Book format used to store audio data on CDs and controls the process of recording the audio clips to the recordable CD. You can then play the CD in a standard audio CD player. (Some newer audio CD players can play MP3 files stored on CDs, making it unnecessary to convert MP3 clips into the Red Book format before burning them on a CD. This enables you to store more than 10 times as much music per CD.)

Before you run out and buy a case of CD-R or CD-RW discs, you should understand the difference between the two types of discs. CD-R discs let you write to the disc only once; you can't erase the data on a CD-R disc and then record over it. With a CD-RW disc, you can record data to the disc, erase the data, and write new data to the disc. This makes CD-RW discs an excellent storage medium for backing up files. However, CD-RW discs are typically less reflective than CD-R discs, making them a poor choice for recording audio CDs. Some audio CD players have a tough time reading a CD-RW disc. When you're burning audio CDs, stick with CD-R discs.

def•i•ni•tion

The surface of a compact disc has smooth, reflective areas and pits or dyed areas that refract rather than reflect light. A **CD drive** or player reads data from a disc by bouncing a laser beam off the surface of the disc and interpreting differences in the intensity of the returning beam. On **CD-RW discs,** the contrast between the reflected areas and the nonreflective dyed areas is less than the contrast found on CD-R discs.

Although MP3 gets all the press, you'll encounter many other audio formats on the web. Some audio formats are designed specifically for streaming audio; that is, they are designed to start playing an audio clip as soon as your computer begins receiving it. Streaming audio, such as RealAudio, is commonly used for online radio stations and "live" broadcasts.

Using Your Computer as a Jukebox

If you insert an audio CD into your computer's CD-ROM drive, Windows should display the Audio CD dialog box, prompting you to specify which action you want Windows to perform: **Play Audio CD** (with Windows Media Player), **Rip Music from CD** (with Windows Media Player), **Open Folder to View Files** (in Windows Explorer), or perform another action with some other audio program that's installed on your computer. To start listening to the CD, click one of the options for playing it and then click **OK.** (The audio CD might begin to play automatically when you insert the CD, depending on how your system is configured.)

Playing an audio CD makes your computer little more than an overpriced CD player. To make your computer a superior overpriced CD player, record your favorite audio clips to your computer's hard drive as files. This provides you with a virtual jukebox, which you can program to play only the songs you want to hear in the order in which you want to hear them.

Inside Tip _____

To check out another popular virtual jukebox, go to www.realaudio.com and click the link for downloading the free RealPlayer. The basic, free version lets you record audio clips from CDs to your hard drive and create custom playlists. With the Premium version ($19.99), you can record your playlist to a CD—assuming, of course, that you have a CD-R or CD-RW drive.

Media Player, included as part of Windows XP, not only plays audio CDs but also can copy entire CDs or selected tracks to your computer's hard drive to create custom *playlists.* To see whether Media Player is installed on your computer, check the Windows **Start, All Programs, Accessories, Entertainment** option. If Media Player is not installed, you can install it from the Windows installation CD or pick up the latest version at www.microsoft.com/windows/windowsmedia and install it.

Creating a Custom Playlist with Windows Media Player

Using Windows Media Player, you can record your favorite CD tracks to your computer's hard drive and create a custom playlist. The following steps are for Media Player 11. If you have a different version of Media Player, run Media Player and press **F1** to call for help:

1. Establish a connection to the Internet, if possible. If your computer is connected to the Internet, Media Player can download the title of the album, the name of the artist, and title tracks for most CDs automatically, so you don't have to enter them manually.

2. Run the Windows Media Player by selecting **Start, All Programs, Windows Media Player.** (Depending on your version of Media Player, it may appear on the Start, All Programs, Accessories, Entertainment menu.)

3. Insert a CD that has one or more tracks you want to record into your computer's CD player. (Your computer might have a program other than Media Player that runs when you insert an audio CD. At this point, you can either use the player that appears or close the player and proceed with these steps.)

4. Click the **Rip** tab. Media Player displays a list of the tracks stored on the CD, as shown in Figure 25.1, and automatically begins ripping the tracks.

Click the Rip tab

Figure 25.1

Windows Media Player makes it easy to copy individual tracks from a CD.

You can click the check box next to a track to omit it

You can click Stop Rip to interrupt the process

5. (Optional) Click the check box next to each track you do *not* want to record to remove the check mark from the box. Or click **Stop Rip** to interrupt the process and then click the check box next to each track you do *not* want to record.

6. Repeat Steps 3 and 4 for each CD that has one or more tracks you want to record.

7. Click the arrow below the **Library** tab and click **Create Playlist.** Media Player displays New Playlist in the right pane.

8. Type a brief, descriptive name for your new playlist.

9. In the list pane (on the left), select a folder or subfolder that has the tracks you want to add to your playlist. (Click the plus sign next to a folder to view its subfolders and then click a folder or subfolder to display its contents.)

Whoa!

If the track names do not appear you can add them later or edit the existing names. The process is identical to renaming files and folders: click once on a track name to select it, click again to highlight the name, and then type the new name.

10. Select the tracks you want to add to your playlist, as shown in Figure 25.2. (To select multiple tracks, click one track and then **Ctrl+click** the other tracks.)

11. Drag and drop one of the selected tracks into the New Playlist pane (on the right). Media player adds the tracks to your playlist.

12. Repeat Steps 10 to 12 to add tracks to your playlist. (You can add tracks from different CDs to create your own custom list.)

13. Drag and drop items up or down in the list to rearrange the tracks in the desired order.

14. Click **Save Playlist.**

Select tracks

Figure 25.2

Drag and drop the audio tracks you recorded to your playlist.

Drag selected tracks here

15. To play your clips, click the clip you want to start playing and then click Media Player's **Play** button (near the bottom of the window). Media Player plays the selected song and then the remaining songs in your playlist.

Changing Media Player's Skin

Many cell phones, handheld computers, and other trendy electronic devices now come with thin, detachable covers called skins. Likewise, most onscreen MP3 players come with their own virtual skins. You simply pick the desired skin from a list to personalize the appearance of your player.

Inside Tip _____

If you don't like the selection of skins, click the **More Skins** button (just to the right of **Apply Skin**). This connects you to Microsoft's website, where you can download additional skins.

To change skins in Media Player, right-click the Media Player window's title bar, point to **View,** and click **Skin Chooser.** The skin chooser appears, as shown in Figure 25.3. Click the name of a skin to preview it. When you find a skin you like, click its name and then click **Apply Skin** (above the list of skins).

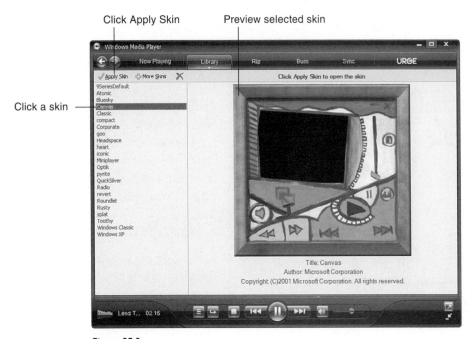

Click Apply Skin   Preview selected skin

Click a skin

Figure 25.3

Give Media Player a new skin to completely redesign it.

I Want My MP3: Downloading Music Clips from the Web

The web is buzzing with companies that sell downloadable music, audio books, and other digital audio. You can go to iTunes, Napster, Sam Goody's, and a host of other music sites, and pack your shopping cart with tracks for under a buck each. You might even be able to pick up a few tracks for free. You can then burn the tracks to CDs, copy them to your iPod or MP3 player, and add them to your growing audio library on your computer.

The following sections take you on a brief tour of music sites and show you how to download and play audio clips using Internet Explorer and Windows Media Player. You also learn how to copy your clips to a portable music player to take them with you wherever you go.

Finding and Downloading Music Clips

Downloading any file is pretty easy. You click a link and follow the onscreen instructions to tell your browser where to save the file. However, before you can download audio clips, you have to find some tunes that are worth downloading. The following sites are popular online stores where you can purchase individual tracks:

Panic Attack

Although downloadable audio files are smaller than their CD counterparts, they're still fairly large. A 4-minute music clip can be more than 4 megabytes, which can take a long time to download over a 56Kbps modem connection. If you plan to download audio clips on a regular basis, you should have a DSL or faster connection.

♦ **iTunes at www.apple.com/itunes.** This is the home of one of the most popular music stores on the Internet. Here you can listen to your favorite tunes, preview recent releases, and purchase and download quality clips online for less than $1 per tune. If you purchase clips at iTunes, Windows Media Player can't play them; you need to download Apple's iTunes to play these files.

♦ **Rhapsody at www.real.com.** The creators of RealPlayer host their own online music store, where you can purchase and download individual tracks to play on your RealPlayer, transfer to portable players, or burn to CDs.

♦ **MusicMatch at www.musicmatch.com.** MusicMatch is one of the most popular online music sites, featuring Internet radio stations. If the MusicMatch station is playing a song you like, you can jump to the online store, order it, download it, add it to your playlist, and then transfer it over to your portable music player or burn it to a CD.

◆ **AOL Music Now at aol.musicnow.com.** Like MusicMatch, AOL Music Now features on-demand Internet radio and customizable, commercial-free listening and enables you to order individual tracks online for less than a buck.

Whoa!

Before you start purchasing audio recordings online, make sure you can play them in Windows Media Player or whatever player you use and on your portable music player. Recordings from iTunes play only on an iPod or a computer running iTunes, and the iPod can't play tunes that you download from Rhapsody. Most sites have a link you can click to learn which portable players and programs are compatible with the service.

Playing Your Clips

As soon as you find a clip you want to download, simply click its link to play it. After your computer is finished downloading the clip, it should run your MP3 player, which typically starts playing the clip. If the clip doesn't start, click the **Play** button.

Copying Clips to a Portable Music Player

Building a huge music library on your computer is cool, but a computer is a bit too bulky to replace your Walkman. How do you take your music collection, or at least a portion of it, on the road? The easiest and lightest way is to purchase a portable music player (often called MP3 players). Portable music players come equipped with enough storage to hold gobs of music. You can rip tracks from CDs or download them from various sources on the Internet and then transfer (copy) them to your player.

Portable music players typically are equipped with the software you need to transfer clips from your computer to your player. Many of the music stores discussed earlier in this chapter also offer free software that can handle the file transfers. However, this software may not enable you to rip music from the CDs you already own.

An alternative is to use Windows Media Player to perform both jobs. This assumes, of course, that you have a portable music player that Windows Media supports. If you don't, you may need to purchase additional software.

In any event, the process of transferring clips to your player is fairly straightforward. The following steps show you how to copy files from your computer to your portable music player using Windows Media Player. If you're using other software, the steps should be similar.

1. Connect your portable music player to your computer as instructed in the player's documentation and turn it on.

2. Run the Windows Media Player as explained earlier in this chapter.

3. Click the **Sync** tab. A pane appears on the right, instructing you to drag tracks into the pane to add them to the Sync list. (If your portable music player or a drive letter for it does not appear, your player may not be supported by Windows Media Player.)

4. From the Library on the left, change to the folder that contains the tracks you want to copy to your portable music player.

5. Drag and drop one of the selected tracks into the Sync pane (on the right).

6. Repeat Steps 4 and 5 to copy any remaining tracks to the Sync pane.

7. Click the **Start Sync** button (near the bottom of the Sync pane).

8. Exit Media Player and disconnect your portable music player as instructed in its documentation.

Burning Your Own Audio CDs

Ever since companies placed the power of recording technology in the hands of the people, people have copied vinyl albums, audiotapes, TV shows, movies, and anything else they can get their hands on. CDs are no exception. As soon as audio CD burners hit the market, people started their own bootleg operations, churning out free CDs for themselves, their friends, and their families.

Computer Cheat

Although Windows Media Player features no command for copying directly from an audio CD to a blank CD-R or CD-RW, you can copy all the songs from the CD, save them in a separate playlist, and then copy the playlist to a CD. See the next section for details.

Some of this copying is acceptable. For instance, if you purchased the entire collection of Beatles CDs and you want to create your own "favorites" CD to play in your car, you won't be prosecuted for copying songs you paid for to another disc for your own use. However, if you copy your entire collection to give as Christmas gifts, you're crossing the line.

Be that as it may, the technology is available for copying CDs and for transferring your collection of MP3s (however you obtained it) to CDs, and I show you how to do it. I'll leave the legal and ethical decisions up to you, the courts, and the music industry.

Duplicating CDs

If your computer is equipped with a CD-R or CD-RW drive and a program for copying CDs, you can duplicate your audio CDs. Most computers that come with CD-R or CD-RW drives have a program for copying CDs. If you don't have a CD copy program, check out Roxio's Easy Media Creator at www.roxio.com. At about $100, it's a little pricey, but Easy Media Creator can help you make the most of your recordable disc drive. It includes features for backing up your computer's hard drive to CDs or DVDs, copying audio or video clips to CDs or DVDs, transferring MP3 clips to CDs, and much more.

With Roxio's Easy Media Creator, you simply insert the disc you want to copy, run Easy Media Creator, and click the **Copy** button. Easy Media Creator copies everything on the disc and then displays a dialog box telling you to insert a blank recordable disc. After you insert the disc, Easy Media Creator transfers everything it copied from the original disc to the blank disc.

Recording a Custom Mix to a CD

Besides the Counting Crows' *August and Everything After* and Tom Waits' *Swordfish Trombones*, I haven't encountered a CD that contains more than three songs I like. Fortunately, with a CD-R or CD-RW drive and the right program, you can pull one or more of your favorite songs off each CD to create and record your own custom mix to a blank CD. You can even add MP3 clips you downloaded from the Internet to the mix.

Again, several programs on the market let you copy tracks from one CD to another and burn MP3 clips to CDs, but because you already have Windows Media Player, you'll probably want to use it for creating your custom CDs.

First, record the desired tracks and copy them to a separate playlist, as explained earlier in this chapter. Click **Burn**. The Burn pane appears on the right, as shown in Figure 25.4. Drag and drop the tracks or playlists you want to burn to the CD into the Burn pane. Insert a recordable CD into your computer's recordable CD drive, and then open the list above the right pane and click the icon for your recordable CD drive. To start copying the playlist to the CD, click the **Start Burn** button (near the bottom of the Burn pane).

Figure 25.4

Windows Media Player can write the tracks in a playlist to a disc.

Click Burn

Drag entire playlists or individual tracks into the Burn pane   Click Start Burn

Playing DVD Movies on Your Computer

Can you watch movies on your computer? The short answer is yes—if your PC has a DVD drive you can watch DVD videos on your PC. However, you probably won't want to watch DVD videos on your PC. I once watched *Apocalypse Now* on my 17-inch monitor and had a headache for two days. The picture was sharp and the sound was incredible—my computer has a better sound system than my TV—but the picture was so dinky I had to press my face to the screen to see anything. Want to watch your movies using the full screen? Try pressing *Alt+Enter*.

At any rate, if your computer has a DVD drive, it probably came equipped with its own DVD video player. If it didn't, Windows Media Player can handle the job.

The Least You Need to Know

◆ To play an audio CD, insert it into your computer's CD-ROM drive, and then when a dialog box pops up asking what you want to do, click **Play Audio CD** and click the **OK** button.

◆ To copy tracks from the CD to the Windows Media Library, click **Copy from CD,** be sure a check mark appears next to only the tracks you want recorded, and then click the **Copy Music** button.

◆ To create a new playlist in Media Player, click the **Media Library** button and then click the **New playlist** button or open the **Playlists** menu and click **New Playlist.**

◆ Go to www.mp3.com for a wide selection of MP3 music clips and links to players, rippers, and MP3 gear.

◆ To take your tunes on the road, copy them to a portable MP3 player.

◆ You can use a CD burner program, such as Roxio's Easy CD Creator, to duplicate audio CDs or to copy MP3 clips to a blank CD to create your own mix.

Chapter 26

Snapping, Enhancing, and Sharing Digital Photos

In This Chapter

◆ Point and shoot with a digital camera

◆ Generating your own photo prints for pennies per print

◆ Placing photos on your web pages

◆ Sending digital photos via e-mail

◆ Making your own photo album

In a few short years, digital cameras have managed to replace the standard 35mm models. You no longer have to fumble with rolls of film, drop them off at the local pharmacy for developing, wait an hour or a day or a week for your prints, or store shoeboxes packed with prints in your closets.

With a digital camera, you get immediate gratification. Right after you take a picture, you can check out the results in the LCD display and then delete the photo and retake it if it didn't turn out. You can plug your camera into a TV set and view the picture, or connect your camera to your computer and print the photo. You don't even have to wait for one-hour service. In addition, digital photography enables you to e-mail photos to your friends and relatives, post them on your website or blog, and pack them away on CDs or DVDs.

In this chapter, you learn the basics of digital photography, including how to take photographs, enhance your photographs with digital imaging software, print and e-mail photos, and even order prints online.

Learning the Lingo

When you're shopping for a digital camera and first learning to use it, prepare yourself to be pummeled by a barrage of new technical terminology. The following list of terms and their definitions can bring you up to speed in a hurry:

- ◆ **Pixel.** Short for *picture element*, a pixel is one of the tiny colored dots that makes up a digital image or photograph. Generally, the more dots you have, the bigger and better the picture.

- ◆ **Megapixel.** A million pixels. Photo size and quality are often measured in megapixels—generally, the more megapixels, the larger the photo and the higher the quality. A 3.1 megapixel camera is considered standard for producing high-quality prints.

- ◆ **Resolution.** Resolution is another term for describing the quality of an image. The higher the resolution, the larger the photo and the higher the quality.

- ◆ **Optical zoom.** The ability of a camera to zoom in on a subject with its lens. Optical zoom is like focusing in with a telescope; it provides you with a clear, up-close view of the subject.

- ◆ **Digital zoom.** The ability of a camera to zoom in closer than what its lens is capable of. With digital zoom, the camera uses a program to magnify the image, which usually results in making the image a little blurry.

- ◆ **Optical viewfinder.** The little window you look through when taking a photograph that you use to frame your subject. An optical viewfinder can be somewhat deceptive—it doesn't always show exactly what will appear in the photograph.

- ◆ **LCD.** Short for Liquid Crystal Display, this is the preview screen on the back of most digital cameras. Unlike an optical viewfinder, the LCD displays the subject just as it will appear in the photograph.

- ◆ **Autofocus.** A feature in many digital cameras that automatically adjusts the lens to bring the subject into focus. To autofocus on most cameras, you hold down the button halfway for a brief moment. When the camera is focused, you then press down the button all the way to snap the photo.

♦ **Memory card.** The equivalent of a roll of film. Instead of storing images on film, a digital camera stores them on a memory card. Most digital cameras use removable memory cards or sticks that typically range in storage capacity from 16MB up to 1 gigabyte. The number of photos you can store per card varies depending on the capacity of the memory card and the size of the photos.

Inside Tip

When shopping for a camera, don't focus exclusively on megapixel ratings. A camera with a lower megapixel rating but a superior lens can often take a better photograph than a camera with a higher megapixel rating and a lower quality lens. Also opt for a higher optical zoom—3X at the very least; 4X–6X for landscapes; or 7X–12X for long-distance shots, sports photos, or wildlife images.

Taking Snapshots

Because digital cameras are modeled off of standard 35mm cameras, snapping a picture is easy. You just point and shoot. If the camera has an autofocus feature, you may need to hold down the button halfway to focus the camera and then press down all the way to snap the shot.

Before you snap too many pictures, check the following camera settings:

♦ **Resolution, image size, or megapixels.** Most cameras enable you to adjust the size and quality of the image. If you plan on printing the photos, choose a higher setting. If you're only going to e-mail the photos or place them on a web page, a setting of 640-by-480 pixels is usually sufficient. Larger images are higher quality, but they're also larger files, taking up more space on the memory card and taking longer to send and receive via e-mail.

♦ **Mode or environment.** Many cameras feature an assortment of modes or environments that automatically adjust the camera settings for different types of photos; for example, parties, landscapes, sporting events, daytime or nighttime portraits, and so on.

♦ **Flash.** In most cases, leave the flash setting at Auto. If you're taking all your pictures outside, turn off the flash. For backlit scenes, turn on the flash.

♦ **Exposure.** Many cameras enable you to bump the exposure up or down for very dark, very light, or high-contrast subjects. (When you're first starting out, you may want to leave this setting alone.)

♦ **Date imprint.** Some cameras can add a date imprint to your photos, so you can tell later the date on which you snapped them. If you find the date imprint more annoying than helpful, turn it off.

Inside Tip

Some digital cameras can capture audio and short video clips as well as take photographs. Check your camera's documentation to determine any additional features it may have.

The procedure for checking the camera settings varies from one digital camera to another. Some cameras have two buttons: one for changing to a feature (such as flash, image quality, timer, and audio) and another for changing the settings. You change to the desired feature (for instance, flash) and then press the other button to change the setting (for instance, Autoflash or Flash On).

Digital cameras that have LCDs typically use a menu system for changing settings. In addition, many cameras come with preprogrammed settings for specific environments; you simply flip a switch or turn a dial to pick the environment (beach, indoor party, night scene, museum, etc.), and then start snapping pictures—the camera adjusts all the settings for you. You can concentrate on centering your subject in the frame rather than worrying about aperture settings and shutter speeds.

Whoa!

As you snap pictures, keep track of the amount of storage remaining. Most digital cameras that have LCDs display the remaining space or display a warning when you're running out of space. You can then insert a blank memory card or disk or delete photos from the memory card that is currently loaded. If your camera does not have an LCD for framing pictures, it may have a small LCD display that shows the number of pictures you've taken and the available storage.

Copying Photographs to Your PC

Digital cameras typically come with their own software that transfers the image files from the camera to your PC. In addition, the camera should include a cable for connecting to one of the ports on your PC (typically the USB port). Some digital cameras require a PC card reader. Other cameras come with their own docking stations; you simply insert the base of the camera into the docking station to connect it to the computer.

To transfer the images, connect the cable to your camera and to the specified port. Run the photo transfer utility and enter the command to retrieve the images. The program retrieves the images from the camera and displays them on screen (see Figure 26.1). You can then delete the images from the PC card or other storage medium.

Most photo transfer utilities double as photo-editing tools. After you retrieve the images from your camera, you can adjust the brightness, color, and contrast of an image; crop it; flip it; resize it; and perform other digital imaging gymnastics. Figure 26.2 shows a sample photo displayed in PhotoImpression, the digital imaging software included with the Nikon CoolPix 3100. If you purchased a special printer for printing photos, it may include its own digital image enhancing software, too.

Inside Tip

Many printers are now equipped with memory card readers. You simply remove the memory card from your camera and plug it into your printer. The memory card reader typically appears as another storage drive on your computer.

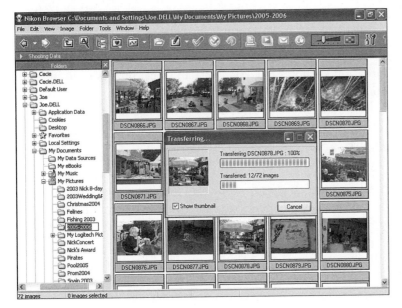

Figure 26.1

The photo transfer utility grabs the photos from the camera and copies them to your computer.

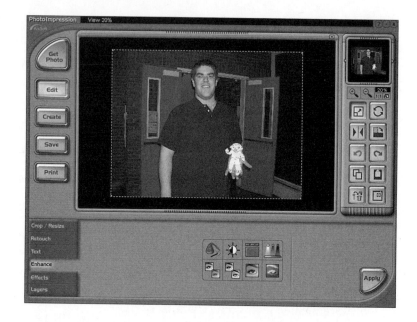

Inserting Digital Images into E-Mail and Web Pages

One of the best features of digital cameras is that they create graphic files that you can immediately use on web pages and in e-mail messages. You don't have to scan the picture after taking it, because it's already in a digital format.

To place a picture on your web page, insert it as you would insert any graphic. In addition, if your e-mail program supports HTML, you can insert images right inside the message area when composing an e-mail message. To insert an image into a message you are composing in Outlook Express, for example, you click in the message area, click the **Insert Picture** button, and then use the resulting dialog box to select the image, as shown in Figure 26.3.

The image management software included with many digital cameras features an option that can automatically prepare images for e-mail by reducing the resolution and file size of the image. This makes the image travel across the Internet much faster and take up less space on the recipient's computer. If you have software that offers this feature, use it instead of inserting high-resolution photos. The people on the receiving end sure will appreciate it.

You can add the file as an attachment

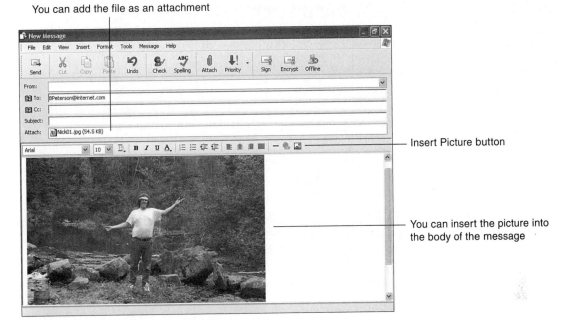

Insert Picture button

You can insert the picture into the body of the message

Figure 26.3
You can insert digital photos right inside your e-mail messages.

Ordering Photo Prints Online

Many new inkjet printers can generate high-quality photo prints on special photo paper. In addition, manufacturers have developed fairly inexpensive printers designed specifically for printing photos. Hewlett Packard's Photosmart, for example, is designed to print exclusively 4-by-7-inch prints. It even has a slot into which you can plug the memory card from your camera, so you can copy pictures directly to the printer without having to connect the camera to your computer.

If you prefer to leave the photo printing up to the professionals, you can order prints online at any of several online film developers, such as Shutterfly (www.shutterfly. com), Snapfish (www.snapfish.com), or Walmart (at www.walmart.com) which can mail prints to your local Walmart for pickup (typically a little cheaper than mailing them to your residence).

The process is pretty simple. You can either e-mail your photo files to the online photo shop or use the online photo shop's software to upload your photo files to the service. For example, at Shutterfly, you simply click Choose Pictures and then select

Inside Tip

Many stores that traditionally processed film now allow customers to upload their images online and pick up their prints at the store or have them shipped to their homes. Check out the website of your favorite local pharmacy to determine if they offer this service.

the pictures you want to order, as shown in Figure 26.4. You then complete an order form, specifying the size and number of prints you want and your billing and delivery information. Shutterfly processes your pictures and then mails them to you.

If you're in a big hurry and need one-hour processing (or faster), take your digital camera to a professional photo shop. Most photo shops have special printers that can transfer your digital photos into high-quality prints in a matter of minutes.

Figure 26.4

At Shutterfly, you drop off your "film" by selecting the photos you want developed and then uploading them to Shutterfly.

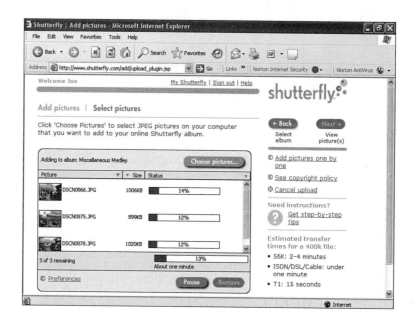

The Least You Need to Know

- Buy a digital camera with a good lens and a rating of 3.1 megapixels or higher.

- Optical zoom uses the camera's lens to zoom in on a subject, resulting in a sharp image. Digital zoom uses computer tricks to blow up an image, commonly making it fuzzy.

- Most digital cameras have an LCD screen on the back that can help you frame your picture and preview it to determine if you want to save or delete it.

◆ Before you take a snapshot with a digital camera, check the settings.

◆ Digital imaging software enables you to crop images, zoom in, adjust the color and brightness, add special effects, remove the red-eye effect, and enhance your photos in other ways.

◆ You can order prints online at any of several processing stores, including Shutterfly and Snapfish.

Chapter 27

Playing Film Editor with Digital Video

In This Chapter

- Transferring video from a camcorder or VCR to your computer
- Working with digital camcorders
- Editing your video recordings
- Adding professional transitions between video clips
- Recording video clips to CDs or VHS tapes

Back in the 1960s and 1970s, 8mm film was the medium of choice for amateur movie makers. I know people who still have boxes of 8mm film cans in their attics and basements. In the 1980s and 1990s, people traded in their 8mm cameras and projectors for VHS and 8mm camcorders. These relatively compact devices made it easy to record video and play it back on a television set, but the tapes were still bulky, and you had to fast-forward through several minutes of tape to find your favorite clips. The new millennium has introduced a new video technology, digital video, allowing us to transfer, edit, and catalog our video clips using a computer. In this chapter, you learn how to take advantage of digital video.

What You Need to Get Started

You can approach digital video from two different directions, depending on how much you have invested in an older camcorder, how many old tapes you have, and how much money you're willing to spend. If you don't have a camcorder or old tapes and you have some cash on hand, purchase a digital camcorder and start filming. Digital camcorders record video in a much higher resolution than analog VHS or 8mm camcorders, and the digital clips won't lose quality when copied to your computer. (The quality of video clips recorded with analog camcorders suffers a little when they are converted from an analog to a digital format.)

When shopping for a digital camcorder, you need to think about how you will connect the camcorder to your computer. Most digital camcorders have an *IEEE-1394* (*FireWire*) or USB connector. If your computer does not have an IEEE-1394 or USB port, you need to install an expansion board to add the required port.

def•i•ni•tion

IEEE-1394 is a standard for transferring data between devices very quickly—at a rate of 400Mbps (megabits per second) or 800Mbps depending on the version. Compare that to the USB standard of 12Mbps and 480Mbps (in USB 2.0), and you can see why IEEE-1394 is the preferred method of transferring video to a computer. IEEE-1394 goes by many names, the most common of which is Apple's **FireWire.** You might also see IEEE-1394 labeled i.link or Lynx.

If you already have an analog camcorder and plenty of old tapes, or if your computer budget is already strained, consider adding a video capture device to your computer. You have several options here. The most convenient way to go is to purchase an external unit that connects to your computer's parallel, USB, or IEEE-1394 port, or into a circuit board that comes with the unit. Figure 27.1 shows a device from Pinnacle Systems, which can capture from digital and analog camcorders and standard VHS tapes. Note that you plug the cables from the camcorder or VCR into the jacks on the front of the unit. To save space on your desk, you can opt for a video capture board, which plugs into an expansion slot inside your computer, but having the jacks right in front of you will make your job much easier.

Video capture boards and external units have special ports that let you connect your camcorder to your computer. They typically capture video at a rate of 15 or more frames per second, and they do a fairly good job of converting your analog clips into a digital format. If you're looking for a way to convert your collection of old camcorder or VHS tapes into a digital format and store them on CDs, this is the way to go.

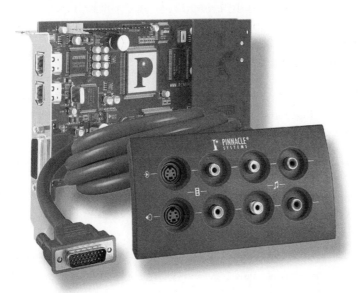

Figure 27.1

An analog-to-digital converter lets you connect a camcorder or VCR to your computer.

(Photo courtesy of Pinnacle Systems, Inc.)

Setting Up Your Audio/Video Equipment

If you're preparing to record and edit video from a digital camcorder, there's not much to setting up your equipment. You simply connect the USB or IEEE-1394 cable to the USB or IEEE-1394 ports on the camera and your computer, and you're ready to roll.

If you're recording from a VCR or analog camcorder, on the other hand, the setup is a bit more time-consuming. You must first install the video capture device and then connect the VCR or camcorder using several cables. The procedure for installing the video capture card or external device varies. The setup might be as simple as plugging the external device into your computer's USB port, or it might require you to install an expansion board inside the system unit. Read and follow the instructions and safety precautions that came with the card or device.

After the video capture device is installed, you can connect your VCR or camcorder to it. The audio and video connections vary, depending on the video capture card, the cables included with it, and the VCR or camcorder. On an external unit, such as Dazzle's Pinnacle Systems' Studio 8 Deluxe, the jacks are color-coded and match up with the standard A/V (Audio/Video) jacks found on most camcorders and VCRs.

def•i•ni•tion

S-video divides the video into two signals—one for color and one for brightness—generating a high-quality image. **Composite video** combines the color and brightness data in a single signal, resulting in a lower-quality display.

Video capture cards typically have a single A/V input jack for audio and video input. You need a four-headed input adapter to make the necessary connections. This adapter contains a single plug for the A/V input jack on your video capture card and four connectors for the camera: one for left audio, one for right audio, one for *S-video*, and one for *composite video*. You use either the S-video or composite video connector, depending on the camera. (S-video produces higher-quality recordings.) See Figure 27.2.

Figure 27.2

Use the proper cables to connect the video player to the A/V-in port on your video capture card.

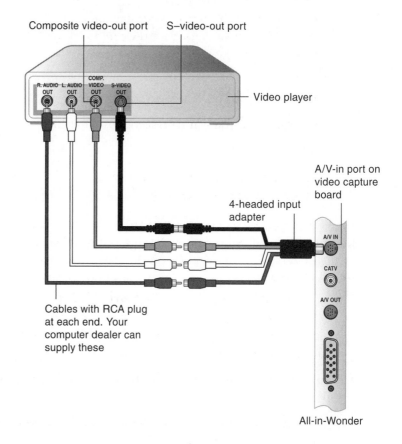

Capturing and Saving Your Clips

Your digital camcorder or video capture device probably came with its own program for recording and editing your video footage. Most of these programs are similar and follow the same overall procedure for recording and editing video. Here's a quick overview of the process:

1. Connect your camcorder or VCR to the video capture device.

2. Run your video recording program and enter the command to start recording.

3. Use your camcorder or VCR controls to play the video you want to record.

4. When you're ready to stop recording, enter the command to stop recording, and then press the **Stop** button on the camcorder or VCR. The video recording program chops the recording into *clips* to make them more manageable. It displays a thumbnail view of each clip.

5. Arrange the clips in the order in which you want them played.

6. Trim the clips. You can trim sections of any clip.

7. Add background music.

8. Add transitions between clips. For example, you can have a clip fade out at the end and fade into the next clip.

9. Save your movie to your hard drive.

10. Record your movie to a CD/DVD or e-mail the movie clip.

Windows XP includes its own video recording and editing software, Windows Movie Maker. To run Movie Maker, choose **Start, All Programs, Accessories, Entertainment, Windows Movie Maker.** Windows Movie Maker appears, as shown in Figure 27.3. You can download a free copy of Movie Maker at www.microsoft.com/windowsxp/moviemaker.

To start recording clips in Movie Maker from a VCR or analog camcorder, follow these steps:

1. Connect your VCR or camcorder to the video capture device.

2. In Movie Maker, click **Capture from Video Device.** The Video Capture Wizard appears, prompting you to select the video capture device that's connected to your computer.

Figure 27.3

Windows Movie Maker.

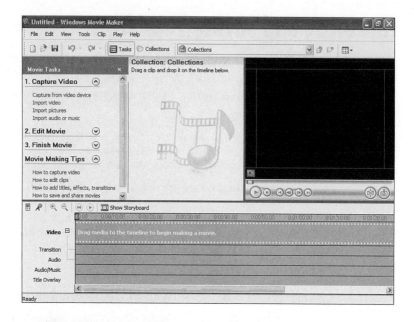

3. Select the video capture device you plan on using (if more than one such device is connected to your computer), and specify the audio device, video input source, and audio input source. Click **Next.** Video Capture Wizard prompts you to enter a name for the video.

4. Type a descriptive name for the video you are about to record and click **Next.** Video Capture Wizard prompts you to specify the desired video quality.

5. Click the option for the desired video quality. By default, Movie Maker is set to record video for optimal playback on a computer. (Higher-quality settings result in larger files.) Click **Next.** Video Capture Wizard displays the controls you need to record the video.

6. To have Movie Maker chop your video footage into manageable clips when you're done recording, make sure **Create Clips When Wizard Finishes** is checked.

7. Use the controls on your VCR or camcorder to locate the beginning of the clip you want to record, and then rewind it slightly. Video Capture Wizard displays a small preview area where you can watch the video, so you can see what you're doing.

8. Press the **Play** button on your VCR or camcorder, and when the video reaches the point at which you want to begin recording, click Video Capture Wizard's **Start Capture** button.

9. When you have reached the end of the clip, click the **Stop Capture** button to stop recording, and press the **Stop** button on your VCR or camcorder.

10. If desired, repeat Steps 7 to 9 to capture additional footage from this tape or from another tape.

11. When you are finished capturing video clips for your movie, click Video Capture Wizard's **Finish** button. If you turned on **Create Clips When Wizard Finishes** in Step 6, Movie Maker automatically chops the footage you recorded into smaller clips to make them more manageable and displays a thumbnail view of each clip, as shown in Figure 27.4.

Movie clips   Preview area

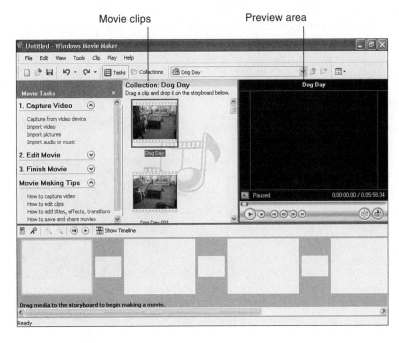

Figure 27.4

Windows Movie Maker chops your film footage into smaller clips.

The procedure for recording from a tape in a digital video (DV) camcorder is a little different, because you can control the camera from Movie Maker. Just connect the DV camcorder to your computer and set the camcorder mode to play your video. In Movie Maker, click **Capture from Video Device.** The Video Capture Wizard appears, prompting you to select the video capture device that's connected to your computer. Select the DV camcorder from the Available Devices list and click **Next.** Type a filename for the recording and click **Next.** Choose the desired video quality and click **Next.** When prompted to choose a capture method, choose **Capture the Entire Tape Automatically** (to have Movie Maker rewind the tape and record it in its entirety) or choose **Capture Parts of the Tape Manually** (to capture selected portions of the tape). When recording from a DV camcorder, you can use the camcorder's controls or the controls in Video Capture Wizard to control the camcorder during the capture.

Splicing Your Clips into a Full-Length Movie

As soon as you have a few clips to work with, you're ready to start your new career as a professional film editor, cutting undesirable footage, trimming clips, and rearranging clips to create your own feature film. The editing procedure is surprisingly simple. You drag and drop thumbnails of your clips onto the storyboard at the bottom of the Movie Maker window, as shown in Figure 27.5.

Drag a clip from this list to the storyboard.

Figure 27.5

Drag and drop your clips onto the storyboard.

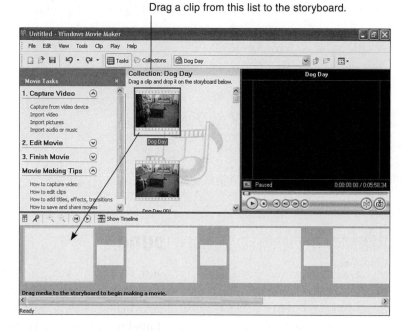

If a portion of a particular clip is out of focus or contains material you do not want to include in your video, you can trim the clip. This process consists of designating a start and end trim point. Movie Maker then cuts the beginning and end of the clip, leaving the portion between the two trim points intact. Here's what you do.

1. In the bar above the storyboard, click **Show Timeline,** to view a timeline that shows how the clips are stitched together. (You cannot trim clips in Storyboard view.)

2. Click the clip you want to trim. The play indicator appears at the beginning of the clip as a blue box in the timeline with a vertical line that illustrates where the clip would start playing if you were to click the Play button.

3. Drag the play indicator to the position where you want the beginning of the clip chopped off.

4. Open the **Clip** menu and click **Set Start Trim Point.** Movie Maker trims the portion of the clip to the left of the play indicator.

5. Drag the play indicator to the position where you want the end of the clip chopped off.

6. Open the **Clip** menu and click **Set End Trim Point.** Movie Maker trims the portion of the clip to the right of the play indicator.

7. Repeat steps 2 to 6 to trim any additional clips in the timeline.

Inside Tip _____

You can add a title frame to your video. Choose **Start, All Programs, Accessories, Paint** to run the Windows graphics program. Open the **Image** menu and click **Attributes.** Type **320** for the width and **240** for the height. Make sure **Pixels** is selected under **Units,** and then click **OK.** Use Paint to draw your title frame, and then save it as a BMP graphics file. Use the **File, Import** command in Movie Maker to bring the file into Movie Maker, and then drag it to the first frame on the filmstrip.

Adding an Audio Background

To give your video another dimension, consider recording some background music or narration. To record narration, first change to Timeline view, if it is not already displayed. If Movie Maker is in Storyboard view, click Show Timeline in the bar above the storyboard. Click the Narrate Timeline button (the button with the microphone on it, in the bar above the timeline). Click the **Start Narration** button and start talking into your microphone. When you're finished, click **Stop Narration** and then name and save your narration.

The easiest way to add background music, assuming you have a CD-ROM drive, is to record tracks from your audio CDs or download some music clips, as explained in Chapter 25. You can then use Movie Maker's **File, Import** command to import the audio clips into Movie Maker.

Panic Attack

Movie Maker might have trouble importing audio clips recorded with Windows Media Player. If you receive error messages when trying to import these clips, try recording your audio clips with a different CD ripper.

After you have imported audio clips into Movie Maker, adding them to your video is a snap. First, make sure the timeline is displayed; if the storyboard is displayed, instead, click Show Timeline (in the bar above the storyboard). Next, drag and drop the desired audio clip over the audio bar, as shown in Figure 27.6.

Figure 27.6

Drag and drop your audio clips onto the audio bar.

Drag an audio clip from this list to the storyboard.

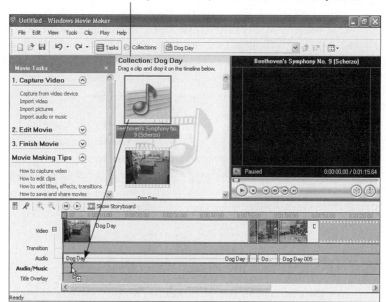

Smoothing Out Your Transitions

When you splice clips and trim sections of clips, some of the transitions might seem a little abrupt and surreal. To reduce the shock, add smooth transitions between clips. With Movie Maker, you can create a transition that makes the end of one clip fade out and the beginning of the next clip fade in.

To create a transition, change to Timeline view, as explained earlier in this chapter. Open the **Tools** menu and click **Video Transitions.** A list of video transition effects appears above the timeline. Scroll down the list to bring the desired transition into view, and then drag the transition from the list and drop it between the two clips where you want the transition to play. To preview the transition, drag the play indicator to a position just before the transition and then click the **Play** button. When Movie Maker reaches the point in the movie clip where you placed the transition, it displays the effect in the preview area.

Inside Tip _____

To add background music and narration, overlap the narration with the background music. You cannot completely overlap the two audio clips, but you can get pretty close.

Saving Your Movie

When your movie is complete, you can save it to your computer's hard drive, transfer it to a recordable disc (if your computer has a recordable CD or DVD drive), e-mail it to a friend or family member, save it to the web, or record it back to your DV camcorder. During the save operation, Movie Maker transforms your collection of clips into a single Movie Maker file. To save your movie, follow these steps:

1. Open the **File** menu and click **Save Movie File.** Movie Maker prompts you to choose what you want to do with the movie file, as shown in Figure 27.7. Save it to your computer's hard drive (using My Computer), transfer it to a recordable disc, e-mail it, save it to a web server, or record it to a tape in a DV camcorder.

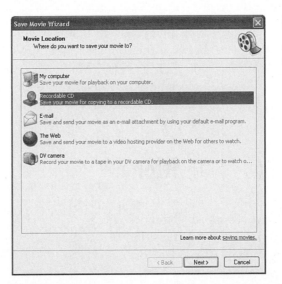

Figure 27.7

Specify where you want your movie saved.

2. If you plan on saving your movie clip to a recordable disc, insert a blank disc into your computer's recordable disc drive. To record to a DV camcorder tape, make sure a blank tape is loaded into the camcorder and that the camcorder is connected to the video capture device's video out port.

3. Choose the desired option to specify where you want the file saved and click **Next.** Movie Maker prompts you to enter a name for the file.

4. Type a file name for your movie and select the desired location where you want it saved. Click **Next.** Movie Maker prompts you to specify the desired video quality for the movie. (Low-quality settings are excellent for playing the video on a computer; if you plan on playing the video on a TV set, choose a higher setting.)

5. Choose the desired quality setting and click **Next.** Movie Maker processes the movie, creates a file, and saves it to the specified destination.

Copying Your Movie to a VHS Tape

If you want to copy your movie to a VHS tape to share it with people who don't have computers or DVD players, good luck. Most video recording devices and programs are much better at pulling video off tapes than recording edited video back to tapes. If your video capture device has an A/V output port, you can connect the device to a VCR to record to tape or a TV set that has RCA jacks. To make the connections, you need an adapter that plugs into the A/V output port on the video capture board and that has the proper connectors for the S-video-in or composite-in jacks on your VCR or TV set (see Figure 27.8).

Panic Attack

Some video cards have a very odd configuration. Some cards have a video-out connector that hooks up to the video-in port on a VCR, but the audio-out jack plugs into the sound card on a computer. So you play the video into the VCR and the audio into the computer, making it impossible to record both the audio and video portions to a tape!

Now that you've made the physical connection between the computer and the VCR or TV, how do you play the video? Movie Maker has no command for sending the video to a VCR or TV. However, if your video card has an option for using a TV as a display device, here's a little trick you can do to record your movie on a tape using your VCR:

1. Connect your VCR to the A/V output port on your video card, as shown in Figure 27.8.

2. Right-click a blank area of the Windows desktop and click **Properties.**

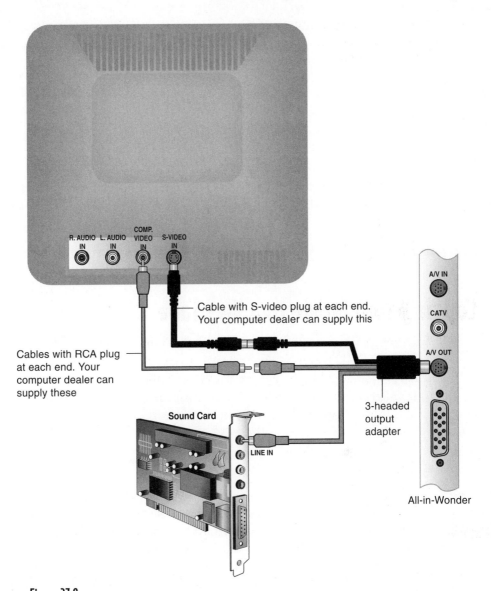

R. AUDIO   L. AUDIO   COMP. VIDEO   S-VIDEO

IN   IN   IN   IN

Cable with S-video plug at each end. Your computer dealer can supply this

Cables with RCA plug at each end. Your computer dealer can supply these

A/V IN

CATV

A/V OUT

3-headed output adapter

Sound Card

LINE IN

All-in-Wonder

Figure 27.8

Some video capture cards allow you to output recorded clips to a TV set or VCR.

3. Click the **Settings** tab and then click the **Advanced** button. This displays advanced options for your particular video card.

4. If you see a **Television** option, turn it on. If no **Television** option is available, this feature might not be available for your video card. Check the card's documentation to be sure.

5. Run Windows Media Player, as explained in Chapter 25.

6. Use the **File, Open** command to open the movie file you created.

7. Press the **Record** button on your VCR, and then perform the next two steps as quickly as possible.

8. Click Media Player's **Play** button.

9. Press **Alt+Enter** to change to full-screen mode.

The Least You Need to Know

♦ You can connect a digital camcorder directly to your computer via an IEEE-1394 port.

♦ To connect an analog camcorder or VCR to your computer, you must install an internal video capture card or an external video capture device.

♦ To run Windows Movie Maker, choose **Start, All Programs, Accessories, Entertainment, Windows Movie Maker.**

♦ To start recording video in Movie Maker, use your camcorder to start playing the video and then click the **Start Capture** button.

♦ To create transitions between video clips, display Timeline view, open the **Tools** menu, click **Video Transitions,** and then drag the desired transition between the two video clips where you want the transition to play.

♦ To save your movie as a file, open the **File** menu and click **Save Movie File,** and follow the onscreen instructions.

Part 6

Maintaining and Upgrading Your Computer

You don't need to be a mechanic to use a computer, but you should perform some basic maintenance tasks on a regular basis to keep your computer in tip-top condition and peak performance.

This part acts as your computer maintenance and upgrade manual. Here you learn how to clean your monitor, keyboard, mouse, printer, and system unit; give your computer a regular tune-up to keep it running at top speed; troubleshoot common computer problems; and find valuable technical support.

Chapter 28

Keeping Your Computer Clean

In This Chapter

- ◆ Sucking the dust from your computer
- ◆ Squeegeeing your monitor
- ◆ Picking hair and other gunk out of your mouse
- ◆ Keeping your printer shiny and new
- ◆ Spin-cleaning your disk drives

One of the best clean-air machines on the market is a computer. The cooling fan constantly sucks in the dusty air and filters out the dust. A monitor acts like a dust magnet, pulling in any airborne particles unfortunate enough to get close to it. And the keyboard and mouse act like vacuum cleaners, sucking crumbs and other debris from your desk. Unfortunately, the dust and smoke that your computer filters out eventually build up on the mechanical and electrical components inside it. When enough dust and debris collect on your computer and accessories, it's time for a thorough cleaning.

Tools of the Trade

Before you start cleaning, turn off your computer and any attached devices, and gather the following cleaning equipment:

- **Screwdriver or wrench.** This is for taking the cover off your system unit. (If you don't feel comfortable going inside the system unit, take your computer to a qualified technician for a thorough annual cleaning. It really does get dusty in there.)

> **Computer Cheat**
>
> You've probably seen floppy disk or CD-ROM cleaning kits, but most likely you don't need one. If your drive is having trouble reading disks, buy a cleaning kit and clean it. If it's running smoothly, let it be.

- **Computer vacuum.** Yes, there are vacuum cleaners designed especially for computers.

- **Can of compressed air.** You can get this at a computer or electronics store. Compressed air is great for blowing the dust out of tight spots, such as between keyboard keys.

- **Soft brush** (a clean paintbrush with soft bristles will do). Use the brush to dislodge any stubborn dust that the vacuum won't pick up.

- **Toothpicks.** The only tool you need to clean your mouse.

- **Cotton swabs.** A cotton swab is another good tool for cleaning your mouse, and it's great for swabbing down your keyboard, too.

- **Paper towels.** You need some paper towels for wiping dust off your equipment and for cleaning the monitor.

- **Alcohol.** This is not the drinking kind; save that for when you're done.

- **Distilled water.** You can get special wipes for your monitor, but paper towels and water do the trick.

- **Radio or CD player.** When you're cleaning, you need music ….

Vacuuming and Dusting Your Computer

Work from the top down and from the outside in. Start with the monitor. (You can use your regular vacuum cleaner for this part; if you have a brush attachment, use it.) Get your vacuum hose and run it up and down all the slots at the top and sides of the monitor. This is where most of the dust settles. Work down to the tilt-swivel base and vacuum that, too. (You might need a narrow hose extension to reach in there.) Now, vacuum your printer, speakers, and any other devices. If dust is stuck to a device, wipe it off with a damp (not soaking wet) paper towel.

Now for the system unit. When vacuuming, make sure you vacuum all the ventilation holes, including the floppy disk drive, power button, CD-ROM drive, open drive bays, and so on. Open the CD-ROM drive and gently vacuum the tray.

Now for the tough part—inside the system unit. Before you poke your vacuum hose in there, you should be aware of the following precautions:

- ◆ Use only a vacuum designed for computers. Don't use a Dust Buster, your regular vacuum cleaner, or your ShopVac. These can suck components off your circuit boards and can emit enough static electricity to fry a component. A computer vacuum is gentle and grounded. You can use a can of compressed air to blow dust off external peripheral devices, such as your keyboard and speakers, but be careful spraying the air against internal components. Compressed air can be very cold and can cause condensation to form on sensitive electrical components.

- ◆ Be careful around circuit boards. A strong vacuum can suck components and jumpers right off the boards. Also be careful not to suck up any loose screws.

- ◆ Touch a metal part of the case to discharge any static electricity from your body, and keep your fingers away from the circuit boards.

Now, take the cover off the system unit and vacuum any dusty areas. Dust likes to collect around the fan, ventilation holes, and disk drives. Try to vacuum the fan blades, too. If you can't get the tip of the vacuum between the blades, gently wipe them off with a cotton swab. Some fans have a filter where the fan is mounted. If you're really ambitious, remove the fan (be careful with the wires) and clean the filter.

Inside Tip

Some PCs have a fan that pulls air from the outside and pushes it through the ventilation holes. If the system unit case has openings near the fan, cut a square of sheer hosiery fabric, stretch it over the openings, and tape it in place with duct tape, keeping the tape away from the openings. Check the filter regularly, and replace it whenever dust builds up.

Wash Me: Cleaning Your Monitor

If you can write "Wash Me" on your monitor with your fingertip, the monitor needs cleaning. Check the documentation that came with your computer or monitor to see if it's okay to use window cleaner on it. The monitor might have an antiglare coating that can be damaged by alcohol- or ammonia-based cleaning solutions. (If it's not okay or if you're not sure, use water.) Spray the window cleaner (or water) on a paper towel, just enough to make it damp, wipe the screen, and then wipe with a dry paper towel to remove excess moisture. *Don't* spray window cleaner or any other liquid directly on the monitor; you don't want moisture to seep in. You can purchase special antistatic wipes for your monitor. These not only clean your monitor safely, they also discharge the static electricity to prevent future dust buildup.

> **Inside Tip**
>
> If you don't want to spend money on antistatic wipes, wipe your monitor with a *used* dryer sheet. (A new dryer sheet might smudge the screen with fabric softener.)

Shaking the Crumbs Out of Your Keyboard

Your keyboard is like a big place mat, catching all the cookie crumbs and other debris that fall off your fingers while you're working. The trouble is that, unlike a place mat, the keyboard isn't flat; it's full of crannies that are impossible to reach. And the suction from a typical vacuum cleaner just isn't strong enough to pull up the dust (although you can try it).

The easiest way I've found to clean a keyboard is to turn it upside down and shake it gently. Repeat two or three times to get any particles that fall behind the backs of the keys when you flip it over. If you don't like that idea, get your handy-dandy can of compressed air and blow between the keys.

For a more thorough cleaning, shut down your computer and disconnect the keyboard. Dampen a cotton swab with rubbing alcohol and gently scrub the keys. Wait for the alcohol to evaporate completely before reconnecting the keyboard and turning on the power.

Panic Attack

If you spill a drink on your keyboard, try to save your work and shut down the computer fast, but properly. Flip the keyboard over and turn off your computer. If you spilled water, just let the keyboard dry out thoroughly. If you spilled something sticky, give your keyboard a bath or shower with lukewarm water. Take the back off the keyboard, but do not flip the keyboard over with the back off, or parts will scurry across your desktop. Let it dry for a couple of days (don't use a blow-dryer), and put it back together. If some of the keys are still sticky, clean around them with a cotton swab dipped in rubbing alcohol. If you still have problems, buy a new keyboard; they're relatively inexpensive.

Making Your Mouse Cough Up Hairballs

If you can't get your mouse pointer to move where you want it to, you can usually fix the problem by cleaning the mouse. Flip the mouse over and look for hair or other debris on the mouse ball or on your desk or mouse pad. Removing the hair or wiping off your mouse pad fixes the problem 90 percent of the time.

If you have a mouse with a ball in it, remove the mouse ball cover. (Typically, you press down on the cover and turn counterclockwise.) Wipe the ball thoroughly with a moistened paper towel. Now for the fun part. Look inside the mouse (where the ball was). You should see three rollers, each with a tiny ring around its middle. The ring is not supposed to be there. The easiest way I've found to remove these rings is to gently scrape them off with a toothpick. You have to spin the rollers to remove the entire ring. Use a pair of tweezers to extract any dust mats that you can't pull out with a toothpick. You can also try rubbing the rings off with a cotton swab dipped in rubbing alcohol, but these rings are pretty stubborn. When you're done, turn the mouse back over and shake it to remove the loose crumbs. Reassemble the mouse.

Cleaning Your Printer (When It Needs It)

Printer maintenance varies widely from one printer to another. If you have a laser printer, you need to vacuum or wipe up toner dust and clean the little print wires with cotton swabs dipped in rubbing alcohol. For an inkjet printer, you might need to remove the print cartridge and wipe the print heads with a damp cotton swab. If you have a combination scanner/printer, you might have to wipe the glass on which you place your documents for scanning. Be sure to check the documentation that came with your printer for cleaning and maintenance suggestions.

You also need to be careful about the cleaning solution you use. Most printer manufacturers tell you to use only water on the inside parts—print rollers, print heads, and so on. In other cases, you can use a mild cleaning solution. Some manufacturers recommend rubbing alcohol on some but not all parts.

Even with these variables, there are a few things the average user can do to keep the printer in peak condition and ensure high-quality output:

♦ When turning off the printer, always use the power button on the printer (don't use the power button on your power strip) or press the **Online** button to take the printer offline. This ensures that the print head is moved to its rest position. On inkjet printers, this prevents the print head from drying out.

♦ Vacuum inside the printer. Open any doors or covers to get inside.

♦ If the ink starts to streak on your printouts (or you have frequent paper jams in a laser printer), get special printer-cleaner paper from an office supply store and follow the instructions to run the sheet through your printer a few times.

♦ Using a damp cotton cloth, wipe paper dust and any ink off the paper feed rollers. Do not use alcohol. Do not use a paper towel; fibers from the paper towel could stick to the wheels.

> **Inside Tip**
>
> Rubbing alcohol is an excellent cleaning solution for most electronic devices, because it cleans well and dries quickly. Use it for your keyboard, plastics, and most glass surfaces (except for some monitors). Avoid using it on rubber (for example, your mouse ball), because it tends to dry out the rubber and make it brittle.

What About the Disk Drives?

Don't bother cleaning your floppy, CD-ROM, or DVD-ROM drives unless they're giving you trouble. If your CD-ROM or DVD-ROM drive is having trouble reading a disc, the disc is usually the cause of the problem. Clean the disc and check the bottom of the disc for scratches. If the drive has problems reading every disc you insert, try cleaning the drive using a special drive-cleaning kit. The kit usually consists of a disc with some cleaning solution. You squirt the cleaning solution on the disc, insert it, remove it, and your job is done.

If you have a floppy disk drive that has trouble reading any disk you insert, you can purchase a special cleaning kit that works like the CD-ROM drive-cleaning kit. Although cleaning the disk drive might solve the problem, the problem can also be caused by a poorly aligned read/write head inside the drive, which no cleaning kit can correct.

The Least You Need to Know

♦ Vacuum your system, especially around its ventilation holes.

♦ Wipe the dust off your screen using a paper towel and the cleaning solution recommended by the manufacturer.

♦ Blow the crumbs out of your keyboard with compressed air.

♦ If you have a mouse with a ball inside it, remove those nasty dust rings around the rollers with a toothpick.

♦ Vacuum any ink dust that accumulates inside your printer.

♦ Clean your floppy or CD-ROM drive only if it is having trouble reading disks.

Chapter 29

Giving Your Computer a Tune-Up

In This Chapter

- ◆ Clearing useless files from your hard disk
- ◆ Streamlining the Windows startup
- ◆ Repairing hard disk storage problems with ScanDisk
- ◆ Doubling your disk space without installing a new drive
- ◆ Getting more memory without installing more RAM

Over time, you will notice that your computer has slowed down. Windows takes a little longer to start up. Programs that used to snap into action now seem to crawl. Scrolling becomes choppy. Your computer locks up almost every day. You might begin to think that you need a new processor, more RAM, a larger hard drive, or even a whole new computer.

Before you take such drastic action, work through this chapter to give your computer a tune-up. By clearing useless files from your disk drive, reorganizing files, and reclaiming some of your computer's memory, you can boost your computer's performance and save a lot of money at the same time.

Clearing Useless Files from Your Hard Disk

Your hard disk probably contains *temporary files* and backup files that your programs create without telling you. These files can quickly clutter your hard drive, taking room that you need for new programs or new data files you create. You can easily delete most of these files yourself.

The easiest way to clear useless files from your hard drive in Windows XP is to let the Windows Disk Cleanup utility manage the details:

1. Click the **Start** button, point to **All Programs, Accessories, System Tools,** and then click **Disk Cleanup.** If your computer has more than one hard drive, Windows prompts you to select the drive you want to clean.

2. If prompted to select a drive, click the arrow to the right of the **Drives** box, click the desired drive, and click **OK.** The utility scans your computer's hard drive for useless files and displays a list of file types you probably will never need, as shown in Figure 29.1.

3. Check the box next to each file type you want Disk Cleanup to sweep off your computer's hard drive.

4. For a more aggressive cleanup, click the **More Options** tab to remove additional items: Windows components, Installed programs, and System Restore points. (If you choose to remove System Restore points, Disk Cleanup removes all but the most recent restore point; so unless you're having serious problems with your computer, this is a safe option.)

5. Click the **Clean up** button next to any of the additional items you want to remove, and use the resulting dialog box or window to enter your preferences. Windows removes any of the selected items immediately, but you still need to run Disk Cleanup to remove the files you selected in Step 3.

6. Click **OK** to commence the proceedings. Windows removes the files you selected in Step 3.

def•i•ni•tion

Temporary files (files whose name end in .TMP) are files that your programs create but often forget to delete. You can safely delete them.

Computer Cheat

You can clear temporary Internet files off your hard drive without having to perform a full disk cleanup. In Internet Explorer, click **Tools, Internet Options.** Under **Temporary Internet Files,** click the **Delete Files** button and then click **OK** to confirm.

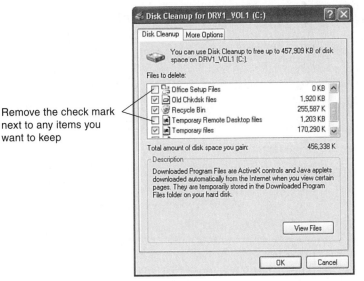

Figure 29.1

Disk Cleanup can remove useless files from your hard drive.

Remove the check mark next to any items you want to keep

Disk Cleanup does not remove copies of old digital photos you never look at, video clips you never watch, or music clips you never listen to. These are the items that really gobble up hard drive space in a hurry. Use My Computer to track down the folders where these files are stored and then delete them or move them to CDs or DVDs.

While you're at it, open your e-mail program and delete any e-mail messages you no longer need, including copies of messages you sent. When you delete e-mail messages, some e-mail programs, such as Outlook Express, stick the deleted messages in a separate folder (called Deleted Items in Outlook Express). Be sure to delete the messages from that folder, too.

Computer Cheat

Disk Cleanup can dump your Recycle Bin and open up a lot of disk space. If you already did this, that's fine, but realize that you can dump the Recycle Bin at any time. Just be sure it doesn't contain something you might need. Open the **Recycle Bin** (by double-clicking its icon on the desktop) and scroll down the list of deleted files to make sure you will never again need anything in the Bin. If you find a file you might need, drag it onto the Windows desktop for safekeeping, or right-click the file and select **Restore** to restore the file to its original location. Now, open the **File** menu and click **Empty Recycle Bin**.

Clearing Space on Your Windows Desktop

The Windows desktop can get as cluttered as a real desktop, and the more icons you have on your desktop, the longer it takes Windows to load them at startup. To clear some space and trim a couple seconds off the time Windows requires to start, you can have Windows clear unused icons off the desktop:

1. Right-click a blank area of the Windows desktop and click **Properties.** The Display Properties dialog box appears.

2. Click the **Desktop** tab.

3. Click **Customize Desktop.** The Customize Desktop dialog box appears.

4. Click **Clean Desktop Now.** The Desktop Cleanup Wizard appears.

5. Click **Next.** The Desktop Cleanup Wizard display a list of all the icons on your desktop along with the dates of when they were last used, as shown in Figure 29.2. Icons you've recently used are not tagged for deletion.

6. Click the check box next to each icon you want to leave on the desktop.

7. Click **Next.** The Desktop Cleanup Wizard displays a list of the icons it is about to delete and asks for confirmation.

8. Click **Finish.** The Desktop Cleanup Wizard removes the selected icons.

Figure 29.2

The Desktop Cleanup Wizard can automatically delete unused icons from your desktop.

Remove the check mark next to each icon you want to leave on the desktop

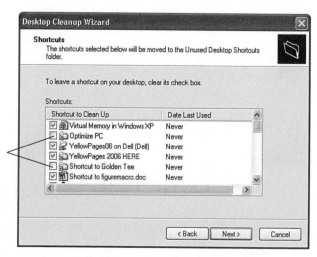

Checking for and Repairing Damaged Files and Folders

Windows comes with a utility called ScanDisk that can test a disk (hard or floppy), repair most problems on a disk, and refresh the disk if needed. What kind of problems? ScanDisk can find defective storage areas on a disk and block them to prevent your computer from using them. ScanDisk can also find and delete misplaced (usually useless) file fragments that might be causing your computer to crash.

You should run ScanDisk regularly (at least once every month) and whenever your computer seems to be acting up (crashing for no apparent reason). Also if you have a floppy disk that your computer cannot read, ScanDisk might be able to repair it and recover any data from it.

To run ScanDisk in Windows XP, follow these steps:

1. Open **My Computer.**

2. Right-click the icon for the drive you want to scan and click **Properties.**

3. Click the **Tools** tab, and (under Error-Checking) click the **Check Now** button. The Check Disk Local Disk dialog box appears, as shown in Figure 29.3.

4. Click the check box next to **Auto-matically Fix File System Errors** to place a check in the box.

5. To check for bad areas on the disk, click the check box next to **Scan for and Attempt Recovery of Bad Sectors** to place a check in the box. (Checking this option tells ScanDisk to do a thorough job, which might take several hours; turn on this option only if you don't plan on using your computer for a while.)

6. When you're ready to begin the scan, click **Start.**

Inside Tip

If you recover files from a damaged floppy disk, don't keep the disk. Transfer the files to another floppy disk or your computer's hard drive for safekeeping. When a floppy disk proves itself unreliable, it goes completely bad in a hurry.

Panic Attack

If Windows shuts down improperly (if you press the power button on your system unit before Windows is ready, if the power goes out, or if Windows locks up), Windows might run ScanDisk automatically when you restart your computer. It reminds you to shut down properly next time, even though this probably wasn't your fault.

Figure 29.3

ScanDisk can repair most disk problems.

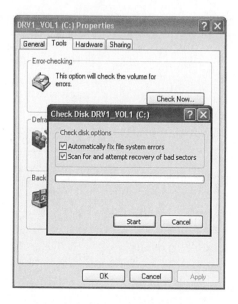

Defragmenting Files on Your Hard Disk

Whenever you delete a file from your hard disk, you leave a space where another file can be stored. When you save a file, your computer stores as much of the file as possible in that empty space and stores the rest of the file in other empty spaces. The file is then said to be *fragmented*, because its parts are stored in different locations on the disk. This slows down your disk drive and makes it more likely that your computer will lose track of a portion of the file or the entire file. Every month or so, you should run Windows Disk Defragmenter to determine the fragmentation percent and to defragment your files if necessary.

Before you start Disk Defragmenter, it's a good idea to disable any power-management utilities that might interfere with Defragmenter and any antivirus programs you're using:

- To disable the Windows power management settings, click **Start, Control Panel,** click **Performance and Maintenance,** click **Power Options,** and then open the **Power Schemes** list, select **Always on,** and click **OK.**

- Save and close all open documents and exit any programs you currently have running.

- To disable an antivirus program, right-click its icon in the system tray, at the right end of the taskbar, and click the option to disable the security features or exit the program.

Now you're ready to have Disk Defragmenter defragment your files. Follow these steps:

1. Open the **Start** menu, point to **All Programs, Accessories, System Tools,** and click **Disk Defragmenter.** A dialog box appears, asking which disk drive you want to defragment, as shown in Figure 29.4.

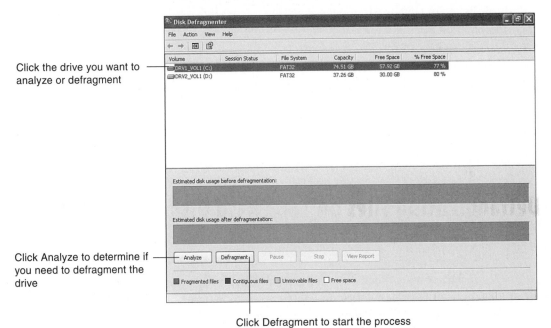

Click the drive you want to analyze or defragment

Click Analyze to determine if you need to defragment the drive

Click Defragment to start the process

Figure 29.4

Defragmenter prompts you to select the drive(s) you want to defragment.

2. Click the icon for the drive you want to defragment.

3. Click **Analyze.** Defragmenter displays both the percentage of file fragmentation on the disk and whether you need to defragment the disk.

4. When you're ready for Defragmenter to start working, click the **Defragment** button. Defragmenter starts defragmenting the files on the disk.

5. Wait until the defragmentation is complete. It's best to leave your computer alone during the process. Otherwise, you might change a file and cause Defragmenter to start over. Don't run any programs or play any computer games. When defragmentation is complete, Defragmenter displays a message telling you so.

Making Windows Start Faster

Windows is a slow starter, even on a quick machine. If you have some power-saving features on your computer, you can make Windows start a lot faster. Instead of turning your PC off and on, use the **Power** or **Power Management** icon in the Control Panel to access the options for placing your PC in sleep mode when you're not using it (rather than shutting it down completely). In Windows XP, display the **Control Panel,** click **Performance and Maintenance,** and click **Power Options.** Enter the desired settings to specify which components you want Windows to power down after a specified period of inactivity. When Windows powers down the computer, you can quickly restart by pressing the **Shift** key or rolling the mouse around rather than by turning on the computer and waiting for Windows to restart. The Power Options Properties has two options that need a little explanation:

♦ **System standby.** In standby mode, Windows turns off your monitor and disk drives to conserve power. When you press a key on your computer or roll the mouse around, Windows quickly snaps out of standby mode. Use this option only if you're going to be away from your computer for a short time. System standby does not save your work to disk, so in the event of a power outage, you can lose any recent work you've done and haven't yet changed.

♦ **System hibernates.** In hibernation mode, Windows saves everything to disk and then shuts down your computer. When you restart, Windows loads everything back into memory, so you can pick up where you left off. Hibernation mode is safer if you plan on being away from your computer for an extended period of time.

Windows features a few other tricks that can help trim time off the Windows startup. Try the following:

♦ To prevent Windows from running programs that are on the Startup menu, hold down the **Shift** key right after you log on to Windows. If you don't log on to Windows, press and hold down **Shift** when you see the Windows *splash screen* (the screen that appears before you get to the desktop).

♦ To remove programs from the Startup menu, click the **Start** button, point to **All Programs, Startup,** and then right-click the program you want to remove and click **Delete.** (Be careful. If you have an antivirus program that runs on startup, keep it on the **Startup** menu.)

◆ To prevent programs from starting when you start your computer, click **Start, Run,** type **msconfig,** click **OK,** click the **Startup tab,** and click the check box next to each item you want to disable on startup to remove the check from its box. (Be careful. If you have an antivirus program that runs on startup, don't disable it.)

◆ To quickly restart Windows XP without turning your computer off and then on, click **Start, Turn Off Computer, Restart.** You can use these same steps to place Windows in Standby mode, but instead of clicking Restart, click **Standby.**

Inside Tip _____

Every computer comes with a set of startup instructions called the BIOS (basic input/output system). These instructions include boot settings that can make your computer start faster. For instance, you can enter a setting to have your computer start directly from drive C (instead of first checking the floppy and CD drives for the operating system). Check the startup screen or your computer's manual for instructions on accessing the BIOS settings, but don't change any settings you are unsure of. Changing the wrong settings can cause serious problems.

Boosting Performance with Shareware Utilities

Does your 56Kbps modem seem slow? Does Windows frequently lock up or display the "insufficient memory" message, even though your computer has more than 256MB of RAM and plenty of free disk space? Has your computer's performance become so degraded that you just can't stand using your computer for another day? Then it's time to bring out the big guns—utility programs designed to optimize your computer automatically.

The following is a list of shareware programs, along with information on where to find out more about them and where to go to download the latest version:

◆ **MemTurbo** is a memory (RAM) optimizer. When you exit some programs, they fail to free up the memory they were using, reducing the amount of free memory available to other programs. MemTurbo reclaims this memory to make programs run faster and prevent Windows from locking up. You can find out more about MemTurbo and download a trial version at www.memturbo.com.

◆ **Magical Optimizer** is designed to pick up where the Windows Maintenance Wizard leaves off. It clears redundant, duplicate files from your system and streamlines the Windows Registry to boost overall system performance. Learn more about Magical Optimizer and pick up a shareware version of it at www.ashampoo.com.

◆ **Registry Clean Pro** safely and automatically deletes entries in your Windows Registry, an enormous, complex file that Windows uses to control nearly every computer component and program. The Windows Registry often becomes cluttered with useless settings and codes that can result in slowing down Windows and making it unstable. You can edit the Registry yourself, but it's a risky activity that can cause all sorts of terrible problems. Registry Clean Pro tidies up the Registry and can significantly improve the performance of your computer. Download a trial version at www.registry-clean.com. (If you use Magical Optimizer, you don't need another Registry cleaner.)

Computer Cheat

If you don't have a utility for reclaiming memory, shut down Windows and restart your computer. You might need to do this every day or two to keep your computer running smoothly.

◆ **TweakDUN** is an Internet connection optimizer for Windows. It automatically adjusts the Windows Dial-Up Networking settings to make Windows transfer data more efficiently over a modem connection. If you're using a 56Kbps modem and you aren't ready to move up to an ISDN, DSL, or cable connection, TweakDUN can improve your current connection speed. Check it out at www.pattersondesigns.com/tweakdun. (You may also want to check out Download Accelerator at www.speedbit.com.)

◆ **SiSoft Sandra** is a system information utility that provides a complete inventory of your system's resources. Sandra shows you the processor's type and speed, the amount of memory, the amount of free storage space, the monitor make and model, and descriptions of all installed peripherals. When you want to know more about your computer, check out Sandra at www.sisoftware.co.uk.

The Least You Need to Know

◆ Clear temporary files; unused photos, videos, music files; old e-mail messages; and temporary Internet files from your hard disk, and don't forget to dump the Recycle Bin.

◆ To avoid system crashes and lost files, run ScanDisk and Disk Defragmenter at least once every month.

◆ If you have an older computer that you're not ready to upgrade or replace, obtain a set of utilities for optimizing performance.

◆ Instead of shutting down the power to your computer when you're done working, use the Windows power-management features to place it in Hibernation or Standby mode.

◆ If your computer seems to be running slowly, exit all programs and restart Windows to clear your computer's memory.

Troubleshooting Common Computer Problems

In This Chapter

♦ Figuring out what to do and not do in a crisis

♦ Sniffing out the cause of a problem

♦ Recovering safely when your computer locks up

♦ Getting your speakers to say something

♦ Making your modem dial

Your computer can be quite moody. One day, all the components run properly and all tasks proceed without a glitch. The next day, your mouse pointer won't budge, your printer refuses to print a document, Windows locks up, or cryptic error messages pop up on your screen. Sometimes, simply installing a program or a new component can bring your computer to a grinding halt. In many instances, the computer provides no clue as to what the problem is, leaving you to troubleshoot on your own.

When problems arise, what should you do? Where do you begin to look for help? How do you track down the root cause of the problem? This chapter is your guide to solving a host of common computer problems.

Here you learn common troubleshooting tactics and do-it-yourself repairs. This chapter won't transform you into a professional computer technician; but with a little practice and a lot of patience, by the end of this chapter, you should be able to solve the most common problems and even help your friends with their computer woes.

Troubleshooting Tactics: Pre-Panic Checklist

When you run into a problem that doesn't have an obvious solution, the best course of action is inaction—that is, don't do anything. If you're fidgeting to do something, take a walk or grab a snack. Doing the wrong thing can often make the problem worse. After you've calmed down a little, come back and work through this checklist:

- **Are there any onscreen messages?** Look at the monitor for any messages that indicate a problem.

- **Is everything plugged in and turned on?** Turn everything off and check the connections. Don't assume that just because something looks connected, it is; wiggle the plugs.

- **When did the problem start?** Did you install a new program? Did you enter a command? Did you add a new device? When my speakers went mute, I realized that the problem started after I installed a new hard drive. I had knocked a tiny jumper off the sound card during the hard drive installation.

- **Is the problem limited to one program?** If you have the same problem in every program, the problem is probably caused by your computer or Windows. If the problem occurs in only one program, focus on that program.

- **When did you have the file last?** If you lost a file, it probably did not get sucked into a black hole. It is probably somewhere on your disk, in a separate folder. Chapter 8 reveals several tricks for tracking down lost or misplaced files.

Whoa!

Keep a running log of the changes you make to your system. It takes a little extra time, but it enables you to retrace your steps later.

- **Realize that it's probably not the computer, and it's probably not a virus.** The problem is usually in the software—Windows or one of your programs. Of the problems that people blame on computer viruses or the computer itself, 95 percent are actually bugs in the software or problems with specific device drivers (the instructions that tell your computer and Windows how to use the device).

Preventing and Recovering from Problems with System Restore

Windows includes a nifty utility called System Restore that can help you return your computer's settings to an earlier time when everything was working properly. System Restore monitors your computer, and when you install a program or a new peripheral device or component, it creates a restore point and saves the current settings to your computer's hard drive. System Restore also creates a daily restore point, just in case something goes wrong during the day. If you install a program or change a setting in Windows that causes problems, you can run System Restore and pick the desired restore point. Here's what you do:

1. Click the Windows **Start** button, point to **All Programs, Accessories, System Tools,** and then click **System Restore**. The System Restore window appears.

2. Click **Restore My Computer to an Earlier Time** and click **Next.** System Restore displays a calendar showing the days of the current month. Dates in bold represent days in which a restore point was created, as shown in Figure 30.1.

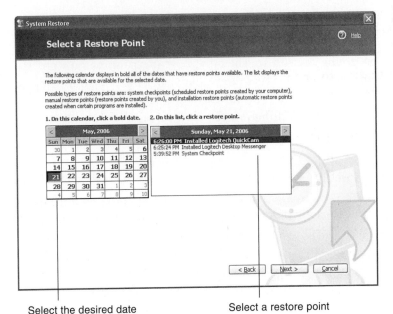

Select the desired date

Select a restore point

Figure 30.1

System Restore enables you to return your system to an earlier time.

3. Click the date that has a restore point you want
to use to restore your system. A list of restore
points created on the selected date appears on
the right. (This is where it's helpful if you keep
a running log of changes.)

4. Click the desired restore point and click **Next.**
System Restore displays a message assuring you
that none of your data files or e-mail will be
wiped out by the restoration, and informing you
that the process is reversible.

5. Click **Next.**

6. System Restore takes a few seconds to collect the information it needs, and then
it restarts Windows and displays the Log on screen. Log on to Windows as you
normally do. System Restore runs automatically and displays a window that
enables you to undo the restoration.

7. Close or cancel the window.

Identifying Troublesome Background Programs

Don't assume that the programs you run are the only programs running on your
computer. Many programs you install or that came already installed on your computer
run in the background. You won't see buttons for them on the Windows taskbar or
even in the system tray, but they're running just the same and can cause conflicts
with Windows and your other programs. They can also consume a great deal of your
computer's resources.

Fortunately, Windows features a configuration tool that enables you to disable these
programs when Windows starts. You can disable most of the programs to prevent
them from running and then enable each program to identify the program that's
causing problems. To prevent programs from running in the background, take the
following steps:

1. Open the **Start** menu and click **Run.** The Run dialog box appears.

2. Type **msconfig** and press **Enter** or click **OK.** The System Configuration Utility
appears.

3. Click the **Services** tab and click **Hide All Microsoft Services** to place a check in its box, as shown in Figure 30.2. By hiding Microsoft services you avoid accidentally disabling a service that's critical for the operation of Windows.

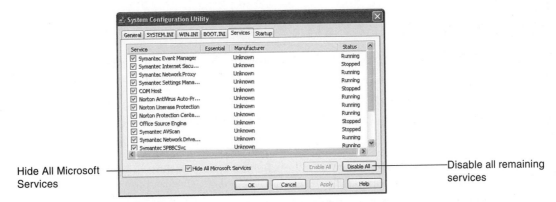

Hide All Microsoft Services

Disable all remaining services

Figure 30.2

The System Configuration Utility enables you to safely disable programs and services that might cause problems.

4. Click the **Disable All** button. This disables all services that are not critical for Windows to function properly.

5. Click the **Startup** tab. A list of all the background programs that run on startup appears.

6. Click the **Disable All** button. This removes the checkmark next to each program.

7. Click **OK.** The System Configuration dialog box appears, prompting you to restart your computer.

8. Exit any programs that are currently running and then click the **Restart** button. Windows restarts and then displays a dialog box indicating that you're running Windows with a selective startup configuration for troubleshooting.

9. Click **OK.** The System Configuration Utility appears.

10. Click **Cancel.**

If Windows and the various applications you use run properly, you know that one of the programs or services that you disabled was causing the problem. Use the System Configuration Utility to re-enable the programs and services one at a time, restarting

Windows after each change. If the problem arises, you know that the program or service you just enabled is the cause, and you can focus your troubleshooting efforts on that program or service.

My Computer Won't Start

A computer is a lot like a car; the most frustrating thing that can happen is that you can't even get the engine to turn over. To solve the problem, consider these questions:

- **Is the computer on?** Make sure the power switch on the system unit is turned on. Some computers have a power button that you have to press and hold for a couple of seconds.

- **Is the surge strip on?** If your PC is plugged into a surge suppressor or UPS, make sure the power is turned on.

- **Is the screen completely blank?** If you heard the computer beep and you saw the drive lights go on and off, the computer probably booted fine. Make sure the monitor is connected and turned on and the brightness controls are turned up. Try moving your mouse or pressing the **Shift** key; your computer may be in sleep mode, and this wakes it up.

- **Is there a disk in drive A?** If you see a message onscreen that says "Non-system disk or disk error," you probably left a floppy disk or CD in one of the drives. Remove the disk or CD that might be loaded, and then press any key to start from the hard disk.

- **Can you start from a floppy disk or CD?** Insert the Windows CD and restart your computer. If you can start from the Windows CD, the problem is on your hard disk. You may need some expert help to get out of this mess.

Inside Tip

Booting from the Windows CD can be a little tricky. Most new computers are set up to check the CD-ROM drive on startup for a bootable CD. When you restart your computer, a message appears asking if you want to start from the CD-ROM drive or the hard drive. Select the option to start from the hard drive. If your computer displays no such message, you may need to enter your computer's setup program and select your CD-ROM drive as the first drive your computer checks for a bootable disc. Watch the screen on startup for a message telling you which key to press to enter your computer's setup.

My Computer Locked Up

The computer might be too busy to handle your request, so wait a few minutes. If it's still frozen, press **Ctrl+Alt+Del.** A dialog box should appear, showing you the names of the active programs. Next to the program that's causing the problem, you should see "[not responding]." Click that program's name and click **End Task.** Frequently, a second End Task confirmation dialog box appears a few seconds after clicking the End Task button; repeat the command to end the task. (You may lose data when you close a program that is not responding.) You should now be able to continue working.

If you close the errant program and Windows is still locked up, press **Ctrl+Alt+Del** again and close any other programs that are causing problems. If you still cannot regain control of your computer, you may have to press **Ctrl+Alt+Del** again or use your computer's Reset or Power button. Do this only as a last resort. Shutting down your system without exiting programs properly causes you to lose any work you had not saved before shutting down. (Files saved to your hard disk are safe.)

It Could Be a Program

Many programs, especially web browsers, games, and antivirus programs, typically are buggy. They have programming code that makes the program conflict with Windows, other programs, one of your hardware devices, or even your computer's memory. One common problem is that the program never frees up the memory it uses.

The only permanent solution is to install a patch or bug fix from the manufacturer, assuming a patch is available. (A patch is a set of program instructions designed to fix a programming bug or add capabilities to a program.) Contact the manufacturer's tech support department to determine whether they have a fix for the problem, as explained in Chapter 31. For a temporary solution, use the program in spurts. Use the program for awhile, save your work, exit, and restart before your computer locks up. If your computer seems to be getting sluggish, try restarting Windows to free up memory.

Check Your Mouse Driver

Windows might be having a problem with the mouse driver (the instructions that tell Windows how to use your mouse). Check to make sure that you don't have two conflicting mouse drivers installed. Right-click **My Computer** and click **Properties** to access System Properties, click the **Hardware** tab, and then click the **Device Manager** button. Click the plus sign next to **Mouse.** If you have more than one mouse listed, you have more than one mouse driver installed. To disable one of the mouse drivers, double-click the mouse that doesn't match the type of mouse you have, click **Disable in This Hardware Profile,** and click **OK.** Click **OK** again and restart your computer.

> **Whoa!**
>
> If you pick the wrong mouse driver, you won't have a mouse pointer in Windows, making it tough to navigate. If you pick the wrong driver, start your computer in Safe mode by tapping the **F8** key during startup (right after the computer beeps) and choosing the option to start in Safe mode. Then pick a different driver. See "Dealing with Windows in Safe Mode" later in this chapter for details.

If that doesn't fix the problem, go to the computer or mouse manufacturer's tech support page on the web and check whether they have an updated driver for the mouse (see Chapter 31). In most cases, the updated driver contains the fix for the problem. (See "Updating the Software for Your Hardware" later in this chapter to learn how to install an updated driver.)

If you cannot obtain an updated mouse driver, try reinstalling the mouse driver. Right-click **My Computer,** click **Properties,** click the **Hardware** tab, and then click the **Device Manager** button. Click the plus sign next to **Mice and Other Pointing Devices** and then right-click the icon for your mouse and click **Uninstall.** Press **Alt+F4** repeatedly to shut down all programs and display the Windows Shut Down window, and then choose the option for restarting Windows. When Windows starts, it installs the required mouse driver.

Check the Windows Graphics Acceleration Setting

Windows is initially set up to exploit the full potential of your computer. Unfortunately, sometimes Windows is too aggressive, especially when it comes to your system's video acceleration. Windows cranks up the video acceleration rate to the maximum, which can sometimes cause your system to crash without displaying an error message. Try slowing it down:

1. Right-click a blank area of the Windows desktop and select **Properties.**

2. Click the **Settings** tab and click the **Advanced** button.

3. Click the **Troubleshoot** tab.

4. Drag the **Hardware Acceleration** slider to the second or third hash mark, and click **OK.**

5. Click **Close.**

6. If Windows asks whether you want to reboot your system, close any programs that may be running, and click **Yes.**

 Inside Tip

Some programs have trouble dealing with a large number of colors. Right-click the Windows desktop, choose **Properties,** and click the **Settings** tab. Choose **256 Colors** from the **Colors** drop-down list. Don't go lower than 256; some programs do not work with a lower setting.

Obtain an Updated Video Driver

Hiding behind the scenes of every video card and monitor is a video driver that tells your operating system (Windows) how to use the card and monitor to display pretty pictures. Occasionally, the driver contains a bug that can lock up your system. More frequently, the driver becomes outdated, causing problems with newer programs. In either case, you should obtain an updated driver from the manufacturer of the video card. You can call the manufacturer's tech support line and have them send the driver to you on a floppy disk or obtain the driver from the company's website. (See "Updating the Software for Your Hardware" later in this chapter to learn how to install an updated driver.)

Dealing with Windows in Safe Mode

Windows typically starts in Safe mode if you install a wrong device driver (especially a wrong video or mouse driver). In Safe mode, "Safe Mode" appears at each corner of the desktop. In most cases, you can simply restart Windows to have it load the previous driver. If on restarting, the Windows desktop is not visible or you cannot use the mouse, restart your computer, wait for it to beep, tap the **F8** key several times, and then choose the option for starting Windows in Safe mode. (You have to be quick with the F8 key—press it before you see the Windows screen.)

Windows loads a standard mouse and video driver in Safe mode, so you can see what you're doing and use the mouse to point and click. This allows you to install a different or updated driver or change settings back to what they were before you encountered problems.

I Can't Get the Program to Run

If you try to run a program using a shortcut icon, the icon might be pointing to the wrong program. Right-click the shortcut, choose **Properties,** and check the entry in the **Target** text box. This shows the path to the program's folder followed by the name of the program file that launches the program. If the text box is blank or points to the wrong file, click the **Find Target** button and use the resulting dialog box to change to the program's folder and choose the right program file.

If the program starts and immediately closes, your computer might not have sufficient memory or disk space to run the program. Right-click **My Computer,** select **Properties,** click the **Advanced** tab, click the **Performance Settings** button, click the **Advanced** tab, and under Virtual Memory, click the **Change** button. Make sure that you have at least 30 megabytes of free space on the disk that Windows is using for virtual memory. Any less, and you have to clear some files from your hard disk.

If the program still won't run, try reinstalling it. If that doesn't work, contact the program manufacturer's tech support department to determine the problem and the required fix. The program may require special hardware or additional software that is not available on your system.

I Have a Mouse, but I Can't Find the Pointer

After you get your mouse working, you will probably never need to mess with it again (except for cleaning it, which we talked about back in Chapter 28). The hard part is getting the mouse to work in the first place. If you connected a mouse to your computer and you don't see the mouse pointer onscreen, you should investigate a few possibilities:

♦ **Is the mouse pointer hidden?** Mouse pointers like to hide in the corners or edges of your screen. Roll the mouse on your desktop to see whether you can bring the pointer into view.

♦ **When you connected the mouse, did you install a mouse driver?** Connecting a mouse to your computer is not enough. You must install a program (called a *mouse driver*) that tells the computer how to use the mouse if the mouse did not come with the computer. Follow the instructions that came with the mouse to figure out how to install the driver.

I Can't Hear My Speakers!

Several things can cause your speakers to go mute. Check the following:

- Are your speakers turned on?

- Is the speaker volume control turned up?

- Are your speakers (or headphones) plugged into the correct jacks on your sound card? Some sound cards have several jacks, and it's easy to plug the speakers into the input jacks instead of the output jacks.

- If you're having trouble recording sounds, make sure that your microphone is turned on and plugged into the correct jack.

- Does your sound card have a volume control? Crank it all the way up.

- Click **Start; Control Panel; Printers and Other Hardware; Sounds, Speech, and Audio Devices.** Click **Adjust the System Volume,** and then go through all options in the resulting dialog box to make sure that every volume control is set at the desired level and nothing is set to mute.

> **Inside Tip**
>
> Windows comes with several hardware troubleshooters that can help you track down problems with your mouse, sound card, monitor, network, and other devices. To view a list of troubleshooters, open the **Start** menu, click **Help,** and search for "troubleshooter."

If you still can't get your speakers to talk, right-click **My Computer,** select **Properties,** click the **Hardware** tab, and then click the **Device Manager** button. Scroll down the list and click the plus sign next to the **Sound** option. If your sound card is not listed, you need to reinstall the sound card driver. If the sound card is listed but has a yellow circle with an exclamation point on it, the sound card is conflicting with another device on your system. Check your sound card's documentation to determine how to resolve hardware conflicts.

I Can't Get My Modem to Work

If your modem can't dial, Windows can help you track down the problem with its hardware troubleshooters. To run the modem troubleshooter in Windows XP, display the Control Panel, click **Printers and Other Hardware,** click **Hardware** (under

Troubleshooters in the left pane), and then click the option button to the left of **I'm Having a Problem with a Modem,** click **Next,** and follow the onscreen instructions to track down the problem, as shown in Figure 30.3.

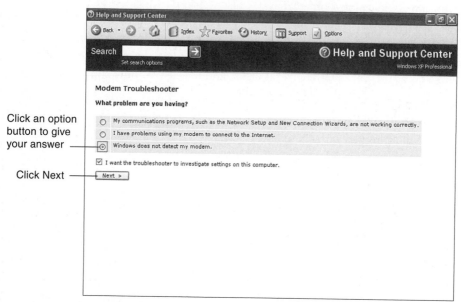

Click an option button to give your answer

Click Next

Figure 30.3

Windows comes with a modem troubleshooter.

My Printer Won't Print

If you run into printer problems, you probably have to do more fiddling than Nero. Look for the following:

- ◆ **Is your printer plugged in and turned on?**

- ◆ **Does your printer have paper?** Is the paper tray inserted properly?

- ◆ **Is the printer's online light on (not blinking)?** If the online light is off or blinking, press the online button to turn on the light.

- ◆ **Is your program set to print to a file?** Many Print dialog boxes have a Print to File option, which sends the document to a file on your disk instead of to the printer. Make sure this option is *not* checked.

- **Is the print fading?** If so, your printer may need a new toner or ink cartridge. If your inkjet cartridge has plenty of ink, check your printer manual to determine how to clean the print head. Inkjet cartridges have some sensitive areas that you should never clean, so be careful.

- **If you have an inkjet printer, check the print head and the area next to the print head for tape, and remove the tape.** Ink cartridges usually come with two pieces of tape on them. You must remove both pieces before installing the cartridge.

- **Is your printer marked as the default printer?** In My Computer, double-click the **Printers** icon. Right-click the icon for your printer and make sure that **Set as Default** is checked. If there is no check mark, select **Set as Default.**

- **Is the printer paused?** Double-click the **Printer** icon in the taskbar, open the **Printer** menu, and make sure that **Pause Printing** is not checked. If there is a check mark, click **Pause Printing.**

- **Is the correct printer port selected?** In My Computer, double-click the **Printers** icon and double-click the icon for your printer. Click the **Details** tab and make sure that the correct printer port is selected—LPT1 or USB in most cases.

- **Did you get only part of a page?** Laser printers are weird; they print an entire page at one time, storing the entire page in memory. If the page has a big complex graphic image or a lot of fonts, the printer may be able to store only a portion of the page. The best fix is to get more memory for your printer. The quickest fix is to use fewer fonts on the page and try using a less complex graphic image.

- **Is it a printer problem?** To determine whether the printer has a problem, go to the DOS prompt (choose **Start, Programs, MS-DOS prompt** or **Start, Programs, Accessories, MS-DOS prompt** or **Start, All Programs, Accessories, Command Prompt**), type **dir > lpt1,** and press **Enter.** This prints the current directory list. If it prints okay, the problem is in the Windows printer setup. If the directory does not print or prints incorrectly, the problem is probably the printer or the connection to the printer. (Many printers have a button combination that you can press to have the printer perform a self-test. Check your printer manual.)

- If error messages keep popping up on your screen, Windows might be sending print instructions to the printer faster than your printer can handle them. In **My Computer,** double-click the **Printers** icon, and then right-click your printer's icon and choose **Properties.** Click the **Details** tab and increase the number of seconds in the **Transmission Retry** text box.

Updating the Software for Your Hardware

Computer hardware and software is in constant transition. Whenever Microsoft updates Windows, manufacturers have to ensure that the hardware they're coming out with works with the new operating system, and Microsoft does its best to make sure that the new operating system can handle most hardware devices. In this rush to get their products to market, the computer industry often releases products that contain bugs—imperfections that cause problems.

Inside Tip

Windows 98 and more recent versions can check for updated drivers at Microsoft's Internet site and download the updated driver for you. To do this, open the **Start** menu and click **Windows Update** or click **Start, All Programs, Windows Update.**

Inside Tip

Some drivers come with their own installation program. Try changing to the disk and folder in which the driver file is stored and running the installation program.

To help make up for these shortcomings, hardware manufacturers commonly release updated drivers for their devices. The driver works along with the operating system to control the device. You can solve many problems with your display, sound card, printer, joystick, modem, and other devices by installing an updated driver. The best way to get an updated driver is to download it from the Internet, as explained in Chapter 31. If you don't have an Internet connection and you suspect that a device driver is causing problems, call the manufacturer's technical support line and ask whether they have an updated driver. They may be able to send it to you on a floppy disk or CD, but they'll wonder why you don't have an Internet connection.

After you have the updated driver, take the following steps to install it:

1. If you have the updated driver on a floppy disk or CD, insert the disk.

2. Right-click **My Computer** and choose **Properties.**

3. Click the **Hardware** tab and then click the **Device Manager** button or click the **Device Manager** tab (in versions of Windows prior to Windows XP).

4. Click the plus sign next to the type of device that requires a new driver.

5. Double-click the name of the device.

6. Click the **Driver** tab and then click the **Update Driver** button.

7. Choose the option for searching for a better driver and click **Next.** If the driver is on a floppy disk, Windows finds it and prompts you to install it. Follow the onscreen instructions and skip the remaining steps.

8. If you downloaded the driver from the Internet, click the **Other Locations** button, choose the disk and folder where the driver file is stored, and click **OK.**

9. Follow the onscreen instructions to complete the installation.

The Least You Need to Know

◆ Use the **Ctrl+Alt+Del** sequence to thaw your computer when it freezes.

◆ Use System Restore to return your computer to an earlier time when it was working properly.

◆ Use the System Configuration Utility to troubleshoot problems caused by programs that run in the background.

◆ Don't go into shock when Windows starts in Safe mode. Shutting down and restarting your PC usually corrects the problem.

◆ If your printer won't print, check the cables and the online indicator. You can avoid most printer problems by making sure your printer has plenty of paper and is online before you start printing.

◆ Check regularly for Windows and device driver updates and install any updated drivers.

Chapter 31

Help! Finding Technical Support

In This Chapter

- ◆ Prepare for your tech support phone call
- ◆ Find answers and updates on the web
- ◆ Have your computer tested online for free at PC Pitstop

In the preceding chapter, you learned how to troubleshoot and correct most common computer problems. Unfortunately, not all glitches are so obvious or so easy to fix. A wrong setting in the Windows Registry can crash your system whenever you run a certain application. A single typo in your Internet setup can prevent your computer from establishing a connection. A buggy device driver can lock up your system. To make matters worse, you might not be able to identify the cause of the problem at all. When a particularly frustrating problem arises, it's tempting to heave your computer out the window or take a sledge hammer to your monitor.

Before you do that, try one other solution: contact the technical support (tech support) department for the program or device that's giving you problems. In this chapter, you learn the ins and outs of tech support—what they can and cannot help you with, what to ask, what information you should have ready, and how to find answers to common questions on the Internet.

Phone Support (Feeling Lucky?)

If you're very lucky, the documentation that came with your program or hardware device contains a phone number in the back for contacting technical support. It's usually printed really small to discourage people from calling. Flip through your manuals to find the number you need.

Before you call, be aware that the quality of technical support over the telephone varies widely from one company to another. Most places have a computerized system that asks you to answer a series of questions, usually leading to a dead end. Other places keep you on hold until you eventually give up and call a relative or friend for help. However, some tech support departments provide excellent, toll-free service, enabling you to talk with a qualified technician who can walk you through the steps required to solve your problem.

Even if you get to speak with a great tech support person, you need to be prepared. No tech support person can read your mind. You must be able to describe the problem you're having in some detail. Before you call, here's what you need to do:

♦ Write down a detailed description of the problem, explaining what went wrong and what you were doing at the time. If possible, write down the steps required to cause the problem again.

♦ Write down the name, version number, and license (or registration) number of the program with which you are having trouble. You can usually get this information by opening the **Help** menu in the problem program and choosing the **About** command. Of course, this assumes you can run the program.

♦ Write down any information about your computer, including the computer brand, chip type (CPU) and speed, monitor type, amount of RAM, and the amount of free disk space. In Windows, open the **Start** menu, point to **All Programs, Accessories, System Tools,** and click **System Information.** The opening System Information screen gives you most of the details you need.

♦ Make sure that your computer is turned on. A good tech support person can talk you through most problems if you're sitting at the keyboard.

- Make sure you're calling the right company. If you're having trouble with your printer, don't call Microsoft. If you even get through to a Microsoft Windows tech support person, the person will tell you to call the printer manufacturer.

- Don't call when you're angry. If you start screaming at the technical support person, the person is going to be less likely to offer quality help.

Finding Tech Support on the Web

Nearly every computer hardware and software company has its own website where you can purchase products directly and find technical support for products you own. If your printer is not feeding paper properly, you're having trouble installing your sound card, you keep receiving cryptic error messages in your favorite program, or you have some other computer-related problem, you can usually find the solution on the Internet.

In addition, computer and software companies often upgrade their software and post both updates and fixes (called patches) on their websites for downloading. If you are having problems with a device, such as a printer or modem, you should check the manufacturer's website for updated drivers. If you run into problems with a program, check the software company's website for an update or a patch—a program file that you install to correct the problem.

The following table provides web page addresses of popular software and hardware manufacturers to help you in your search. Most of the home pages listed have a link for connecting to the support page. If a page does not have a link to the support page, use its search tool to locate the page. You might also see a link labeled FAQs (frequently asked questions), Common Questions, or Top Issues. This link can take you to a page that lists the most common problems other users are having and answers from the company, as shown in Figure 31.1.

Computer Hardware and Software Websites

Company	Web Page Address
3COM	www.3com.com
Acer	global.acer.com
Adaptec	www.adaptec.com
Adobe	www.adobe.com

continues

Computer Hardware and Software Websites (continued)

Company	Web Page Address
ATI Technologies	www.ati.com
Brother	www.brother.com
Canon	www.usa.canon.com
Compaq	www.compaq.com
Corel	www.corel.com
Creative Labs	us.creative.com
Dell	www.dell.com
Epson	www.epson.com
Fujitsu	www.fujitsu.com
Gateway	www.gateway.com
Hewlett-Packard	www.hp.com
Hitachi	www.hitachipc.com
IBM	www.ibm.com/support/us
Intel	www.intel.com
Intuit	www.intuit.com
Iomega	www.iomega.com
Maxtor	www.maxtor.com
Microsoft	www.microsoft.com
Motorola	www.motorola.com
NEC	www.nec.com
NVidia	www.nvidia.com
Packard Bell	www.packardbell.com
Panasonic	www.panasonic.com
Sony	www.sony.com
Texas Instruments	www.ti.com
Toshiba	www.toshiba.com
Western Digital	www.westerndigital.com

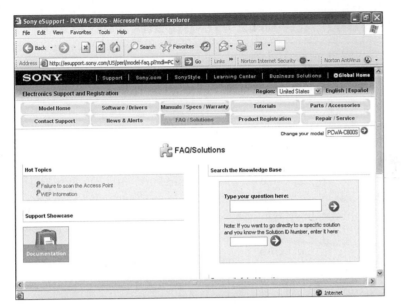

Figure 31.1

Check out the FAQs or Top Issues link for answers to common questions.

If the manufacturer you're looking for is not listed in this table, don't give up. Connect to your favorite web search page and search for the manufacturer by name or search for the problem you're having. You should also seek help from online computer magazines. Here are some excellent resources:

- ◆ **Help.com at help.com** is a great place if you need technical support for Internet problems as well as hardware and software issues. It's also a great place to check out gaming information and obtain shareware programs.

- ◆ **Protonic at www.protonic.com** is a free online technical support service staffed by qualified volunteers who are eager to help other computer users solve their problems. Post your question and then check the site for answers.

- ◆ **Help2Go.com at www.help2go.com** is maintained by a community of computer users and features free tutorials, a Q&A area, and live support for your computer problems.

Inside Tip

Although manufacturers like to keep the tech support phone number a secret, they want you to know their web page address so that you can check out their other products. The website's technical support areas also cut down on calls to tech support.

Troubleshooting Problems with Diagnostic Software

When you purchase a computer, it doesn't come with its own technical support expert, but the manufacturer may include a diagnostic program that can identify common hardware problems. Gateway computers, for example, include a program called PC Doctor that examines the various components and settings, identifies defects, and offers to help you tweak your system to improve performance (check the **Start, All Programs, PC Doctor** menu). Dell computers include a Resource CD that features a diagnostics program for testing the various components that comprise the computer: memory, video card, disk drives, monitor, network card, modem, and so on. Most manufacturers also place an icon on the Windows **Start, All Programs** menu for accessing their online help system. Check the Windows menus and desktop for a support icon.

If your computer does not include a diagnostics program, you can purchase such a program or even have your computer examined on the Internet. An industrial-strength program, such as PC Doctor Service Center, can be a little pricey (about $500); but if you plan on becoming a service technician or sharing the cost with some friends, it is well worth the investment. You can learn more about this program at www.pc-doctor.com. For a more affordable solution, check out TuffTest Pro at www.tufftest.com.

To have your computer examined on the Internet, go to www.pcpitstop.com. PC Pitstop can run a full series of tests on your computer and provide you with a run-down of problem areas and security issues, as shown in Figure 31.2. Best of all, the test is free. PC Pitstop also provides links to online technical support (for a fee).

Figure 31.2

Drive your computer into PC Pitstop to have it examined online.

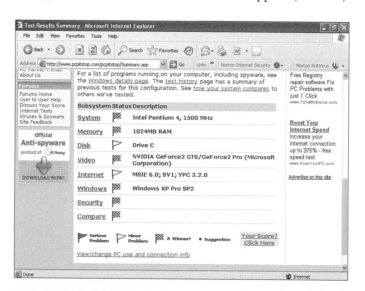

The Least You Need to Know

♦ Prepare for a productive phone conversation with a tech support person by having as much specific information as you can about your PC and the problem before calling.

♦ Check out your computer manufacturer's tech support web page.

♦ Find technical support using computer magazines and support sites on the web.

♦ Use the diagnostics program that came with your computer, if you're fortunate enough to have such a program.

♦ Obtain a computer diagnostics program or have your computer tested online at PC Pitstop.

Speak Like a Geek: The Complete Archive

ADSL (asynchronous digital subscriber line)   A communications technology that allows fast data transfers over standard copper phone lines. "Asynchronous" indicates that the system uses different data transfer rates for upstream and downstream communications—typically 32Mbps for downstream traffic and 32Kbps to 1Mbps for upstream traffic.

BIOS (basic input/output system)   The built-in set of instructions that tells the computer how to control the disk drives, keyboard, printer port, and other components that make up your computer. Pronounced BUY-ose.

bit   The basic unit of data in a computer. A computer's alphabet consists of two characters: 1 and 0. 1 stands for on, and 0 stands for off. Bits are combined in sets of eight to form real characters, such as A, B, C, and D.

bits per second   A unit for measuring the speed of data transmission. Remember that it takes 8 bits to make a byte (the equivalent of a single character). Modems have common bps ratings of 28,800 to 56,600.

boot   To start a computer and load its operating system software (usually Windows).

BPL (Broadband over Power Line)   A relatively new and not widely available technology that enables computers to connect to the Internet over existing electrical cables at speeds ranging from 500Kbps to 3Mbps.

bus   A superhighway that carries information electronically from one part of the computer to another. The wider and faster the bus (speed is measured in megahertz [MHz]), the faster your computer.

byte   A group of 8 bits that usually represents a character or a digit. For example, the byte 01000001 represents the letter A.

cable modem A modem that supports high-speed connections to the Internet via a TV cable connection. (To use a cable modem, you must have a cable company that offers Internet service.)

cache A temporary storage area in memory or on disk that computer components and various programs use to quickly access data. Pronounced cash.

CD burner A disc drive that lets you copy CDs and record tracks from audio CDs to blank CDs.

CD ripper A program that reads tracks from an audio CD and converts them into a digital file format that your computer can store.

CD-R (compact disc recordable) A storage technology in which a CD drive not only reads data from compact discs but also writes data to compact discs (special CD-R discs). A standard CD-ROM drive can only read data from a disc.

CD-ROM (compact disk read-only memory) A storage technology that uses the same kind of discs you play in an audio CD player for mass storage of computer data. A single disc can store more than 600MB of information. Pronounced see-dee-rahm.

CD-RW (compact disk rewritable) A storage technology in which a CD drive reads data from a compact disc, writes data to a disc, and erases data from discs (CD-RW discs) to make them reusable.

cell The box formed by the intersection of a row (1, 2, 3 …) and column (A, B, C …) in a spreadsheet. Each cell has an address (such as B12) that defines its column and row. A cell might contain text, a numeric value, or a formula.

client Of two computers, the computer that's being served. On the Internet or on a network, your computer is the client, and the computer to which you're connected is the server.

Clipboard A temporary storage area in Windows that holds text and graphics. The Cut and Copy commands put text or graphics on the Clipboard, replacing the Clipboard's previous contents. The Paste command copies Clipboard data to a document.

COM port Short for communications port. A receptacle, usually at the back of the computer, into which you can plug a serial device such as a modem, mouse, or serial printer.

context menu A list of commands or options that pops up on the screen when you right-click a selected object or highlighted text. Context menus contain only commands that pertain to the selected object or text.

cookie   An electronic identification "badge" that many websites store on your computer to help identify you when you return to the site or to record items you buy as you shop online.

CPU (central processing unit)   The computer's brain.

crash   The failure of a system or program. Usually, you realize that your system has crashed when you can't move the mouse pointer or type anything. The term *crash* is also used to refer to a disk crash (or head crash). A disk crash occurs when the read/write head in the disk drive falls on the disk, possibly destroying data.

database   A type of computer program used to store, organize, and retrieve information. Popular database programs include Access, Approach, and Paradox.

default   The initial state of a setting or option. Most word processing programs, for example, are set up to print documents in portrait mode rather than in landscape mode. Portrait mode is said to be the default setting.

desktop   The main work area in Windows. The desktop displays several icons for running programs and accessing common Windows tools.

desktop publishing (DTP)   A program that lets you combine text and graphics on the same page and manipulate the text and graphics onscreen. Desktop publishing programs are commonly used to create newsletters, brochures, flyers, resumés, and business cards.

dialog box   An onscreen box that lets you enter your preferences or supply additional information. You use a dialog box to carry on a "conversation" with the program.

directory   A division of a disk or CD that contains a group of related files. Think of your disk as a filing cabinet, and think of each directory as a drawer in the cabinet. Directories are more commonly called folders.

disk   A round, flat, magnetic storage medium. A disk works like a cassette tape, storing files permanently so that you can play them back later. See also *diskette, hard disk*.

disk drive   A device that writes data to a magnetic disk and reads data from the disk. Think of a disk drive as a cassette recorder/player for a computer.

diskette   A wafer encased in plastic that stores magnetic data (the facts and figures you enter and save). You insert diskettes (also called floppy disks) into your computer's diskette drive (located on the front of the computer).

download   To copy files from another computer to your computer, usually through a modem.

DSL (digital subscriber line)   Uses standard phone lines to achieve data transfer rates of up to 1.5Mbps (9Mbps if you're within 2 miles of an ADSL connection center).

DVD (digital versatile disc or digital video disc)   Discs that can store more than seven times as much data as a CD, making them useful for storing full-length movies and complete multimedia encyclopedias. DVD drives are designed to handle DVDs and are also designed to play CDs.

DVD-R (digital versatile disc recordable)   A storage technology in which a DVD drive not only reads data from discs but also writes data to discs (special DVD-R discs). A standard DVD drive can only read data from a disc.

DVD-RW (digital versatile disc rewritable)   A storage technology in which a DVD drive reads data from a disc, writes data to a disc, and erases data from discs (DVD-RW discs) to make them reusable.

e-mail   Short for electronic mail. E-mail is a system that lets people send messages to and receive messages from other computers.

emoticon   A text-only symbol commonly used in e-mail messages and chat rooms to quickly express an emotion or physical gesture. :), for instance, represents a smile.

Ethernet   A common local area network (LAN) protocol developed by Xerox Corporation that allows computers to communicate over network connections.

Ethernet adapter   An expansion card that allows a computer to be connected to an Ethernet local area network.

expansion board   A printed circuit board that plugs into a computer's motherboard and is designed to add a specific capability to a computer. Common expansion boards include modems, sound cards, and video accelerators.

expansion slot   An opening on the motherboard (inside the system unit) that lets you add devices to the system unit, such as an internal modem, sound card, video accelerator, or other enhancement.

extension   The portion of a file name that comes after the period. Every file name consists of two parts—the base name (before the period) and the extension (after the period). The extension (which is optional) almost always consists of three characters.

field   A blank in a database record into which you can enter a piece of information (such as a telephone number, a ZIP code, or a person's last name).

file   A collection of information stored as a single unit on a floppy or hard disk. Files always have a file name to identify them.

file format   An organizational scheme for the data that makes up a file. The simplest file format is text-only, which stores data as typed characters. You can determine a file's format by looking at its file name extension. A graphics file, for instance, might be stored as a PCX, GIF, or JPG file.

File Transfer Protocol (FTP)   A set of rules that governs the exchange of files between two computers on the Internet.

flame war   A war of words between two or more people, typically waged in newsgroups or via e-mail.

folder   The Windows name for a directory, a division of a hard disk or CD that stores a group of related files.

font   Any set of characters of the same typeface (design) and type size (measured in points). For example, Times New Roman 12-point is a font, Times New Roman is the typeface, and 12-point is the size. (There are 72 points in an inch.)

format (disk)   To prepare a disk for storing data.

format (document)   To establish a document's physical layout, including page size, margins, headers and footers, line spacing, text alignment, graphics placement, and so on.

function keys   The 10 or 12 F keys on the left side of the keyboard, or the 12 F keys at the top of the keyboard (some keyboards have both). F keys are numbered F1, F2, F3, and so on; and you can use them to enter specified commands in a program.

gigabyte   A thousand megabytes. Often abbreviated as GB.

hard disk   A disk drive that has an unremovable disk. It acts as a giant floppy disk drive and usually sits inside your computer.

highlight   To select text in order to cut, copy, delete, move, or format it. When you highlight text, it typically appears white on a black background.

history list   A list of the names and addresses of websites and pages you've accessed with your web browser. Your web browser keeps a history list so that you can quickly return to sites even if you've forgotten a site's address.

hotspot   A wireless adapter that is hardwired to the Internet and allows wireless-enabled computers within its range to connect to the Internet.

HTML (Hypertext Markup Language) The code used to create documents for the World Wide Web. These codes tell the web browser how to display the text (titles, headings, lists, and so on), insert anchors that link this document to other documents, and control character formatting (by making it bold or italic).

hyperlink Icons, pictures, or highlighted text commonly used on web pages and in help systems that point to other resources. On web pages, text hyperlinks typically appear blue and underlined.

icon A graphic image onscreen (a tiny picture) that represents another object, such as a file on a disk. Icons can be found almost everywhere in Windows: on the desktop, on toolbars, on menus, and in dialog boxes.

IM (instant message) A private message that reaches the recipient almost immediately after the user sends it. IMs are commonly used in America Online to communicate privately with other users.

insertion point A blinking vertical line used in most Windows word processors to indicate the place where any characters you type are inserted. An insertion point is equivalent to a cursor.

interface A link between two objects, such as a computer and a modem. The link between a computer and a person is called a user interface and refers to the way a person communicates with the computer or a program.

Internet A group of computers all over the world that are connected to each other. Using your computer and a modem, you can connect to these other computers and tap their resources.

Internet service provider (ISP) The company that you pay to connect to their computer and get on the Internet.

ISDN (Integrated Services Digital Network) A system that allows your computer, using a special ISDN modem, to perform digital data transfers over special phone lines. ISDN connections can transfer data at a rate of up to 128Kbps, compared to about 56Kbps for the fastest analog modems.

Kbps (kilobits per second) A unit used to express data transfer rates, typically for modems. A kilobit is equivalent to 1,000 bits.

keyboard The main input device for most computers. You use the keyboard to type and to enter commands.

kilobyte A unit for measuring the amount of data. A kilobyte is equivalent to 1,024 bytes. (Each byte is a character.) Kilobyte is commonly abbreviated as K, KB, or Kbyte.

LAN (local area network)   A system of interconnected computers designed to let users share hardware, software, and data and to communicate with each other via e-mail. A LAN is typically confined to a limited area, such as an office, building, or small group of buildings.

laptop   A small computer that's light enough to carry. Notebook computers and sub-notebooks are even lighter.

LCD   Short for Liquid Crystal Display, this is the preview screen on the back of most digital cameras. Unlike an optical viewfinder, the LCD displays the subject just as it will appear in the photograph.

log off   To disconnect from a network or from the Internet.

log on   To enter your user name and password to establish a connection to a network or the Internet.

mail server   A computer on a network whose job it is to receive and store incoming mail and route outgoing mail to the proper e-mail boxes on other mail servers.

Mbps (megabits per second)   A unit used to express data transfer rates for high-speed communications. A megabit is equivalent to 1,000,000 bits.

megabyte   A standard unit used to measure the storage capacity of a disk and the amount of computer memory. A megabyte is 1,048,576 bytes (1,000 kilobytes). Megabyte is commonly abbreviated as M, MB, or Mbyte.

megapixel   A million pixels. Photo size and quality are often measured in megapixels—generally, the more megapixels, the larger the photo and the higher the quality.

memory   An electronic storage area inside the computer used to temporarily store data or program instructions when the computer is using them. Also referred to as RAM.

menu   A vertical listing of commands or instructions displayed onscreen. Menus organize commands and make a program easier to use. Most applications' menus appear on a menu bar, a band near the top of the application's window. To open a menu, you click its name on the menu bar.

microprocessor   Sometimes called the central processing unit (CPU) or processor, this chip is the computer's brain; it does all the calculations for the computer.

modem   A piece of hardware that converts incoming signals (from a phone line, cable service, or other source) into signals that a PC can understand and converts outgoing signals from the PC into a form that can be transmitted.

monitor   A televisionlike screen on which the computer displays information.

motherboard   The main printed circuit board inside a computer through which all other devices communicate.

mouse   A handheld device that you move across a surface to move an arrow, called the mouse pointer, across the screen. You can use the mouse to move the insertion point (or cursor), select and move items (such as text and graphics), open menus, execute commands, and perform other tasks.

MP3   Short for MPEG audio layer 3. A digital audio format that compresses audio files to one twelfth of their original size with an imperceptible loss of quality.

MPEG   Short for Moving Pictures Experts Group. An assembly that sets standards for digital video recording and file formats.

network   A system of interconnected computers designed to allow users to share hardware, software, and data.

newsgroup   An Internet bulletin board for users who share common interests. Newsgroups let you post messages and read messages from other users.

NIC (network interface card)   An expansion board that plugs into your computer and enables it to be connected to other computers on a network.

notebook   A portable computer that weighs between 4 and 8 pounds.

online service   A network, such as America Online, that allows members to obtain information, communicate, and get files via a modem connection.

parallel port   A connector used to plug a device, usually a printer, into the computer.

partition   A section of a disk drive that's assigned a letter. A hard disk drive can be divided (partitioned) into one or more drives, which your computer refers to as drive C, drive D, drive E, and so on.

patch   A set of program instructions designed to fix a programming bug or add capabilities to a program. On the Internet, you can often download patches for programs to update the program.

path   The route that the computer travels from the root directory to any subdirectories when locating a file.

PC (personal computer)   A computer designed to help a user perform practical tasks, such as typing documents and performing calculations.

PC card   An expansion card that's about the size of a credit card, but thicker. It slides into a slot on the side of a notebook computer. PC cards let you quickly install RAM or a hard drive, modem, CD-ROM drive, network card, or game port without having to open the notebook computer.

PCMCIA (Personal Computer Memory Card International Association)   An organization that sets standards for notebook computer expansion cards.

peripheral   A device attached to the computer but not essential for the computer's basic operation. Any devices attached to the system unit are considered peripheral, including a printer, modem, or joystick. Some manufacturers consider the monitor and keyboard to be peripheral, too.

pixel   A dot of light that appears on the computer screen. A collection of pixels forms characters and images on the screen.

PnP (plug-and-play)   PnP lets you install expansion cards in your computer without having to set special switches. You plug it in, and it works.

port   A receptacle at the back of the computer. It gets its name from the ports where ships pick up and deliver cargo. In this case, a port allows information to enter and leave the system unit.

PPP (Point-to-Point Protocol)   A language that computers use to talk to one another. What's important is that when you choose an Internet service provider, you get the right connection—SLIP or PPP.

program   A group of instructions that tells the computer what to do. Typical programs are word processors, spreadsheets, databases, and games.

prompt   A computer's way of asking for more information. The computer basically looks at you and says, "Tell me something." In other words, the computer is prompting you or prodding you for information or a command.

protocol   A group of communications settings that controls the transfer of data between two computers.

random access memory (RAM)   A collection of chips your computer uses to store data and programs temporarily. RAM is measured in kilobytes and megabytes. In general, more RAM means that you can run more powerful programs and more programs simultaneously. Also called memory.

record   Used by databases to denote a unit of related information contained in one or more fields, such as an individual's name, address, and phone number.

Recycle Bin   A virtual trash can into which Windows places files and folders when you choose to delete them. It also acts as a safety net for deleted files. If you delete a file or folder by mistake, you can usually retrieve it from the Recycle Bin.

resolution   A term for describing the quality of an image. The higher the resolution, the larger the image and the higher the quality.

scanner   A device that converts images, such as photographs or printed text, into an electronic format that a computer can use. Many stores use a special type of scanner to read bar code labels into the cash register.

screen saver   A program that displays a moving picture on your computer screen when the computer is inactive. Screen savers are typically used as decorative novelties and to prevent passers-by from snooping.

Screen Tip   A small text box that displays the name of a button when you rest the mouse pointer on the button. Screen Tips help you understand what a button does when you can't figure it out from the picture. Also known as a ToolTip.

scroll   To move text up and down or right and left on a computer screen.

scrollbar   A band, typically displayed along the bottom and right edge of a window, used to bring the contents of the window into view.

SDSL (synchronous digital subscriber line)   A communications technology that allows fast data transfers over standard copper phone lines. "Synchronous" indicates that the system uses the same data transfer rates for both upstream and downstream traffic.

server   Of two computers, the computer that's serving the other computer. On the Internet or on a network, your computer is the client, and the computer to which you're connected is the server.

shareware   Computer programs you can use for free and then pay for if you decide to continue using them.

shortcut   A cloned version of an icon that points to a document or program on your computer. Shortcuts let you place programs and documents in more than one convenient location on your computer.

software   Any instructions that tell your computer (the hardware) what to do. There are two types of software: operating system software and application software. Operating system software (such as Windows) gets your computer up and running. Application software lets you do something useful, such as type a letter or manage your finances. Other types of software include games and utilities (programs for maintaining and optimizing your computer).

spreadsheet   A program used for keeping schedules and calculating numeric results. Common spreadsheets include Lotus 1-2-3, Microsoft Excel, and Quattro Pro.

status bar   The area at the bottom of a program window that shows you what's going on as you work. A status bar might show the page and line number where the insertion point is positioned and indicate whether you are typing in overstrike or insert mode.

style   A collection of specifications for formatting text. A style might include information on the font, size, style, margins, and spacing. Applying a style to text automatically formats the text according to the style's specifications.

surge suppressor   A device that prevents power spikes and dips from damaging a computer and its peripheral devices.

system tray   The area on the right end of the taskbar that displays the current time, as well as icons for programs that are running in the background.

system unit   The central component of any computer, the system unit contains the computer's CPU, memory, disk drives, and other essential components. See also *CPU*.

tab stop   A setting commonly used in a word processor that specifies where the insertion point will land when you press the Tab key. Tab stops are typically set at a half-inch, unless you change them.

taskbar   A fancy name for the button bar at the bottom of the Windows desktop. The taskbar includes the Start button (on the left) and the system tray (on the right).

TCP/IP (Transmission Control Protocol/Internet Protocol)   A set of rules that governs the transfer of data over the Internet.

thumb drive   A storage device that's about the size of an average human thumb and plugs into the USB port on a computer.

toolbar   A strip of buttons typically displayed near the top of a program window, below the menu bar. The toolbar contains buttons that you can click to enter common commands, allowing you to bypass the menu system.

undo   A feature in most programs that lets you reverse one or more actions. For example, if you delete a paragraph by mistake, you can choose the Undo command to get it back.

uninterruptible power supply (UPS)   A battery-powered device that protects against power spikes and power outages. If the power goes out, the UPS continues supplying power to the computer so that you can continue working or safely turn off your computer without losing data.

upload   To send data to another computer, usually through a modem and a telephone line or over a network connection.

URL (Uniform Resource Locator)   An address for an Internet site.

USB (Universal Serial Bus)   The ultimate in plug-and-play technology, USB lets you install devices without turning off your computer or using a screwdriver.

utility   A program designed to optimize, protect, or maintain a computer rather than perform a task for the user. Utilities include backup programs, antivirus software, and memory optimizers.

video capture   The process of transferring video clips to your computer (using a camcorder or VCR) and storing the video as a file on a hard disk or CD.

virtual   Not real. Virtual worlds on the Internet are three-dimensional computer-generated areas that you can navigate but never physically enter.

virtual memory   Disk storage used as RAM (memory).

virus   A program that attaches itself to files on a floppy or hard disk, duplicates itself without the user's knowledge, and might cause the computer to do strange and sometimes destructive things, such as reformatting your hard drive.

VoIP (Voice over Internet Protocol)   A technology that enables you to place phone calls over the Internet less expensively than you can by using your phone company's equipment.

wallpaper   A graphic design that appears as the background for the Windows desktop.

WAN (wide area network)   A system of interconnected LANs (local area networks) typically set up to let users exchange e-mail and share data over greater distances than covered by LANs.

web browser   A program that lets you navigate the World Wide Web (the most popular feature of the Internet).

web server   A computer on a network whose job it is to make web pages available upon request. When you use a web browser to open web pages, you connect to a web server.

Wi-Fi   A wireless network standard for connecting computers via radio-frequency signals rather than network cables.

windows   A way of displaying information on different parts of the screen. When spelled with an uppercase *W*, used as a shortened form of Microsoft Windows.

wireless Ethernet   Networking technology that enables you to network two or more computers housed in nearby rooms without having to connect them with cables.

wizard   A series of dialog boxes that lead you step by step through the process of performing a task.

word processor   A program that lets you enter, edit, format, and print text.

worksheet   See *spreadsheet*.

World Wide Web   A part of the Internet that consists of multimedia documents interconnected by links. To move from one document to another, you click a link, which might appear as highlighted text or an icon. The web contains text, sound and video clips, pictures, catalogs, and much more.

Index

S

s emoticon for e-mail, 248
S-video, 334
Safe mode, 375
satellite connections, 222
Save As dialog box, 145
Save command (Word File menu), 145
saving
  movies, 341-342
  Word documents, 145-146
ScanDisk, 359
scanning images, 187, 188
screen resolution, 70
screen savers
  passwords, 79
  selecting, 78
  turning on/off, 79
Screen Saver tab (Display Properties dialog box), 78
ScreenTips, 33
Scroll Lock key, 17
scrollbars, 37
SDSL (Symmetric DSL), 221
Search command (Help menu), 130
Search Results dialog box, 99-100
security
  browser settings, 297-299
  cookies, 302
  files
    decrypting, 111
    encrypting, 110-111
    hiding, 108-109
    write-protecting, 109
  firewalls
    hacker prevention, 300-301
    Internet connection problems, 302
  networks, 124-125

  private folders, 106-107
  virus protection, 299-300
Security tab (Internet Options dialog box), 298
see you later (CUL8R), 248
selecting. See choosing
sending
  e-mail messages, 241
  files with AIM, 257
serial printers, 204
servers
  mail, 240
  news, 266-267
setting up
  browser start pages, 236
  e-mail, 240-241
  ISPs, 225
  margins, 207-209
  .Net passport accounts, 94-95
  networks, 118-119
  news servers, 266-267
  newsreaders, 266-267
  paper size, 209
  paper sources, 209
  personal finance accounts, 196
  power-saving options, 362
  print direction, 209
  printers, 204-205, 211
  recurring entries, 199
  screen resolution, 70
  time/date, 83
  video equipment, 333-334
shapes, 189-190
sharing
  files/folders, 119-120
  Internet connections, 123-124
  printers across networks, 120
  private folders, 107
sheet fed scanners, 187

Sheet tab (Page Setup dialog box), 167
shortcuts
  keyboard
    opening menus, 31
    Windows commands, 18
  programs, 63-64
Shutterfly, 327
significant other (SO), 249
signing on
  AIM, 253
  Yahoo! Messenger, 259
Simple Mail Transfer Protocol (SMTP), 240
single-click to open icons, 29
SiSoft Sandra, 364
size
  clip art, 185
  desktop icons, 71
  floppy disks, 44
  taskbar, 72-73
  windows, 35
sleep mode, 13
slide shows, 180-181
sliders in dialog boxes, 33
Small Icons command (View menu), 52
smart menus, 32
SMTP (Simple Mail Transfer Protocol), 240
Snapfish, 327
SO (significant other), 249
software. See programs
Sony website, 386
sorting
  database records, 175
  files/folders, 51
sound
  adding to video clips, 339-340
  CDs
    burning, 308, 316, 317
    custom mixes, 317
    data storage format, 308